T
LUCIFERIANS
THE SERVANTS OF EVIL

DICTATED BY THE SPIRIT

JOHN WILMONT
EARL OF ROCHESTER

VERA KRYZHANOVSKAIA

Adapted to English language by
Beatriz Stella –Limeira, SP, August 2023

The Luciferians Book I

©Vera Ivanovna Kryzhanovskaia; 1904

Translation by Victor Sillin

Revision and adaptation to Portuguese

Margareth Rose F. A. Carvalho

Translated to English from the Portuguese 2nd edition.

World Spiritist Institute
Houston, Texas, USA
E–mail: contact@worldspiritistinstitute.org

About the Medium

Vera Ivanovna Kryzhanovskaia, (Warsaw, July 14, 1861 - Tallinn, December 29, 1924), was a Russian psychographer medium. Between 1885 and 1917 she psychographed a hundred novels and short stories signed by the spirit of Rochester, believed by some to be John Wilmot, second Earl of Rochester. Among the best known are "The Pharaoh Mernephtah" and "The Iron Chancellor."

In addition to historical novels, in parallel the medium psychographed works with "occult-cosmological themes." E. V. Kharitonov, in his research essay, considered her the first woman representative of science fiction literature. During the fashion for occultism and esotericism, with the recent scientific discoveries and psychic experiences of European spiritualist circles, she attracted readers from the Russian "Silver Age" high society and the middle class in newspapers and press. Although he began along spiritualist lines, organizing séances in St. Petersburg, he later gravitated toward theosophical doctrines.

Her father died when Vera was just ten years old, which left the family in a difficult situation. In 1872 Vera was taken in by an educational charity for noble girls in St. Petersburg as a scholar, St. Catherine's School. However, the young girl's frail health and financial difficulties prevented her from completing the course. In 1877 she was discharged and completed her education at home.

During this period, the spirit of the English poet JW Rochester (1647-1680), taking advantage of the young woman's mediumistic gifts, materialized, and proposed that she dedicate herself body and soul to the service of the Good and write under his direction. After this contact with the person who became her spiritual guide, Vera was cured of chronic tuberculosis, a serious illness at the time, without medical interference.

At the age of 18, he began to work in psychography. In 1880, on a trip to France, he successfully participated in a mediumistic séance. At that time, his contemporaries were surprised by his productivity, despite his poor health. His séances were attended at that time by famous European mediums, as well as by Prince Nicholas, the future Tsar Nicholas II of Russia.

In 1886, in Paris, her first work was made public, the historical novel "Episode of the life of Tiberius", published in French, (as well as her first works), in which the tendency for mystical themes was already noticeable. It is believed that the medium was influenced by the Spiritist Doctrine of Allan Kardec, the Theosophy of Helena Blavatsky, and the Occultism of Papus.

During this period of temporary residence in Paris, Vera psychographed a series of historical novels, such as "The Pharaoh Mernephtah", "The Abbey of the Benedictines", "The Romance of a Queen", "The Iron Chancellor of Ancient Egypt", "Herculaneum", "The Sign of Victory", "The Night of Saint Bartholomew", among others, which attracted public attention not only for the captivating themes, but also for the exciting plots. For the novel "The Iron Chancellor of Ancient Egypt," the French Academy of Sciences awarded him the title of "Officer of the French Academy," and in 1907, the Russian Academy of Sciences awarded him the "Honorable Mention" for the novel "Czech Luminaries."

About the Spiritual Author

John Wilmot, Earl of Rochester was born on April 1 or 10, 1647 (there is no record of the exact date). The son of Henry Wilmot and Anne (widow of Sir. Francis Henry Lee), Rochester resembled his father in physique and temperament, domineering and proud. Henry Wilmot had received the title of Earl because of his efforts to raise money in Germany to help King Charles I regain the throne after he was forced to leave England.

When his father died, Rochester was 11 years old and inherited the title of Earl, little inheritance, and honors.

Young J.W. Rochester grew up in Ditchley among drunkenness, theatrical intrigues, artificial friendships with professional poets, lust, brothels in Whetstone Park and the friendship of the king, whom he despised.

He had a vast culture, for the time: he mastered Latin and Greek, knew the classics, French and Italian, was the author of satirical poetry, highly appreciated in his time.

In 1661, at the age of 14, he left Wadham College, Oxford, with the degree of Master of Arts. He then left for the continent (France and Italy) and became an interesting figure: tall, slim, attractive, intelligent, charming, brilliant, subtle, educated, and modest, ideal characteristics to conquer the frivolous society of his time.

When he was not yet 20 years old, in January 1667, he married Elizabeth Mallet. Ten months later, drinking began to affect his character. He had four sons with Elizabeth and a daughter, in 1677, with the actress Elizabeth Barry.

Living the most different experiences, from fighting the Dutch navy on the high seas to being involved in crimes of death, Rochester's life followed paths of madness, sexual abuse, alcoholics, and charlatanism, in a period in which he acted as a "physician."

When Rochester was 30 years old, he writes to a former fellow adventurer that he was nearly blind, lame, and with little chance of ever seeing London again.

Quickly recovering, Rochester returns to London. Shortly thereafter, in agony, he set out on his last adventure: he called the curate Gilbert Burnet and dictated his recollections to him. In his last reflections, Rochester acknowledged having lived a wicked life, the end of which came slowly and painfully to him because of the venereal diseases that dominated him.

Earl of Rochester died on July 26, 1680. In the state of spirit, Rochester received the mission to work for the propagation of Spiritualism. After 200 years, through the medium Vera Kryzhanovskaia, the automatism that characterized her made her hand trace words with dizzying speed and total unconsciousness of ideas. The narratives that were dictated to her denote a wide knowledge of ancestral life and customs and provide in their details such a local stamp and historical truth that the reader finds it hard not to recognize their authenticity. Rochester proves to dictate his historical-literary production, testifying that life unfolds to infinity in his indelible marks of spiritual memory, towards the light and the way of God. It seems impossible for a historian, however erudite, to study, simultaneously and in depth, times and environments as different as the Assyrian, Egyptian, Greek and Roman civilizations; as well as customs as dissimilar as those of the France of Louis XI to those of the Renaissance.

The subject matter of Rochester's work begins in Pharaonic Egypt, passes through Greco-Roman antiquity and the Middle Ages, and continues into the 19th century. In his novels, reality navigates in a fantastic current, in which the imaginary surpasses the limits of verisimilitude, making natural phenomena that oral tradition has taken care to perpetuate as supernatural.

Rochester's referential is full of content about customs, laws, ancestral mysteries and unfathomable facts of History, under a novelistic layer, where social and psychological aspects pass through the sensitive filter of his great imagination. Rochester's genre classification is hampered by his expansion into several categories: gothic horror with romance, family sagas, adventure and forays into the fantastic.

The number of editions of Rochester's works, spread over countless countries, is so large that it is not possible to have an idea of their magnitude, especially considering that, according to researchers, many of these works are unknown to the general public.

Several lovers of Rochester's novels carried out (and perhaps do carry out) searches in libraries in various countries, especially in Russia, to locate still unknown works. This can be seen in the prefaces transcribed in several works. Many of these works are finally available in English thanks to the *World Spiritist Institute.*

Preface

Thanks to the World Spiritist Institute, is pleased to present the reader with two more unpublished works by the spiritual author the Count of Rochester. These are the historical accounts The Luciferians and The Templars, which together make up the collection *The Servants of Evil*, rescued from anonymity and which will certainly become another masterpiece of spiritist literature.

The plot of The Luciferians is set in the Tyrol, a mountainous region between Austria and Italy, which was once the scene of many macabre rituals in the undergrounds of medieval castles between the 13th and 14th centuries, a time of remarkable events in human history. This time, the victims are a young couple, Raymond and Elisa, whose bonds were linked from an early age by an important engagement.

After the mysterious death of Paola, the "fiery Italian", Count Ervin, unmotivated, decides to join the Templar and entrusts his only daughter, Eliza, to his faithful friend, Count Wolfram. Then, to ensure the future of his friend's daughter, he decides to unite her in marriage to his son Raymond when they are still children. Marriages of this nature were common among the ancient nobility, but not always successful. It is exactly at this point that the plot really begins due to the intrigues and jealousy that this premature union provokes in several characters in the story.

Due to their youthful immaturity, Raymond and Eliza do not realize the great danger they are in. Will they overcome all the obstacles and free themselves from all the evil that surrounds them?

Those were tough times in Europe, during the Middle Ages. Sometimes Ervin had to leave for the East to accompany expeditions that sought to free the Holy Land from the hands of the infidels. The Jewish people were also targeted since Western Christians considered them to be the real culprits for the crucifixion of Jesus.

During this period much of the Jewish population was persecuted and decimated, both in Europe and in the East. Discriminated, they could not participate actively in feudal society, and they were left with the economic world of loan sharking. In fact, this was one of the reasons that encouraged the persecution of the Christian nobles against the Jews, motivated by the interest of getting rid of their enormous debts.

Unfortunately, this mutual hatred between Christians and Jews leads our hero Raymond to be imperceptibly introduced into the mysteries of the obscure sect of the Luciferians, whose historical records are scarce, since little is known about its exact origin. It was probably an idolatry of the controversial character from the legend of the Fallen Angels - Lucifer.

In ancient Roman times, the word "Lucifer" was used to designate the planet Venus when it was positioned west of the sun, in the morning before its birth. It meant "light bearer" (from the Latin lux = light and ferre = to bear) and was also known as the "Morning Star".

However, Lucifer seems to have entered the history of religion when in the Bible the expression in Hebrew appears " How have you fallen from heaven, Morning Star, daughter of the dawn!" (Isaiah 14:12). In the Greek version of the Old Testament, the term was translated as " Phosphorus" (the Greek word for "Venus" or "Morning Star") and "Lucifer" for the Latin version. Scholars explain that the parable of the prophet Isaiah referred to the arrogance of a Babylonian king who was thrown down from heaven by God, since he dared to compare himself to the "Morning Star".

Origenes Adamantius (185 - 254), a prominent Christian of the Greek Church, and Augustine of Canterbury (in the sixth century), founder of the Christian church in southern England, interpreted the use of the Latin term "Lucifer" as a reference to the devil or Satan himself. Since then, the term has been generalized in a negative way.

In the fourth century, Bishop Lucifer of Cagliari in Sardinia, a vehement opponent of Arianism,[1] created a sect whose followers came to be called "Luciferians". Making every effort to fight it, as can be seen in the famous dialogue " The Dispute between the Luciferians and the Orthodox", St. Jerome was also one of those responsible for the association of Lucifer with Satan.

However, the sect to which Rochester refers in the title of this work had its expansion in Europe between the 13th and mid-14th centuries. In 1223, the inquisitor Conrad of Marburg, noting the unusual growth of heretics [2] in Germania and Austria, especially of the sect of these "Luciferians", began a series of persecutions.

In Byzantium and in various parts of Europe, legends arose that this highly secretive faction was dedicated to Lucifer, the infernal angel, who had been expelled from Paradise by God. These demon worshipers believed that their master was the true creator of the world and that he had been unfairly imprisoned in the abyss by his enemy, an unfair and vengeful god whom Lucifer was supposed to worship. The Luciferian prophecies preached that one day he would reconquer Paradise, defeat Jehovah, and grant eternal life to all his followers.

As in the case of the Templars and the witches, their confessions were obtained by the Inquisition through torture. They confessed that during the initiation ritual of the neophytes, in underground temples, Lucifer showed himself as a man whose upper body radiated light, but from the waist down was dark as

---

[1] Arianism - Doctrine of Arius, a famous Alexandrian heretic (280-336), according to which Christ was a creature of an intermediate nature between divinity and humanity.

[2] Heretic - A person who professes a doctrine contrary to what has been defined by the Church as a matter of faith.

night. The end of the ritual was celebrated with a feast and concluded with orgies, in which virgin novices were offered.

These reports are confirmed in detail in this amazing narrative by Rochester, an audacious spirit, sagacious and skilled scholar of occult mysteries, whose competent historical records make us relive important events lost through the dust of time...

The dénouement of this enigmatic story and the fate of Eliza and Raymond can be found in the second volume, The Templars, in which historical facts about this important order of medieval knights are described in detail.

Enjoy your reading!

Antonio Rolando Lopes Junior

"Beware of false prophets who come to you disguised as sheep, but inwardly they are predatory wolves. You shall know them by their fruits. Do you gather grapes from thorn bushes or figs from thistles?

Even so, every good tree brings forth good fruit, but a corrupt tree brings forth evil fruit."

(Matthew, Ch. VII, vv. 15, 16 and 17)

Chapter 1

The narrow, rocky trail meandered capriciously, sometimes bordering deep chasms, sometimes running between rocks. The views around the curves were simply magnificent. Far away, on the misty horizon, stretched the fertile valleys of the Tyrol,[3] covered with lush vegetation. The sun was burning brightly, and the proximity of blessed Italy could be felt in everything.

Up this picturesque, steep path followed a group of five riders trotting or slow stepping, depending on the steepness of the terrain. The exhausted horses and completely dusty clothes indicated a long and difficult walk.

A handsome young man in his late thirties, wrapped in a dark cloak, was leading the way. Under his hat stood out locks of abundant curly hair, as black as a raven's wing, framing a pale face with perfect features.

The thoughtful look in his dark eyes reflected intelligence and perseverance. But the charming facial features were his thin,

---

[3] Tyrol - A province now belonging to Austria, bordered by Germany to the north, Italy to the south, and Switzerland to the west. It is in the Alpine region, cut by the Inn River and famous for its idyllic beauty. Its capital is Innsbruck. The history of this province is somewhat complicated. During the 14th century, North Tyrol, at first divided into small counties, was united and ceded to Austria. At the time of this account, the southern part was governed by the bishoprics of Brixen and Trento. Later, in the early 19th century, it was ceded to Austria because of a treaty between France and Austria itself. In 1810, Napoleon annexed South Tyrol to Italy, but in 1815 both parts were returned to Austria through the Congress of Vienna. In 1919, South Tirol was definitely incorporated into Italy.

well-defined lips and the charming smile that illuminated his face, showing sympathy, although sometimes it seemed a bit arrogant.

Behind the handsome knight, two well-armed warriors and two squires, one of whom carried the knight's helmet and sword, and the other the spear and light armor, lined up along a very narrow path. Then, at one of the bends in the path, a small castle appeared on the top of the mountain like an eagle's nest, and an hour later, the travelers were already in front of the gates.

Now it could be perceived that the castle differed from buildings of that time. The stone building, which had a tall quadrangular tower, was protected neither by moats nor drawbridges. It was surrounded only by a thick wall and massive cast-iron gates. Under a canopy was a bell hung with a long rope that descended to the foot of the wall, giving the castle the appearance of an abbey. One of the warriors jumped off his horse and rang the bell, whose shrill, trembling sound propagated far into the mountains.

After a few minutes, a small door opened and in it appeared a gray-haired gentleman who cast a dark and suspicious look at the road. When he saw the travelers, a happy smile lit up his face.

The trapdoor closed immediately, and then the gates creaked open. The porter, with deep reverence, approached the knight who was leading the small convoy.

- Welcome Mr. Wolfram! - he said, looking fondly at the knight.

- Greetings, old Bertrand! - replied the young man, extending his hand, which the old man kissed respectfully.

- How is my master's health?

- Thank God, he is well and has just returned from the garden with Mr. Ervin who arrived here yesterday.

During the conversation, the knight got off his horse and went into a low-ceilinged room that served as a lobby. There, he was greeted by another gentleman who, like the porter, was also pleased with his arrival.

[14]

- Cristofor, get my men settled! They are tired and hungry - asked Wolfram with a friendly smile, handing his cloak to the old servant.

- The Baron must be in his office, right?

- He is, my lord. I will now carry out your order right away and get your men and horses settled.

The young knight seemed to know the house very well, since without the slightest hesitation he entered the building and climbed the stairs that were dimly lit by narrow windows built into the wall.

The stairway led to a large, vaulted room, modestly furnished, which probably served as a library, since the walls were occupied by shelves with scrolls, books, and manuscripts. There, the windows were wider and taller, and the sun's rays streamed through the tinted glass, reflecting diverse colors on the floor. From one of the opened windows there was a beautiful view of a canyon and a lake that shone like a mirror from afar.

Wolfram stopped for a moment and stood for a while in thought, appreciating that beautiful picture.

-How everything here breathes silence and peace of mind!" he murmured with a sigh.

Then he moved forward at a quick pace and knocked gently on a small door.

-Come in! - answered in a sonorous voice.

Wolfram opened the door and entered the room, which was even more luxuriously appointed than the previous ones. The walls were covered with carved dark oak and the windows were draped with heavy velvet curtains. In the background, a wide curtain covered the entrance to the adjoining room. In the center was a table covered with scrolls and astronomical instruments, and beside it, in a high-backed chair, sat a young man, thin and pale, dressed in robes of the Templars[4]. Leaning against the table, was a tall gentleman in a long, wide suit. His long hair and beard were white as snow, but his large blue eyes reflected a freshness in his gaze. The beautiful features of his face showed a majestic and indescribable peace.

Upon seeing Wolfram, he quickly went to meet him and embraced him lovingly.

- Welcome, my son! What a happy day I am having today. My two favorite disciples are under my roof again, said the elder, with a friendly smile.

Wolfram shook his head in surprise and observed:

- So, you ended up disguised as the Templars? That means it's all over for you! Have you said goodbye to life?

- Yes, I took the vows! But why do you say that means saying goodbye to life? Do you find worldly life so good, to the point of complaining about it? How much happiness has it brought you, for example? - replied the Templar, and a sad smile spread across his suffering and bitter face.

Wolfram lifted his wig proudly.

- Not much! But it does not matter. In any case, I prefer this life to that of a monk.

- My children, stop arguing about the pleasures of life," interrupted the old man with a smile, "life is a traitor that promises much and offers nothing; in the end it destroys everything we have in us and around us, if we do not know how to get out from it in time, what it cannot take from us: knowledge and wise submission. Although I do not approve of Ervin's decision, I would be happy to keep him here, but...he does not have the researcher's vein. Let's eat now! Wolfram is probably hungry. Since he is neither an old

---

[4] The Templars - It was founded in 1119 in Jerusalem by Hugues de Payns, they were originally called the "Poor Knights of Christ" and were destined to guard the Holy Land (Palestine). Baldwin II, King of Jerusalem, installed the Knights in a palace next to the ancient Temple of Solomon, from which came the new name.

bookseller, like me, nor a monk, like you, then there is no need to make him fast.

The visitors laughed and followed the elder to the dining hall where a simple but well-served table awaited them. Cheerful and interesting conversation enlivened the meal, to which Wolfram did the honors. Afterwards, the three of them went out into a small, shady garden. As the sun began to decline over the horizon, the old host stood up.

- Are you leaving Uncle Conrad? - asked Ervin, taking him by the hand.

- Yes, I have some work to do. In the meantime, my children keep talking! It has been a long time since you have seen each other, and of course you have a lot to tell each other.

Baron Conrad von-Vart was the last descendant of a line of rich and noble feudal knights. Like his ancestors, he started out as a brave warrior; but after he was seriously injured in a tournament, he was doomed to solitude for a long time.

At that time, his only sister married an Italian courtier and he, still weak and not recovered from his injury, accompanied them to Venice. There, he met an old scientist who not only cured him but made him interested in his strange and mysterious science to such an extent that the Baron became his disciple and devoted himself entirely to his studies. He then began to live alternately between Venice and the small castle where we now find him, devoting his time to science and dodging people.

When they were alone, the friends kept silent, and each of them immersed themself in their own thoughts. Wolfram was the first to break the monotony. He took a sip of wine, put the goblet away and, leaning his elbow on the table, stared for a moment at the pale, tired face of his friend, whose sad gaze seemed lost. Then he put his hand on his shoulder and said:

- Ervin, tell me, wasn't your entrance into the Order triggered by the death of your wife? What did Paola die of? She was so young and healthy!

[17]

The Templar shuddered and straightened up.

- What did Paola die of? Ah! I wish I knew! - he replied with a heavy sigh. - Some unknown disease, which had no treatment, destroyed her in a few months; she melted like wax in the sun, and nothing could reveal the cause of her illness. I confess that at first, I suspected that my stepmother Ortrude had poisoned her. But since she had never been near Paola, I dismissed this possibility, especially since Ortruda, after such a misfortune, treated me with the most respectful condolences. So, I thought that Paola might have been the victim of some sorcery. She always complained that a dark haze enveloped her, suffocating her, and sucking the energy out of her. As death approached, she said, the haze became thicker and blacker.

- But who would cast a spell against such a lovely creature? - Wolfram remarked.

- Paola liked to be nice and many women hated her. Today, more than ever, I am convinced that it was Ortruda herself, and nobody else, who killed Paola with poison or sorcery. This is because a few months after my wife's death, she confessed that she was very much in love with me. Can you understand the horror I felt at this confession that turned my suspicions into certainty? The despicable woman tried to convince me to move into her house with Eliza. But after such a confession, I could not stay a single day in her house, so I left that afternoon. On the way, my daughter caught a cold and I also felt so bad that I had to take shelter in the monastery of St. Bridget. Now imagine my amazement when I realized that Mother Vilfrida, the abbess of the monastery, was Hildegarda!

- I guess! It must have been "terrible" to see the girlfriend you cheated on! - said the knight with a sad smile.

The Templar blushed.

- You are incorrigible! Hildegarda abandoned earthly sensations long ago and we both consecrated ourselves to God.

- How can I doubt "your holiness"? - Wolfram interrupted, laughing. - I just think that now Mother Vilfrida will sing her psalms more peacefully, knowing that handsome Ervin is serving the Lord and not the beautiful ladies. But go on!

- When I realized she was my former fiancée, I was so embarrassed that I wanted to leave immediately, but she stopped me and said - By withdrawing from the world, I also abandoned all the anger and affronts of the past. Stay gentleman! You look sick! I will take care of your daughter as if she were my own. May God accept this dedication as proof that I humbly submit to his Will.

- I was deeply touched, and that same night I fell sick. It seemed that Ortruda's poisonous breath had hit us: my daughter Eliza and I were on the verge of death. Father Romualdo's art and the nuns' care saved us.

- During my convalescence, I once managed to be alone with Hildegarda. I was able to say a few words to her about the past and asked her to forgive me for my betrayal. She smiled sadly and replied, "You did well! I would always rather lose you than share your heart with someone else. I confess that there were moments when neither the vows nor this habit could bring me inner peace, preventing me from praying. But now I have overcome my earthly feelings and I see you only as a brother. So, Ervin, if you can be happy with another wife, I will pray without any resentment for your happiness."

I was deeply embarrassed and touched by that magnanimous self-sacrifice. From that day on, a very different feeling awakened in me than the one I had for Paola. I realized that by giving up Hildegarda, I had given up the true and quiet happiness that only a loving and faithful wife can give to a husband until death.

Ervin fell silent and bowed his head sadly.

- Now I understand why you became a Templar; you were unhappy with Paola - Wolfram said.

- Yes, I decided to consecrate myself to God and Hildegarda too. My four years of marriage passed like an intoxicating and feverish dream. Paola allowed herself to be admired: she saw my love as a deserved gift to her beauty. Possessive and capricious, she was jealous of any woman I treated kindly. Then she would immediately begin to punish me with her typically Italian rage, turning her attention to the most beautiful admirers, of whom she always had a large number. You yourself knew the charm she had over them all. So, she created a hell of jealousy for me. Eliza inherited her beauty. She has the same elegance, the same eyes full of warmth and ardor. She has gotten only a more serious, tranquil face, and an air of sadness, which her mother never showed.

- That means I will have a lovely daughter-in-law - Wolfram said, laughing.

- So, if you agree with my proposal to unite our children, we can perform the wedding without further delay. Five-year-old Eliza and eleven-year-old Raymond will make a lovely couple.

- It has been a long time since I have seen your son! Does he look like you?

- He will not be as handsome as me, because he looks like his mother - Wolfram replied with a grimace.

- In any case, he will be a beautiful boy!

- I will be happy knowing that Eliza is under the guardianship of my best friend and that her future is secure. It would be difficult for me to leave her with Hildegarda because I am deeply guilty before her. Besides, I would not want my daughter to be drawn into monastic life. I confess, in all honesty, that I do not like your wife very much, although I know that she is kind and will not neglect the child as perhaps Ortruda would have done. You too, Wolfram, seem tired to me. It seems that your life with a woman who does not understand you is not easy at all.

Wolfram's face turned grim, and he ran his hand through his full, black hair.

- Yes, my family life is very difficult. Anna loves me and is jealous of me, and I can barely stand the repulsion she provokes in me. I got married on my father's orders; I respect her as the mother of my only child, but my heart has never beaten strongly for her. Anna does not forgive me for this and tries to keep Raymond's heart away from me, over which she has great influence. Also, to make me angry, she is friends with all the people who are unpleasant to me. She has even become friends with her stepmother Ortruda, whom I have always instinctively hated, and also with her son Guntram, who has that blessed face and those snake eyes. But enough about that! So, when are you leaving and where?

- First, I go to Maine[5] and from there probably to Cyprus[6] together with my prior who takes instructions to the Master, thanks to whom I was accepted in the Order. Tomorrow, I will give you a letter for Hildegarda, reporting on Eliza's marriage.

The next morning, after bidding a fond farewell to their old friend, the knights set off and they would travel together to the nearest village.

---

[5] Maine - Former province in northwestern France and south of Normandy. It passed definitively to the French crown in 1548 with the death of the Duke of Alencon. Le Mans, its capital, is an important industrial and commercial center.

[6] Cyprus - Island located in the eastern Mediterranean Sea, 60 km south of Turkey and 100 km west of Syria. Nowadays, Republic of Cyprus, whose capital is Nicosia.

Chapter 2

Wolfram von- Reifenstein and Erin von- Finsterbach were neighbors and childhood friends. Even though they had very different personalities, they were inseparable. One was courageous, impetuous, and bold; the other was dreamy, timid, and indecisive. One completed the other one. Both were happy when circumstances brought them together for a few years under the same roof. Ervin was fifteen when his father married a sixteen-year-old girl for the second time, with whom he had fallen passionately in love and who dominated him completely.

From the first days of the marriage, frequent confrontations between stepmother and stepson began to occur. Old Finsterbach, tired of the constant fighting, gladly accepted his cousin Conrad Vart's proposal to take over Ervin's education. The boy also felt very comfortable in the scientist's quiet residence. By chance, a few months later he was joined by his friend Wolfram. At that time, the boy's father, fulfilling an old promise, went on a pilgrimage to the Holy Land and during his absence also entrusted his son to Conrad Vart, an old friend, and comrade-in-arms.

Wolfram, whose mother had died long ago, and Ervin, who had become a stranger in his father's house because of his stepmother's hostility and the birth of his brother, became attached to the scientist who, in turn, reciprocated them in the same way. The boys' minds developed under Conrad's guidance. They received an education far superior than the one given to most of the noble youth of the time.

The Baron's ostensible tranquility acted beneficially on Wolfram's explosive nature, while Ervin's docile soul was fortified by contact with von-Vart's energetic and rigid character. The return of Count Reifenstein separated the friends once again. Wolfram then returned to his father's home, who was feeling ill. A year later the Count married his twenty-year-old son to a wealthy widow of good family who was a mother of a seven-year-old boy.

Ervin continued to live in the Baron's house and accompanied him to Venice. There he met Paola Aldini, whom he married and lived in Italy until his father's death forced him to return to his homeland.

When they reached the nearest village, they became apart, and Wolfram then went on his way alone, but his face grew darker and darker as he got closer to home. The usual disgust he felt whenever he returned to the castle was mixed with dissatisfaction at having to endure his wife's inevitable scene when she learned of the decision about his son's marriage without her approval. Moreover, the bride would be hateful to her, since she was preparing as a wife to her son, a little orphan girl educated in the castle itself, named Margarita Raments, the daughter of one of her friends who, upon her death, had entrusted her with the girl she was very fond of.

Countess Anna always hated Ervin because Wolfram had so much affection for him. She was jealous of any smile or kind word her husband said to another human being. She was jealous even of her own son and felt that he was stealing her husband's love. With such contradictory feelings, she either pampered or tyrannized the boy, depending on her mood at the time.

Countess Reifenstein was ugly, eight years older than her husband, and she knew that he simply put up with her. She was dying of passion for the charming man whose name she bore. She watched him with a sick jealousy and took revenge for his indifference, demeaning everything that was dear to him. She had a particular hatred for Paola, the beautiful Italian woman, and called her "the adventuress who caught the idiot Finsterbach in her net".

The countess Anna sought in religion for solace for her marital unhappiness and the way she fawned over Father Gregory, her chaplain and confessor, was repulsive to Wolfram.

Lunchtime was approaching when the drawbridge lowered in front of the castle owner. With a heavy sigh, Wolfram entered the house, where he felt like a stranger and where only feelings such as family duty and love for his son took him.

The family was gathered in the small room attached to the dining hall when the sound of the horn announced the lord's return. The countess put aside her embroidery and slowly walked out to meet her husband. The blush on her cheeks revealed her emotion. She was a tall woman, strong, but slender, and without any grace or delicacy. Her face was pale; her dark eyes showed pride and seriousness, while her full lips, behind which shone white teeth, gave her physiognomy a sensual and cruel expression.

The chaplain interrupted the reading of his breviary and also went to the door, while the children ran into the vestibule and jumped on the Count, who kissed his son, a handsome, strong boy with big dark eyes, and then Greta (as Margarita Raments was called), a little girl of ten years old, white, ruddy, and chubby, with full blond hair.

The wife received the Count by the entrance of the dining hall. Shadowy and serious, like a Byzantine icon, she held out her hand, which her husband kissed.

A little later, everyone sat down at the table. Recounting the details of his trip to the Baron's house, Wolfram said that in two days he would be traveling again and that he intended to take Raymond with him. Then he asked them to prepare everything that was necessary for the child.

The countess was extremely intrigued by the sudden trip and thought that the decision had been prompted by her husband's visit to the "old sorcerer," as he called Baron Vart. But she did not dare to question him directly and did not want to discuss her husband's true desire to take the child with him. At the end of dinner, Wolfram sat by the window and watched the children play.

Raymond knew that his mother was preparing Greta to be his wife and eventually got used to the idea. His childish flirtation with the supposed bride elicited a mischievous smile from the Count.

"You will soon, soon have your first disappointment, my poor boy," he thought, "but you will only gain by this change! If, at eleven years old, you are so enchanted by this fat blonde, then at twenty you will prefer the elegant and graceful Eliza. You would not be my son if you had no taste for beauty and could not tell the rose from the cabbage!"

On the appointed day, Wolfram traveled with his son, accompanied only by a page, a stableman, and two armed men. The group stayed overnight at an inn, and on the second day, after lunch, they left the main road and took a side road that led straight to the monastery.

Raymond did not dare inquire of the knight about the reason for that trip, whose unexpected amusement, unlike his monotonous life in the castle, excited him a lot. So, he kept chattering to the father he adored. But when the Count became silent and thoughtful, the boy, frightened, followed beside him also silent. Upon seeing the monastery, Raymond could not bear it and asked:

- Dad, what is the name of that monastery? I have never seen it before. Why are we going there?

- It is the monastery of Saint Bridget. We are going to visit Abbess Vilfrida. You, Raymond, will kiss her hand and treat her with respect. She is a holy woman, despite her youth and beauty! I hope you will be obedient and do everything she tells you to do.

Raymond raised his head and gave his father a worried and suspicious look. The tone in which the Count spoke those last words was well known to him: it meant the unwavering "I want", which his father imposed on the countess in her fights, and against which there was no use for resistance or tears. But Raymond also knew that obeying his father against his mother's will foreshadow very unpleasant consequences in the form of undeserved

[25]

punishment, dissatisfaction, and resentment on the part of his mother. The countess, irritated with life and people, rarely left the castle, and had full authority over the boy during the frequent absences of the father, who spent whole weeks at the Court of the Count of Tyrol, or hunting, or at the house of his friend.

All these thoughts were reflected so clearly on the boy's expressive face that Wolfram, who was watching him, laughed happily.

- Fear not! Your mother will not punish you for following my orders. I will explain everything to her.

Raymond turned red when he realized his father had read his thoughts. Then he recovered his good humor.

Several times he confessed to his father how unfairly he was treated in his absence; but of course, he told him this, under the condition of great secrecy so as not to attract a new storm to himself. Each time this happened, his father did not betray him, and even rewarded him for the injustice by taking him hunting with him, or to one of his friends' houses, where he met boys of the same age, so he could rest easy; it did not matter what he demanded of him.

As for Wolfram, he was soberly thoughtful. He was seized by a bitter feeling, brought on by his own married life. The deaf and constant fighting with his hateful wife and the harm this was causing his only son drove the Count to despair. Then, his impetuous character pushed him into various sprees, amorous adventures, and madness with which he tried to silence the suffering and emptiness in his heart. Sometimes he was overcome by a dark state of mind, during which he avoided people, locked himself away in a secluded castle pavilion, or hunted alone in the farthest corners of the mountains.

An hour later, they finally arrived at the monastery and were led to the visitors' room. The carved oak walls and dark curtains gave the room a somber impression. Raymond, who was examining everything with curiosity, saw his father take a small box out of his shirt pocket and place it on the table, and thought he was going to give the abbess a present, but had no time to ask, because at that moment Vilfrida entered, accompanied by two nuns who stood respectfully by the door.

Count Wolfram and the mother had known each other since the days when the beautiful Hildegarda reigned supreme in tournaments, and the promise that had bound her from childhood to Ervin Finsterbach provoked pity and jealousy among the most noble knights.

The first meeting after so many years and, moreover, in such a situation, thrilled them both. Tears clouded the abbess' beautiful blue eyes when the Count kissed her hand and handed her the letter from her former fiancé.

After reading the correspondence, Mother Vilfrida called one of the nuns and gave her an order. Then, after half-voiced confabulation, she asked Raymond to come closer. Then, he bowed to the abbess, as his father had taught him, and stood timidly in the corner. But the extraordinary kindness that lit up the nun's face made him regain his self-control. A mischievous smile passed across his rosy lips as Mother Vilfrida said:

- Your son is very handsome, Mr. Wolfram, but... - she smiled - is he less dangerous than you?

The Count laughed, but his attention was drawn by the nun arriving and carrying a little girl in a white dress. Quickly approaching the little girl, the Count took her in his arms and covered her with kisses.

At first, she was startled; but that impression soon passed. And, wrapping her little arms around the count's neck, the girl confidently pressed her velvety cheek against the bearded face of her new friend. She was a charming child, extraordinarily delicate, with big blue eyes and hair as full and black as a raven's wing. The Count looked at her with admiration.

- She will be prettier than Paola and has another character; you can see it in her eyes! Forgive me for reminding you of that - Wolfram added, realizing in time what he had already commented.

- I no longer have any sorrow for the memory of Ervin's wife," replied the abbess.

- But, Count, you are right! This girl has got a personality. She knows what she wants, and sometimes her answers are incredible.

Raymond watched this scene with curiosity. He even felt jealous seeing his father lovingly kissing the little stranger. Then his attention was attracted by the arrival of an old priest accompanied by a nun, a squire, and a page.

- Come closer Raymond! - said the Count. This is little Eliza, daughter of my friend, the Knight Finsterbach. She is your fiancée and we have come here to perform your engagement.

The boy was so stunned by these words that he was speechless, and let himself be led, without reacting to a large crucifix hanging on the wall, near which the priest stood.

Wolfram put the two children in front of him and said:

- Before Our Lord Jesus Christ and in the presence of Venerable Father Romualdo, Mother Abbess, Sister Treasurer, and everyone else here present, I am performing the engagement of my son Raymond Reifenstein to Elizabeth Finsterbach and assume the obligation to marry them within six weeks.

During this speech, the boy's cheeks turned red. When his father wanted to put the ring he took from the box on his finger, the boy backed away and quickly hid his hands behind his back. The Count frowned and gave his son a look that he had never seen before. Then he took Raymond's hand, placed the ring on his finger, and, handing him the other ring, added sternly:

- Put the ring on your fiancée's finger now! This is my will, do you understand?

Raymond, intimidated, put the ring on Eliza's finger, who looked in awe at the strange boy who was twice her size.

- Now, kiss her! - ordered the Count.

The children obeyed without question, and the chaplain blessed them. Suddenly Eliza ripped her hand from Raymond's and threw herself into the arms of the abbess, who looked on sadly at the scene.

- The main thing is done - the Count remarked cheerfully.

- Raymond and Eliza are engaged to be married. In six weeks, I will come to fetch the future Countess Reifenstein and officially take her to the castle. Now, most worthy Mother Vilfrida, I would be most grateful if you would invite us for a meal.

- You are incorrigible, Wolfram! - said the abbess, smiling. But, come with me! The meal awaits us. I only apologize for not being as refined as I would like to offer an old friend.

Everyone went to the abbey refectory, where a bountiful table awaited them, around which Mother Vilfrida, the priest, the Count, and the children were seated. The conversation was very lively, for Wolfram had inexhaustible subjects about the news of the Court and the surrounding area. His stories were intelligent and cheerful and captivated his listeners, except for Eliza who, tired, fell asleep before the end of the meal, and the nanny had to take her away, while Raymond, worried and sulky, forgot the food, wrapped up in his unpleasant thoughts.

The unexpected engagement to a stranger, small and veiled in comparison to Greta, offended and frightened him. He counted himself almost a knight, and it was embarrassing to him to see that his future wife had fallen asleep at the table and needed to be taken to bed by a nanny. What would he say to his mother, and especially Greta, who was offended by any pleasant words he directed at her little friends? He could soften the countess, claiming he could obey his father; but he would grieve with his former fiancée. When the meal was over, the Count talked a little more with the abbess, said goodbye, and left with his son.

Gloomy and worried, Raymond stood silently beside his father. The Count, who was watching his son, and apparently amused by his dissatisfaction, was the first to break the silence:

[29]

- Well, my boy? Now you know why we went to St. Bridget Monastery? You are growing and it is time to prepare for your future.

Raymond's inner irritation spilled over:

- Don't laugh at me, Dad! - he exclaimed, in an intermittent voice. There is nothing funny about getting me engaged to a pale, thin, and disgusting girl who can barely reach my elbow. I do not want her! Greta is much prettier. With her I can talk and play. But this one does not understand anything and still needs a nanny...

The tears stopped him from continuing.

The Count bit his whiskers and a wry smile passed his lips.

- Calm down, my son! If you don't like your fiancée now, that does not mean anything. At eleven years old, you will forget a good cheese sandwich for the beautiful Greta. But wait until you are twenty! You will gladly trade a hundred cheese sandwiches together with Greta for Eliza Finsterbach. Trust me and my taste. However, now – the Count put his hand on his son's shoulder and looked at him decisively, - you will see for yourself that it is not pleasant to be the center of a brilliant ceremony. I will have the silver shirt you have always wanted made for the wedding. Don't be afraid of your mother if she makes any noise when we tell her the news, because I will take all the blame!

The prospect of winning a sweater and especially the Count's last words made Raymond's despair disappear as if by magic. His little face could not seem to clear up, and he started asking his father about the details of the ceremony in which he would play the main role.

When our travelers arrived at the castle the next day, the countess, who was waiting impatiently for them, welcomed them into the foyer along with the father and Greta.

The Count kissed his wife with the usual cool friendliness that characterized their relationship. Then he spoke loud enough to be heard by the squires, knights and servants who had gathered to welcome their lord.

[30]

- We have come back very well, and we bring you good news: at St. Bridget's monastery I have arranged the engagement of our son Raymond to my friend's daughter, the knight Finsterbach. Father Gregory, you cannot imagine how happy I am about this brilliant and noble union! I have scheduled the wedding for six weeks from now. So, I decided to throw a big party for our vassals and the servants.

Listening to her husband, the countess turned green with rage; her lips moved tremblingly, but no sound escaped from her blocked throat. Her tall, strong figure staggered, almost losing her balance; fury practically suffocated her. Wolfram had dared to perform his son's engagement behind her back and look who it was with! With the daughter of the detestable Italian woman, who turned all men's heads, and of Finsterbach, whom the countess also detested.

- Anna, take my hand and let's go to my chambers. We must discuss this good news – said the Count, looking subtly into the countess' misty eyes. The joy that fills your mother's heart has touched you too much.

Unable to retort to the teasing, as her heart wanted to burst under the narrow bodice, the countess took her husband by the arm and began to climb with him the staircase leading to his chambers.

Raymond followed them quietly and gloomily, but margarita, dumbfounded and red, grabbed him by the sleeve.

- Tell me, what did your father say? Does he intend to throw a party on the occasion of our wedding?

Raymond stopped on the platform and, pulling away his former fiancée hand, replied with the solemnity befitting the moment:

- First of all, do not tear my shirt sleeve! It is certain that my marriage will be celebrated, but not with you. Did you not happen to hear that I got engaged to Eliza Finsterbach? Look, here is the ring.

With these words, he placed in front of Greta's nose the hand in which the ring with an emerald shone.

- Ah, what a beautiful ring! - she exclaimed, but almost immediately realizing the situation, she continued:

- What? Did you really dare to get engaged to the knight Finsterbach daughter, despite our agreement?

Of course, I did! Didn't you notice how angry my mom was when she heard that Dad and I had decided this? My engagement to Eliza was blessed by the monastery chaplain. My father will have a silver sweater made for me for the wedding. But you can also dress up and enjoy the delicious dishes they will prepare for that day.

But Greta no longer listened to the jeers. The idea of playing a secondary role in the ceremony in which she felt she was entitled to take first place excited her indignation.

- Oh, you wicked traitor! - she shouted, falling on top of Raymond, and giving him a loud slap, followed by a punch.

That unexpected offense to his masculine dignity, the boy responded no less forcefully and grabbed Greta by the thick braids. Cussing rained down and the fight probably would not have ended so quickly had it not been for the interference of the countess's maid and the old squire, who were watching Raymond, and separated the children.

While the agitated understandings between the former bride and groom were taking place, the Count took his wife to his office, a long, vaulted-ceilinged room adorned with expensive weapons; the tall, narrow windows were fully open at that hour. Wolfram threw himself into the high-backed chair, which was near the window and the table, and invited the countess to sit down, but the countess could no longer contain herself, and the anger that had been smothering her finally overflowed. Pushing the chair back, she exclaimed in a broken voice:

- By what right did you dare to arrange the engagement of my son with the daughter of that Italian adventuress and even do it behind my back? Or do you imagine that I will agree with that? Never! I will throw myself between the altar and my son and stop this hateful marriage. My son's happiness and his future belong to me. His wife will be Margarita! I will be able to defend my maternal dignity, which you repress by openly mocking me in front of the servants.

Leaning back on the table and looking at the panorama of the surroundings that could be seen from the window, the Count listened indifferently to the countess' outburst. Her last words made him turn around and observe coldly:

- You talk about your son as if I had no part in it. Not only do you forget that my rights over him outweigh yours, but you dare to call a woman of noble family, the wife of my best friend, an adventurer. You hate her as you hate everything that is young, alive, and beautiful. I naturally don't intend to change your tastes, but I forbid you to intervene in my decisions. I know well your method of arranging your son's happiness: you sneakily tyrannize him and set him against me. I have left the heir to my name under your evil influence for too long! However, don't forget that my patience has limits. Raymond's marriage to Eliza is definitely decided, and if you dare to go against my wishes or show your anger at the wedding party, you will regret it!

The countess suffered a nervous breakdown and collapsed helplessly in the chair. But since Wolfram did not do anything about it, she stood up suddenly and started pacing the room like a tiger in a cage, covering her husband with curses and threats.

The Count listened to her for some time without answering anything. But you could sense his inner emotion by the nervous curling of his beard; suddenly, a dark blush covered the Count's face. He jumped up from his chair and punched the table.

- Shut up, you worthless woman! Stop torturing me. Enough of this hell for me! If our son's wedding is so hateful to you, then I will celebrate it without you. Tomorrow I will leave tomorrow with Raymond and go live with the two children on another property of mine, so you will never see us again. Then you

[33]

can whine about how you drove me away with your anger, but for me, this separation will be a liberation.

The Count turned his back on his wife and, breathing heavily, leaned on the table.

Countess Anna stood on the spot and her red face paled immediately. Her gaze fixed on her husband denoted anger, fear, and passion. She then instinctively realized that she had overstepped the mark and that the Count could really use this opportunity to get rid of her.

The thought of losing forever the man she had worshiped with insistent and wild passion and loved in her own way made the countess fall into the other extreme. Running to her husband, she fell to her knees and took him by the hand.

- Forgive me Wolfram! Stay here! - she begged - I will die if you abandon me and take my son. See how I am suffering! Is my unhappiness still not enough? Haven't you torn my heart apart with your indifference and coldness?

The countess's unexpected contact made Wolfram shudder and try to free his hand, but he was so good and magnanimous that Anna's rebuke stirred his conscience. In fact, he was always harsh and cold with the wife he was repulsed by. Perhaps she could be quite different if he tried to awaken the good feelings hidden in her soul.

Turning to the Countess, who was still on her knees and covered in tears, he said in a tired voice:

- Anna, get up and let's end this discussion; it is up to you whether I stay here. You must respect my decisions. I gave Ervin my word. Marriage is definitely decided and that is the end of it! I did not mean to be cruel, but you have made me angry. Now that is enough! Let's make peace and discuss our son's marriage calmly.

- All right, all right! Whatever you want, just do not leave me! - stammered the countess, embracing her husband and pressing him to her breast.

Wolfram offered no resistance. Only his lips trembled nervously, as the arms that wrapped him seemed like iron chains choking him and preventing his path to freedom and the sun.

He had married the young widow Anna, who even then was completely indifferent, submitting to his father's tyrannical will. Because of his carefree character, he agreed to the marriage without imagining the consequences of such an obligation. As for Anna, she accepted the marriage doubly happy, because she had gotten rid of her old husband thanks to his death, and almost immediately she had found another young husband, the attractive Count Reifenstein, whom she had adored from the moment she met him at a tournament.

Forcing his own nature, Wolfram leaned toward his wife and lightly brushed his lips against her forehead. Then, pulling her away, he said in a low voice:

- Calm down Anna! Try to avoid these agitated scenes, which force me to say unpleasant things to you. As for our son's marriage, it was instilled in me by circumstances. Ervin, who has entered the Templars, is leaving the country, and has entrusted his daughter to my care as proof of his friendship. He could not leave the girl with Ortruda. You know her, and despite the good relations between you, you yourself condemn her way of life. By uniting our children, I reassure Ervin and best secure the future of Eliza and our Raymond. Rest assured that this choice will bring us happiness, the little girl is beautiful, and in time will become a woman as intelligent and charming as her mother. I know you did not like Paola, even if you have no reason to. But you cannot be jealous of a dead woman. Besides, she was Finsterbach's wife, and for me that is enough. No criminal feeling ever clouded his friendship with me. Well, now that I have explained to you what motivated me to make such a decision, I hope you will give up your prejudices and be a real mother to little Eliza. In six weeks, we will officially hold their wedding. And we will never again have scenes like the one we had here.

The countess answered nothing. Grabbing her husband's head, she kissed him impetuously and then left the room almost running.

Being left alone, Wolfram threw himself into the chair and clasped his head with his hands.

- This hell has been going on for twelve years without any hope of change! - he murmured with despair. Fate has been good to her, getting rid of the old Baron for her, but it has shown no mercy to me. If I am doomed to drag this wife, who I do not love, to the end of my days, then I had better throw myself out of this window!

Immersed in his own dark thoughts, he did not notice the small door opening and his favorite stableman appearing in it, who looked at the Count with indescribable sensitivity and pity. He was a tall, strong man of about forty, his pleasant face exuded kindness and intelligence. His name was Lucien, son of the old forester. The late Count Reifenstein had taken him as a servant to his son Wolfram, who was about ten years old at the time. Since then, they have never been separated.

Lucien adored his lord; he was faithful to him like a dog, shared with him the likes and even the dislike of the countess. He served the Count with proven fidelity both in war and in love affairs. Only an accidental sprained foot prevented him from accompanying Wolfram to the monastery and Baron Vart's house.

The slight noise caught the Count's attention. Wolfram raised his head and, recognizing his faithful servant, smiled, and held out his hand.

- Is that you, my friend? What is up? How is the sick foot? - he asked.

- Ah, that damned foot! I have just learned that I will not be able to attend to Sir Raymond's engagement. Now, however, I am completely cured and happy to be able to accompany you on hunts in the mountains, where the air is so clean and where one could forget everything by chasing the game.

[36]

Wolfram stared at him, amazed at the special intonation of those words. But when he met the intelligent and mischievous gaze of the stableman, his face lit up in a smile. Then he stood up, tapped Lucien on the shoulder and said cheerfully:

- You are right, my faithful friend! A hunt will only do me good and dispel the sadness that has taken hold of me in this heavy and suffocating castle atmosphere. Prepare everything, we will leave at dawn.

At night, during dinner, the Count informed his wife that the next day he would be going away for a few days to hunt in the mountains.

Upon hearing of the unexpected departure, Countess Anna was taciturn, but in view of the recent scene, she refrained from any reproaches. She felt a great hatred for those distant and prolonged hunts, which had always seemed suspicious to her, but whose secret she had never discovered, because she could get nothing out of the wretched Lucien.

Chapter 3

The first rays of sunlight were barely illuminating the horizon when Wolfram mounted his horse and left the castle at a gallop accompanied by Lucien. As they rode away from home, his face cleared, and he was happy. The next day, with the coming of night, they penetrated a dense forest. Wolfram took a full breath and impatiently spurred his tired mount.

An hour later, the two riders left the shade of tall trees and stopped for a moment, admiring the surprising view illuminated by the silvery blue light of the moon. A large lake lay in front of them, surrounded by high hills covered with dense vegetation, and a fresh, aromatic wind was blowing on their faces. On a small islet was an inviting white building that looked as much like a castle as an Italian villa. Next to the quadrangular tower, covered in the dark green of Ivy, was a building with an open terrace, from which a staircase descended to the water's edge, adorned at the foot by two stone lions. Silence and peace reigned in that enchanting corner:

- We are not expected – said Wolfram. Then he took the hunting horn[7] and blew a signal. A few minutes later, from behind the island a boat appeared and headed in the direction of the newcomers.

- It is Ludovico! - said the knight, getting off his horse and handing the reins to the stableman.

- Lucien, you will have to wait a bit.

The rower was a middle-aged man, but still strong, of the purely Italian type. He greeted the rider, waving his red beret at

---

[7] Hunting horn - A rudimentary horn, bugle of pastoral use.

him. Without stopping to row towards the terrace, he cheerfully answered the impatient questions of Wolfram.

- Yes, yes Sir! Madame Giovanna is well. Her sadness and longing will disappear as soon as you arrive. There she is! - he added, pointing to the woman who appeared on the terrace staircase.

She was a tall and elegant young woman, with perfect classical features, big shining dark eyes, and magnificent golden hair, immortalized by Titian[8].

Beautiful as a dream in her dress of light blue brocade and a small hat embroidered with pearls, she stood on the last step of the staircase, waving her veil and greeting the knight with a smile.

The impatient Wolfram, in one bold leap, overcame the distance that separated the boat from the shore and silenced with a kiss the scream of terror that escaped the young woman.

- You careless man! You could have fallen into the water.

- So what? It would be impossible to fall into the water before embracing you! Your image gives me wings! - replied the Count, smiling.

Then he grabbed her by the waist, and they quickly went up to the terrace.

At the bottom of the terrace, in the benign shade of the bushes and trees, there was a bench where they sat. Giovanna took the cap off the Count's head, lifted with her thin fingers the black locks from his forehead, looking at him lovingly.

- You have suffered, my dear! I see a wrinkle which, more than words, tells me that you were tortured there, where you are chained by law and duty, but not by heart.

Wolfram sighed.

---

[8] Titian (1487-1576) - Titian Vecellio, the greatest and most successful painter of the Venetian school. His patrons were the Pope and the kings of France.

- I always suffer away from you, Giovanna, and the idea of not being able to call you mine in front of the whole world has cost me many sleepless nights. Oh, there are moments when I hate to death that wicked creature who takes your place.

The young woman shook his hand.

- Put those bad thoughts away! - she said with a smile. As long as you are with me, I forbid you to think about that woman. I don't envy her for having your name and your noble title. I only want to possess exclusively your heart that belongs to me, doesn't it?

You are my good angel!

- Naturally! Now I'm going to remove that horrible wrinkle with a kiss. I don't want you to grow old and be covered with wrinkles, my Wolfram. I like everything about you, except that barbaric name of yours. But wouldn't you like something to drink?

- A glass of wine served by those pretty little white hands wouldn't go amiss! But first I would like to dust myself off from my trip, so I don't look barbaric in both name and appearance.

The young woman smiled. Then the knight went to his quarters, while Giovanna went to a small dining room, whose decoration was a mixture of Italian luxury and 13th century European simplicity. Thus, on an old solid black oak sideboard shone antique-style silverware along with Venetian crystals, the joy of the antique dealers of that time. The furniture in the other rooms also matched this strange mixture of styles.

On the hostess's orders, an old servant quickly began to prepare the table for dinner, which was soon full of plates and jugs of old wine. Giovanna herself placed a bouquet of flowers in the crystal vase.

Giovanna Faleri was the daughter of a wealthy Venetian merchant who died a few years ago. Of all Giovanni Batista's numerous offspring, only left Fulvio, the eldest son, and the youngest, Giovanna, whose birth cost her mother her life. The old man spoiled and idolized the youngest and, on his deathbed, left

[40]

her, besides her mother's inheritance, a large fortune, which would reward her with her independence.

Fulvio was absent when Giovanni Faleri died: he had traveled to Levant[9] on business. Until his return, his sister stayed at the home of her friend Paola, married to the knight Finsterbach. Wolfram, while visiting his friend Ervin and his master and tutor Baron Vart, met the siblings Fulvio and Giovanna.

Count Reifenstein was overshadowed by the incomparable beauty of the young Venetian girl, who at the time was only fifteen years old. The impression he himself made on the girl was no less. Giovanna knew that Wolfram was married. He himself was aware that he was engaged and tried to fight against that passion that dominated him.

He even left Venice. But such an intention seemed like a drunken promise, that is, it came to nothing. After a few months, overcome and blinded by passion, Wolfram returned to Venice and his first meeting with Giovanna decided their fate.

Despite her indomitable pride, the fiery Italian was so much in love that she decided to run away with her lover and settle somewhere near him so she could see him without arousing suspicion. Two of Giovanna's closest people opposed this decision: one of them was her uncle Conrad Vart, who said that she sinned doubly by accepting the love of a married man and getting in the way of his married life under his wife's nose.

The brother, who had returned from a trip at the time, was outraged by his sister's dishonor and only Conrad's interference prevented his duel with Wolfram. Fulvio Faleri was twenty-five years old at the time. He was severe, cold, and indifferent to the women he attracted by his rare beauty and repelled by his cold discretion. Ever since he was a child, he showed great interest in his uncle's studies and devoted himself to them.

---

[9] Levant – Generic name given to the countries situated on the eastern shore of the Mediterranean Sea, from Egypt to Turkey.

The divisions made in France's rule over Syria and Lebanon were also called Levant states, and the term is still sometimes applied to these two nations.

On his last trip he brought with him an old Indian man with extraordinary knowledge. The man's company and lessons absorbed him so much that at first, he did not notice what was happening to his sister. But her intention to leave eventually woke him up. There was an agitated scene, during which Fulvio severely criticized his sister for the shame with which she covered their name. He even declared that if she left the paternal home to publicly become Count Reifenstein's mistress, he would disown her forever, but Giovanna was that kind of person that any opposition made her even more unshakable.

- You condemn me because your heart is dead, and you love no one or nothing - she answered her brother with contempt.

True to her own decision, she left and settled in the small castle near the lake where we found her.

Giovanna had been living in that retreat for three years now, without seeing or receiving anyone, content with the happiness of Wolfram, who was resting from his marital troubles in the enchanted retreat, which until then had escaped the surveillance of Countess Anna.

The happy young hostess was finishing the preparations for dinner when Wolfram entered the dining hall. He had exchanged his usual black attire for a luxurious violet sweater of Italian cut. His face had also changed.

There was not even a sign of that somber concentration and cold irony that exuded in Castle Reifenstein. There he was happy, carefree, kind and loving.

His dark eyes were refulgent and the enchanting smile that subdued the hearts of women did not leave his lips.

- Wolfram, you were an unexpected joy! I did not expect to see you for another three weeks – remarked Giovanna, pouring the wine.

[42]

- Oh! I have news to tell you. Soon I will have my son married. Cheers to you, Giovanna, and to the future couple – he added, laughing, and emptying the goblet.

Noticing her surprise, Wolfram told her everything that had happened.

Poor Paola! She would be very happy with this union. But tell me, was the countess pleased with the marriage? I remember hearing that she did not like my late friend.

I care little for Countess Anna's whims. She must obey me and only obey me – said the Count, and his voice sounded in a harsh and contemptuous tone. Her influence on the boy is bad. She either flatters him and spoils him too much, or she tyrannizes him and treats him badly, taking out on him her own marital dissatisfaction. Such an upbringing has already made Raymond stubborn and reserved. At least I saved him from a disgrace: I got rid of the wife his mother was preparing for him, little Greta, in time, will be the faithful portrait of the countess. She is mean, lecherous and a liar, and already with great skill she can adapt herself to Anna's tastes. But enough about that! Darling, wouldn't you like to go for a walk on the lake? It is a lovely afternoon!

But Giovanna was very interested in what he had said and did not stop inquiring him about the planned marriage.

- God wants the children to be very happy and to realize, in time, the grace the Lord has given them to belong to each other without having to be ashamed of it.

- Let's hope so! Of course, the future is uncertain, but I think I did well and saved Raymond from a disgrace like mine, that is, a marriage to a woman he could not love for a long time.

An hour later they sat in a boat and sailed for a long time on the lake.

The beautiful and fragrant night fell. The full moon illuminated everything as if it were day. The huge, luminous stars stood out in the blackness of the sky and trembled in the reflection on the lake's tranquil surface. All around, the outlines of beautiful mountains and woods were visible. Giovanna took the laud with her and with her clean, powerful voice sang songs from her homeland.

Enraptured by happiness, the couple did not even suspect that, as they passed near the shore, two bright eyes followed them with avid curiosity, and that they hid themselves as soon as they moored the boat at the stone steps.

Those curious eyes belonged to a small, curved creature that for several hours sat behind the bushes, watching everything that happened in the village.

When Wolfram and Giovanna disembarked, the dwarf abandoned his hiding place and ran down the trail to the place where he had tied up his horse. Grabbing it by the mane, he climbed into the saddle like a cat and sneaked forward, soon disappearing into the dense vegetation.

Four days later, Countess Reifenstein was in her oratory in the evening after having had a long talk to her chaplain. She was sitting there, unconsciously turning over the rosary beads, but her thoughts were far away. Suddenly she threw the rosary away and, clasping her hands to her chest, murmured quietly:

- This mystery is killing me! Where is he going with the excuse of hunting? He must be hunting for a skirt! My heart does not deceive me. Wretched Lucien is his partner, and I will never find out anything about him, while Khinko has been watching them for more than a year and cannot find out where the Count has been. Is it incompetence or treason?

Very agitated, the countess left the oratory and began pacing impatiently around the dormitory. At that instant, the maid appeared at the door.

- Khinko arrived - she said timidly - and insisted so much on seeing the lady that I did not dare dismiss him.

The countess frowned, thought for a moment, and then spoke:

- The timing is very inappropriate! But so be it! Let him in.

[44]

A moment later, the dwarf entered and kissed the tip of the countess's dress. After bowing deeply, he whispered:

- I found what the lady ordered me to find.

Anna shuddered.

- Accompany me to the oratory! - she said cheerfully.

- Now speak! Do you know where the Count is? - she added, carefully lowering the curtain.

- My patron saint helped me in this discovery - began the dwarf, twinkling his eyes. A few days ago, I went to visit one of my relatives who has married an innkeeper, whose house is about twenty metric *lieue*[10] from here. I was there chatting with Gerda, when suddenly I heard from the inn's entrance the voice of our master, who came asking for a glass of water. I ran out the back door and up into the attic. I watched from there and saw that it was really the Count accompanied only by Lucien. When they left, I took a horse from the innkeeper Jacob and followed them from afar. Several times I lost track of them because the Count was riding very fast. But God helped me.

After passing through a dense forest, we finally came out to a large lake that I had never seen before. In the middle of the lake, on a large island, there was a small castle. I do not know how the Count managed to get there, but when I approached, Lucien, along with the two horses, were already crossing it by raft. I, naturally, hid in the bushes and decided to sit there for even two days to see who lived in that palace. But I did not have to wait that long to see the Count taking a boat ride on the lake with a lady...

The countess let out a restrained cry.

- Have you seen the woman? What does she look like? Did you hear anything they were talking about? - she asked in a hoarse voice.

---

[10] Metric *lieue*- French mile equivalent to four kilometers, about 2.5 miles.

- Oh! I saw everything perfectly since the boat passed just two steps from my hiding place and the moon was illuminating everything. I could not understand what they were saying, because they were talking in a language I do not know, but it was clear they were talking about love. The lady was young and beautiful like a fairy. She was blonde and looked very rich, since her costume and the ornament she wore on her head were entirely embroidered in gold. When she began to sing, I thought I was hearing the singing of angels. Even the Count looked at her as if she were the Virgin Mary.

Anna threw herself on the back of the chair and closed her eyes, overwhelmed by anger and jealousy. Finally, pulling herself together with difficulty, she took out a gold coin and tossed it to the dwarf.

- Thank you Khinko! My gratitude will not be limited to that. Tomorrow I will send a little cow to your old mother so that she can have milk and get better. Can you find that castle again?

- But of course! "Whenever you want, my benefactor - replied the dwarf, beside himself with such joy and enthusiasm.

The countess spent an agitated night. The awareness of her own powerlessness and mad jealousy took away her reason. Days passed and the Count did not return. So, Anna decided to prepare Raymond to oppose her father's will and the marriage that was now even more hateful to her.

Every time she met her son, Countess Anna began to cry and call him "poor boy". She frightened Raymond so much, with her sighs, sad looks, and mysterious hints, that the idea of marriage to Eliza came to an end, it caused him superstitious terror that it would bring him obvious misfortune.

In such a state of mind, the boy allowed himself to be convinced of the need to rebel openly and declare at the altar, in front of the guests, that he did not want to marry the daughter of an adventurer. Anna knew that such a scandal, even if it did not stop the wedding, would greatly irritate Wolfram.

[46]

To keep Raymond motivated in her favor, the countess showered him with gifts and promised him much more. Thus, prepared by his mother and Greta, seduced with gifts and flattery, the little Count swore he would not marry.

At that time, Wolfram was away longer than usual. When he finally returned home, he was so busy with the preparations for the ceremony that he paid no attention to his wife's silent irritation or his son's silent dissatisfaction.

On the eve of the wedding, the Count brought the little bride from the monastery. Eliza was completely intimidated before the tall, stern, cold woman, who barely touched her forehead with the lips. Raymond stubbornly remained silent, while Greta cast evil glances at the girl. At first, Eliza sought protection in the Count's arms, and then hid behind the nanny, who took her to sleep, claiming that the child was tired from the trip.

The next day, from the morning, the castle was filled with a noisy and adorned crowd. All the knights from the surrounding area attended with their wives and were welcomed by the castle owners on the grand staircase of honor. Some young ladies from noble families wanted to dress the bride personally. The beauty and docility of the little girl, who let herself be adorned like a doll, enchanted them. Eliza really looked like a doll in her silver brocade dress, with a long train that was to be carried by the pageboy, with her jeweled belt and her long black hair adorned with a small heraldic crown, from which a silver veil descended.

Margarita also dressed up herself, wearing a light blue dress with gold stripes and a garland of flowers in her loose blonde hair. But her face was dark as a storm cloud, her eyes red and swollen from crying. Her glances at Eliza, the unworthy rival who had stolen her happiness, did not bode well. Only Raymond, the hero of the day, paid no attention to the ceremony. The groom remained in bed despite the constant sound of horns announcing the arrival of new guests and the noise of the bishop's arrival to bless the wedding. Laying over the cushions and staring stubbornly at the wall, he was answering all the arguments of the old landowner, Ekgardt, and the page who was supposed to dress him.

I am telling you, Ekgardt, I am not getting married, and I am not going to church. You do not seem to understand? You, thank God, are intelligent! So, leave me alone!

In vain, the page tried to convince him that the Count would be angry and that it was time to get dressed. Unsuccessful were his attempts to lure the boy with the beautiful sweater and the small sword with a hilt adorned with precious stones. Raymond seemed deaf and stubborn. The decisive moment was approaching. Despite everything, the boy was afraid of causing a scandal in front of the bishop and the guests, but he wanted to keep his word and win the armor of Damascus[11] that his mother had promised him. So, he tried to stand firm and even invented a compromise that, in his childish imagination, he considered to be the best way out of that tricky situation. Therefore, he decides to stay in bed and not go to church, so the wedding could not take place, even if the bishop tried to convince him.

Tired of his attempts to overcome Raymond's stubbornness and fearful of wasting time with useless conversation, Ekgardt rushed to the great hall, asked the pageboy to call the Count, and when he arrived, he told him in a half voice what was happening.

A dark blush covered Wolfram's face, and he cast an angry glance at Countess Anna who was talking to the bishop. She did not let her husband out of her sight and when their gazes met a wicked, ironic smile passed her lips.

- Ekgardt, go and bring me some quince sticks – ordered the knight, quickly leaving the room.

---

[11] Damascene Armor – Damascene steel was one of the most famous materials of the pre-industrial era, highly used for the manufacture of weapons and armor, and appreciated for its beauty, durability, and elasticity. Its manufacture consisted of a process that joined wrought iron and various carbonic materials by smelting. Found by the Europeans during the Crusades, steel received the name Damascus steel, because it was forged in the city of Damascus, Syria.

Seeing that the squire faltered, he frowned and added imperiously?

- Did you hear me? I do not like to repeat orders. I will get Mr. Raymond out of bed and show him what happens to people who make up stories and disobey my orders.

The Count stopped by the door to his son's room, waiting for Ekgardt, who already appeared at the end of the corridor, hiding under his cloak a thick bundle of quince sticks.

- Countess Anna, for your intrigues your son will pay with his back – grumbled Wolfram, opening the door.

There was the page and another servant trying to convince the little Count to obey.

Wolfram ordered them both out and approached the bed. Raymond, spoiled by his father who had always treated him with condescension, did not even suspect the danger of the moment and saw the Count approaching but he just closed his eyes with an air of boredom.

- You worthless brat. How dare you disobey me and stay here in bed, when the guests are already gathered, and the bride is already dressed up? Get up now and get dressed! Do you hear me? ...I did not come here to play.

- I do not want to marry Eliza... I want to marry Greta! Replied Raymond stubbornly, covering his face with his pillow.

- I will teach you to want what I want and not what your decent mother teaches you! - said Wolfram, red with rage.

Before Raymond could even imagine what would happen, as he had never seen punitive measures from his father, the Count grabbed him by the neck and lifted him off the bed like a puppy. Then the thing that definitely convinced the reticent groom, who was struggling with loud cries at his father's hands. But any reaction was useless in Wolfram's iron hand.

The lashes fell one after another. Wolfram, furious, felt no pity and wanted to prove to his son once for all that he had to pay, with his back, for his mother's kind instructions.

- So? Now are you going to church without stubbornness? - asked the Count, ending the punishment.

- Yes, yes! - moaned Raymond in tears.

- In that case, get dressed then!

The Count let go of him and sat down in the chair, putting his hands in his lap.

Ekgardt dressed the groom, in an instant, who could not stop sobbing and did not feel well, even in his new outfit.

- If you repeat this scene during the ceremony, I will punish you even more painfully in front of everyone. Ekgardt will take the quince sticks to the church and leave them at hand. I can expel you from the castle because I do not want to have a disobedient son- said the Count, rising to his feet.

- Now stop shouting! - continued Wolfram, tapping his foot. Aren't you ashamed to cry like an old woman for a few lashes? And you want to be a knight!

Raymond had no doubt that his father would carry out his threat. So, he vigorously suppressed his crying, washed his red face with cold water, and ten minutes later appeared in the hall together with his father who introduced him to the guests.

The bishop went to the chapel. Obediently, but without casting any glance at the bride, Raymond took her by the hand and the procession went on. Everyone admired the beauty of the children and predicted that in time they would be a beautiful couple.

The praise reached Raymond's ears but did not convince his self-love. Shame, anger, and pain tortured him, instilling in him almost repulsion at the innocent creature, the unwitting cause of his misfortunes. Never, perhaps, had a groom knelt at the altar with such troubled feelings.

[50]

On the other hand, Eliza was dazzled, neither suspecting nor understanding the storm she had unwittingly provoked. As a future woman, she was happy in her gala outfit. Moreover, everything pleased her: the multitude of smiling guests, the church setting, the luxurious vestments of the bishop, her little fiancé with a gold chain around his neck and a sword which hilt sparkled with precious stones.

Fortunately for the good outcome of the sacred ceremony, Eliza's childish heart was still asleep and unaware of the groom's humiliating and hostile indifference. She was just surprised that at that happy moment her little ceremony companion looked so sullen. Leaning forward, the little girl looked curiously and innocently into Raymond's dark eyes. Raymond, at first, looked surprised at the rosy face that smiled at him with shining eyes. Then, overcome by the charm that exuded from that beautiful being, he forgot his anger and the terrible event caused by that little Eva. A smile lit up his face. He felt something like unconscious pride and squeezed harder the tiny little fingers he held in his hand.

Eliza, unknowingly, had won her first victory.

At that instant, the bishop began to speak. The children raised their eyes to him and listened intently to his words, which invoked heavenly blessings on their heads, urging them to love each other for life and to share faithfully their misfortunes and joys.

Barely containing the anger that agitated her inside, the countess, all pale, followed the bridal ceremony with icy eyes. Raymond's incomprehensible submission made her feel almost hatred for her son. Meanwhile, Wolfram prayed fervently, begging God to grant peace and love to his son and friend's daughter, and to free Raymond from the conjugal hell he himself endured, so that he would not have to search outside the house, in various follies, to fill the emptiness in his life.

At the end of the ceremony, the newlyweds received their presents. The solemn attitude of the two children at that moment caused general merriment, and Wolfram could hardly disguise the urge to laugh when he looked at Raymond.

[51]

"If in ten years Eliza hears about the forceful measures with which I forced her fiancé to attend church, she won't be flattered at all," he thought. "The silly Raymond can thank God forever that I made him happy. I can swear that, in time, this little one will be a real treasure."

Amused inside by the imposing air of the groom who avoided looking at his father, the Count served so many goodies and wine to the young couple that they, satisfied and tired of the ovations and kisses, eventually fell asleep.

Among the guests were also Ortruda, Ervins' stepmother, and her son Guntram, Ervin's younger brother. Wolfram hated them both, but he was too hospitable and kind to the host not to propose they stay a few days in his house. As for Countess Anna, she was always friendly with the Finsterbachs.

Two days after the wedding, while the Count, Guntram and two other knights were hunting nearby, Anna and Ortruda were sitting talking in the countess' bedroom.

Ortruda, comfortably reclining in her high-backed chair, listened to the countess' complaints. The countess, with a flaming look in her eyes, told her all the bitterness of her marital life: her husband's eternal coldness, the recent discovery of the Count's infidelity, and her indignation at her son's marriage to the daughter of the "Italian adventuress".

Ortruda listened to her friend, without interrupting. She was a thin, very blonde woman, about thirty-five years old, with a pleasant face and large gray eyes, smart and energetic. Her mouth, with full lips, indicated a lascivious nature, and her hooked nose with mobile and enlarged nostrils gave her physiognomy a somewhat sensual and cruel expression.

The mark left by nature on Ortruda's appearance corresponded to her inner world. Full of tyrannical, impetuous, and proud wills, adoring any kind of "forbidden fruit," she did not know how to restrain her desires and did not admit obstacles in the satisfaction of these. She completely dominated her old husband: since she became a widow, the whole neighborhood followed her various blatant amorous adventures. Serious and restrained women hated Ortruda, but they did not dare to treat her with overt hostility, fearing her, because they said she possessed the "evil eye". Furthermore, it was rumored that she possessed terrible diabolical powers.

When the countess finished her accusations, Ortruda straightened up.

- I can see that you are not happy in this marriage - she said thoughtfully. Of course, you could have chosen a better bride for your son than the daughter of that detestable Italian woman, who did a lot of harm to my relations with my stepson. But she died, and I hope God has mercy on her soul! It seems that, thanks to Paola, I can tell you who the mysterious lady your husband visits is. One day she told me that one of her friends, Giovanna, fell madly in love with Mr. Wolfram during her stay in Venice and, to the great scandal of her entire family, ran away with him. At that time, I did not give much importance to this fact and now your story reminds me of this story.

- Oh, if I could grab the wretch who stole my husband's love from me, I would strangle her with my bare hands - exclaimed the countess, clenching her fists.

Ortruda hid her face with her handkerchief to disguise the smile that flashed across her face. She examined the countess's strong figure and her red face with a wry look.

- Don't get emotional, Anna! However righteous your anger may be, there is no point in getting your hands dirty if there are better ways to get rid of unpleasant people. If you like, I can take you to a person who will help you get rid of your rival without spilling a drop of poison or blood.

- Do I want to? I will be eternally grateful for that good advice.

Sitting very close to each other, they continued their conversation in whispers. Anna decided to visit her friend to spend a few days at her house. In the meantime, Ortruda would take her

[53]

to a man who, in exchange for gold, would give the determined person an invisible but fatal force that would undermine her life until it killed her.

A week later, as evening approached, a closed sedan chair, accompanied by two well-armed men, stopped in front of an old house located on the outskirts of a small town.

The city had no suburbs, but a certain block was preferentially inhabited by Jews and therefore avoided by the Christian inhabitants.

The house was old, blackened, and semi-derelict. There was only a barred window and a massive iron-clad door leading to it. On either side was a high, thick wall, completely concealing what lay behind it.

One of the warriors struck the door with the hilt of his sword. A few minutes later, a small door with a thin iron grille opened and the head of an old man in a black hat appeared in it. Seeing the hooded woman disembarking from her sedan chair, the old man shouted:

- Hold on! I will open the door in a moment!

You could hear how the old man opened the bolts and pushed the heavy latch. Then the door creaked open.

Two hooded women got out of their sedan chairs and entered the house.

- The master of the house awaits you, noble ladies - said the old man.

Then, lifting the sooty, greasy lamp, he led the visitors down the long corridor and through a large kitchen into a room that probably served as a store, as it was crammed with various objects: old clothes, instruments, and a variety of weapons.

Another gentleman was sitting near the table, busy finishing a sword. The pronounced features of his face and his hooked nose clearly showed his Semitic origin.[12]

Seeing the two women, he stood up and made a respectful reference.

- I received your message, noble lady, and I am ready to serve you and your companion as well - he said.

In that case, Mr. Markhodey, take us to the room where we once talked and where, away from any prying ears, we can tell you the reason for our visit - requested Ortruda.

The Jew nodded silently, lit a candle on an iron candlestick, and, pushing aside a leather curtain that covered the door at the back of the room, gestured for the ladies to follow him.

Ortruda bravely went ahead, but Anna faltered for a moment. She was still on the verge of her first crime and her surroundings filled her up with superstitious terror.

They passed through a room full of miscellaneous objects, like the previous one, then a second corridor at the end of which the Jew opened a small door, so cleverly concealed behind shelves full of dusty jars that its existence was not even suspected.

To her great surprise, Anna entered a room luxuriously furnished in Asian style and lit by lamps hanging from the ceiling. A thick fabric covered the walls, and a thick carpet covered the floor. The air was permeated with a strong but pleasant smell.

- Be so kind as to sit down, noble ladies, and explain to me what I can do for you - said the old man with a kind smile, pointing to the pile of cushions spread along the walls - I think I have always fulfilled all the missions entrusted to me.

---

[12] Semitic - An ethnic and linguistic group to which Shem (one of Noah's three sons) is attributed as an ancestor, and includes the Hebrews, Assyrians, Aramaic, Phoenicians, and Arabs. Or members of that group relative to the Jews.

- Yes Mr. Markhodey! You have done me a great favor. I did not forget that, and I brought one of my friends here. She is very unhappy because of a woman who steals her husband's heart. If you help her, she will reward you generously.

The Jew's eyes, which were fixed on Countess Anna, sparkled with greed.

- All my knowledge is entirely at the disposal of Countess Reifenstein! Even through the thick veil I recognize that beautiful and sad face. No doubt her unhappiness is legitimate.

A restrained scream escaped Anna's lips. Her confidence in the wizard was immediately strengthened by the fact that he recognized her despite her covered face. She removed her veil and placed a well-stuffed purse on the table, which she took from her purse.

- I leave that as a sign, Mr. Markhodey! I will give you double, if you destroy my hateful rival and give me back my husband's heart.

An imperceptible mocking smile flashed across Markhodey's face as he stored the wallet in a carved wooden cabinet.

- Kindly follow me to the shrine! - he then said. Only there can I begin to act and see the person you intend to hit.

The three of them went into the adjoining room, whose strange appearance made the countess shudder. It was a rounded, windowless room, whose walls were occupied by shelves full of tins, jars, and bundles of dried herbs. In the center, on a black marble table, was a seven-headed candelabra with seven black candles, a copper container filled with water, and some scrolls. In front of the table, in the center of the triangle formed by the three tripods, was a metal statue of a half human, half animal being. On the human torso, with large wings on its back, there was a horned goat's head with empty eye sockets. At the foot of the demon image sat a magnificent black cat, whose eyes burned like embers in the dimness of the room.

The wizard picked up a short wand from the table and began rubbing it with his hands. From his fingers came a spark and all seven candles in the candelabra were lit with an ominous crackling. In the statue's empty eye sockets a flickering, bluish flame was lit.

Anna let out a deafened cry and stepped back.

- Fear not, noble lady! - said Markhodey. By any chance, has your friend told you that I need some object belonging to the person you want to get rid of?

- I know - replied Anna, handing the wizard a package containing a scented glove and dried roses tied with a ribbon. After a long and careful search, the countess managed to find these objects in one of Wolfram's jewelry boxes.

- This is more than necessary - said Markhodey, leaning over the glove and flowers and strongly inhaling their scent.

Then he placed the glove and flowers on a metal tray, doused them with a colorless liquid, and set it on fire.

When everything burned, the Jew carefully gathered the ashes with an ivory spatula, macerated them with soft wax, and from the mass formed, he made a candle, whose polished surface glowed with all the colors of the rainbow.

Picking up his wand again, the wizard stood in front of the mirror and with a measured voice began to recite incantations, waving the lit candle he had just made in his hand. Under the dim light of the candle, the surface of the mirror seemed to sparkle. These sparks united into a single bluish flame and drew cabalistic signs that then disappeared.

Anna and Ortruda were watching with superstitious horror. But when the wizard, in a deaf voice, pronounced "Giovanna!", Anna shuddered, convulsively squeezed her friend's hand, and her gaze seemed to fix on Markhodey's pale, sweaty face.

Suddenly, the Jew directed his glassy eyes at the countess, seized her by the hand and pushing her in front of the mirror, said imperiously:

[57]

- Take the candle and look!

The countess obeyed, clutching the candle with trembling fingers, she bent towards the mirror. From the sling of the metal surface appeared before her astonished gaze a black cloud that quickly widened and turned into a bluish mist. As if in a frame, the image of a lake appeared, surrounded by wooded hills. In the center of the lake, on an island, stood a small castle, which began to grow and soon took up almost the entire screen. Then a terrace surrounded by rare plants appeared, on a bed, between pillows, was sleeping a young, beautiful, blond woman.

Seeing the girl, at the height of her youth and beauty, the countess's heart was gripped by a jealousy so wild that she let out a shriek and staggered backward. She would have fallen if Ortruda had not held her.

The magic picture quickly faded away.

Markhodey carefully covered the mirror. Then, turning to Countess Anna, who was trying to recover herself, he asked:

- Noble lady, what do you want to happen to the person who appeared in the mirror?

- I want her dead if it is in your power to kill her! - replied the countess in a hoarse voice.

- If that is your wish, then it will be fulfilled - stated the wizard calmly.

Taking the candle, he carved with extraordinary skill a human figure, on the chest of which he pressed the lit end of the candle itself. Then he placed the remaining ashes of the glove and the wax figure in a tiny coffin and fixed it between the horns that adorned the goat's head of the statue. On the lid of the little coffin, he placed a metal circle with zodiacal symbols engraved on it and lit a small piece of bread crumb, which burned with a greenish flame. All done, Markhodey prostrated himself before his god, muttering some unintelligible words that he accompanied with imperative gestures.

At the end of the incantations, the Jew turned to Countess Anna and said in a solemn tone:

- Exactly one year from now, on this very day and at this very hour, the woman named Giovanna will die! Noble lady, you will reward me for my service only when my words are fulfilled.

A smile of satisfaction appeared on Anna's lips. Taking from her finger a ring with an expensive ruby, she handed it to the wizard.

- Please accept this as a token of my appreciation, Mr. Markhodey.

With deep bowing, the Jew escorted the visitors out.

Chapter 4

Life at Reifenstein Castle entered its normal routine. Upon returning from Ortruda's house, Anna was in a very good mood. Not only had she eliminated her hateful rival, but she came to better enjoy the company of Wolfram who was now staying at the castle longer than usual.

The reason for the sedentary lifestyle was Eliza, for whom the Count not only felt a deep affection, but also feared leaving her alone because of the ostentatious hostility that surrounded her. Even the little girl herself, with her impressionable spirit, realized that she was not welcome in that house.

Eliza became quiet and avoided the stern and taciturn Countess, who never gave her a word of affection or attention. The poor little girl did not even dare to play with the children, because Greta's hateful glances and Raymond's hostility kept her away from them.

Such a hostile atmosphere silenced her clear laughter that only sounded in Wolfram's room. The Count was her best friend. He knew how to amuse her, always inventing new jokes or telling her fairy stories so amusing that the girl could not get enough of them. She felt happy sitting on the Count's lap, resting her little head on his chest and listening to his tales without blinking.

Between Wolfram and his son, a cold relationship was established. Since the wedding day Raymond was angry with his father and avoided him, especially after his mother, to whom he confessed everything, grumbled to each other between teeth:

- That poor boy! They are treating you worse than a slave. All this to turn the adventurer's daughter into a Reifenstein Countess!

From that moment on, Raymond considered himself a victim of his father's tyranny, and he vented on Eliza all the dissatisfaction that he did not dare to show to his father. The father was also unhappy with Raymond because he had not asked for forgiveness and given his son's stubbornness, he did not say a word to him.

However, one night, when crossing paths with Raymond in the corridor, and seeing that the boy lowered his eyes and let him pass, the Count stopped.

- Don't tell me that your mother has managed to confuse you to such an extent that you even lower your sight when you run into me! Will it be that you, the only reason for my staying here, also wish me to leave? - he asked in his sonorous voice.

Without waiting for an answer, Wolfram walked past his son, into the room, and dropped into the chair, covering his face with his hands. Sad thoughts went through his head. He thought about the divorce with his wife, who became more hateful every day. The only thing that stopped him was the worry of damaging his son's mind.

The Count's thoughts were interrupted by Raymond, who followed him excitedly. By the door, the boy stopped indecisively, but, noticing his father's somber and thoughtful look, he ran to him. Hugging him by the neck and leaning his head on his chest, the boy repeated through tears:

- Stay!... Stay, father!... Forgive me! I did not think I would bring you so much grief!

The Count shuddered and a smile lit up his worried face.

- No, no my boy! I know and have never doubted that you love me!

The Count lifted his son up, sat him on his lap and gave him a big kiss:

- So, let us forget that detestable moment when I was forced to punish you even though it pained my heart. I know that it was your mother's advice that incited you to disobey me and caused all that scandal - he added.

- Now, can we make up? You will not think about leaving anymore? - asked Raymond fearfully.

The Count smiled and then sighed.

- Calm down! I will not leave you. But since we have made up, let us then talk about an important matter that concerns you personally. I am talking about Eliza. You are still a child, but you already understand that this union gives you certain obligations towards Eliza. She is your wife. According to divine law you must love and protect her. She is still very small and lonely here, where nobody likes her. Do you promise me that you will defend her?

- Yes, Dad! I promise you, even though Mom and Greta always tell me that when I grow up, I should hate her and take her away from me.

- My boy, never listen to this nonsense! - said Wolfram, scornfully.

- Rest assured, father! I will keep my promise.

As Raymond made up with his father, he felt a great relief as if a great weight had been lifted from his back. And with impetuous courage, he murmured:

- You will see, Dad, how I will defend Eliza. Today she has already gone to sleep, but starting tomorrow I am going to play with her, and woe to Greta if she messes with my wife!

The next day, when the children went out into the garden, Eliza stayed away as usual. Sitting next to the nanny, she was playing with her kitten when Raymond approached.

- Eliza, come and play! - he said amiably. I will show you my toys, I will take you for a ride in the buggy, and then we will play hide-and-seek.

[62]

The little girl raised her eyes in surprise, but meeting the boy's friendly gaze, she smiled, held out her hand, and let herself be kissed. Raymond liked that kiss very much. Eliza had a small mouth with cool pink lips, unlike Greta's thick, moist lips which, besides everything else, had an ugly habit of licking them. The children began to play, happy and carefree.

The countess was extremely irritated by the good relationship that had been established between Eliza and her little husband. She did not dare say anything openly, but inside she decided to get rid of the girl at any price.

But how was she going to do it? She was afraid to appeal to Markhodey again, fearing that the Count was secretly watching her, and she could not eliminate her openly either. She would have to wait for the appropriate moment. For now, it was necessary to get rid of the nanny, whose dedication to the little one embarrassed her, and then set the two playmates against Eliza. It would be difficult to convince Raymond, because he had grown accustomed to his little wife and valued her good qualities. Thus, Eliza was more docile, less quarrelsome, and especially less greedy than Greta, who never shared with him any piece of candy she could eat alone. Eliza, however, always gave her young husband most of the goodies Wolfram gave her.

An unexpected event favored the countess's plans: the Count began to disappear again for days on end, returning home so worried that he did not even notice what was happening around him.

The reason for the Count's frequent absences and worries was Giovanna's unexpected illness, whose strange symptoms no one could understand. She began to waste away, and the Count's heart was filled with sadness and despair.

The countess guessed the cause of her husband's sadness and felt satisfied. At the same time, she decided to take advantage of the relative freedom and get rid of Eliza and her nanny.

Taking great precautions, she contacted Markhodey and obtained a certain potion from him, thanks to which the nanny,

[63]

Brigitte, suffered a brain inflammation and had to be separated from the child. The countess treated her with great consideration and even sent for the doctor from the neighboring town.

Putting that troublesome witness away, Anna went on to teach Greta the plan to eliminate the girl. To her, Greta was her accomplice and the tool she needed, the girl also hated and was jealous of Eliza. If Greta was by nature stupid and lazy to study, in compensation she possessed cleverness and rage above her age.

One morning, when Wolfram was gone again for an indefinite period, Countess Anna called Greta into her room and began to question her about her studies, while she passed from one jewelry box to another the family jewels and handled the cases with objects left for Eliza from her late mother's inheritance.

Greta could not take her eyes off the jewelry that glittered in multiple colors in the countess's hand.

- My poor girl, all this I was saving for you! "My heart bleeds to think that the nosy little rascal is going to adorn herself with these jewels - said the countess with a sigh.

The girl's face blushed and her eyes sparkled with hatred.

- Oh, Godmother! If you only knew how much I hate her for taking everything away from me, even Raymond's friendship. Now we are always fighting. Yesterday, when I broke the doll that Uncle Wolfram gave as a present to Eliza, Raymond hit me and pulled me by my braids.

The countess kissed her and wiped away the tears streaming down the girl's face.

- You poor girl! Wipe away those tears, today I am going to talk to Raymond and tell him that he will be severely punished if he dares to do it again. I deeply regret that we cannot get rid of that worthless creature, who hovers over our house like a curse. If she died, you would marry Raymond and all the jewels would belong to you. Imagine the wedding we would celebrate!

On Greta's face came a mixed expression of anger and eagerness.

- Someday I am going to push her into the moat so she can drown! - exclaimed the girl, furious.

- Have you gone mad? Ekgardt or some other servant will hear her screams, save her, and you will be punished. No, no! If God wanted to get rid of her, he would make her get lost in one of the empty rooms of the north tower. In addition, if the heavy door was closed behind her, she could even scream, but no one would hear her and end up staying there until the Final Judgment.

Margarita looked at the countess. Something cruel and mean shone in her aunt's eyes.

- Sometimes we play near this tower. If I can, I will lock Eliza up there. I am just afraid that Raymond will let her go.

- Of course, he will let her go. In any case, she will be punished by fear for all the harm she has caused us. However, Greta, I must warn you that even if we wish her death, killing her would be a sin.

Margarita answered nothing, but the seed of evil had already fallen on fertile ground.

From that day on, the dedicated ward of the countess waited for the opportunity to execute the plan that had been instilled in her.

Eliza did not like to play near the castle. She always tried to keep her distance from the countess, who never gave her a caress or a smile, even though she spoiled her son and Margarita in her presence in every way.

One day, Margarita managed to direct their games in such a way that they stopped by the north tower, an old, long-uninhabited building from the early years of the castle's existence.

From a low-ceilinged room, dimly lit by narrow, deep-seated windows, a massive door led into the tower. A large key protruded from the lock.

The children played for more than an hour in that room, where no one forbade them to move the old, vermin-corroded furniture.

Suddenly Margarita asked pointing to the locked door:

- Raymond, where does that door lead to? I have never been inside.

- Me neither! But I know that behind it there are two small rooms of very bad reputation. Let's go, that is not forbidden.

The boy ran to the heavy oak door and opened it. The girls followed him curiously. The three of them entered a semicircular room, barely lit by the narrow window with colored glass. Everything was covered with a thick layer of dust and cobwebs.

At the back of the room, on a raised shelf, was a bed with faded, rat-corroded curtains. A few chairs and a large closet completed the furniture. Next to this room was another room, almost empty. The air was heavy, permeated with a musty smell.

- Let's get out of here, I am scared! This place is ugly and dark - said Eliza.

- Yes, I have already told you that this place has a very bad reputation. The wife of the guard on the drawbridge told me that a murder took place here - Raymond revealed.

- Ouch! I am trembling with fear. But who was killed here? - asked Margarita shuddering.

- One of our ancestors killed a knight. My great-grandfather was very old. He was at least forty years old. Suddenly, he decided to marry a very young girl who didn't love him because she liked a young knight. On their wedding day, this knight and his bride hid in this room. The husband surprised them here, killed the knight and seriously wounded his wife, who survived. Later, he forgave her. She was the mother of my father's grandfather! Look, on that step, on the floor and on the curtain, you can still see the signs of the crime. Those splashes and the big dark stain must be the blood of the traitor. Come over here! - added Raymond, fearlessly climbing the bed steps.

- Oh, how horrible it all is! I am shaking like a leaf, and there is no way I am going there," exclaimed Greta, backing away quickly.

- You are afraid because you are a woman - Raymond remarked with contempt. I am a man and a future knight, and I am not afraid of the sight of blood. Who knows...maybe even one day I will have to do the same thing that was done here?

- You? But who do you want to kill? - asked Eliza in surprise.

- You, of course, because you are his wife! - interrupt Margarita, with a wicked smile.

Eliza did not even blink.

- He would not dare kill me! Uncle Wolfram would not allow that! Not even his evil great-grandfather dared to kill his wife! Why did that old fool marry the poor woman who loved someone else?

- A woman has no right to prefer another one! The wife must love her husband. My great-grandfather had every right to kill the traitor! - exclaimed Raymond, tempestuously.

The boy's anger only amused the mischievous and stubborn Eliza.

- Maybe that knight was more handsome than your great-grandfather! Who knows, maybe when I grow up, I will end up liking someone more than you, too! For example, Ziguebert. He is elegant, blond, calm, and not quarrelsome like you. You are very fat and have huge legs.

Raymond's face turned dark red. For a moment he stared in surprise at his own legs, but he was too angry to recognize the truth of Eliza's comment. He felt offended. How could she criticize him and find someone more beautiful than him?

- I will teach you now to prefer Ziguebert, that thin, dry mongrel! I will forbid you to look at other men and find them handsome. Apologize right now and kiss my hand like my mother does!

- Do not even think of it! Your father's hands are white and clean while yours are red and are always dirty - said Eliza with disdain.

- Eliza, I command you; you must kiss my hand! I am your husband, and you must respect and obey me! - exclaimed Raymond, furious.

But Eliza was bold and proud. Without answering anything, she turned her back on him and went into the other room.

- Do you know what you can do, Raymond? Lock Eliza in here to punish her for this disobedience. Leave her locked up alone until she asks for forgiveness and kisses your hand like any obedient wife - said Margarita maliciously, who remembered her conversation with the countess and decided to take advantage of the discussion.

Raymond was so angry that he liked the suggestion. In a flash he appeared by the door, and after Greta had left, he slammed it shut. Then they both quickly left the tower.

- Just don't say anything to Ekgardt! Otherwise, he will let her go immediately. Moreover, he will tell Uncle Wolfram. That rude girl deserves to be locked up there until the night.

- I won't say anything to him. Let her stay there! I will teach her to respect her husband's will! After this lesson, she will never disrespect me again, nor will she think that silly Ziguebert is better looking than me - answered Raymond with a flaming face.

Margarita, all happy, immediately ran to see the countess and told her about Eliza's arrest.

Anna pretended to be amused by the event and laughed heartily at the just punishment of her reluctant daughter-in-law but ordered her goddaughter not to tell anyone about it and, as far as possible, to feed Raymond's anger.

An hour later, Ekgardt was sent to Ortruda's house with a message. That mission would keep him away from the castle for at least three days. The countess then went to the north tower, locked the door to Eliza's dungeon and took the key with her. For a few

[68]

minutes she listened with a smile to the poor girl's desperate screams and cries.

The rest of the day was spent in unrest. Brigitte was dying and the countess obliged the chaplain to solemnly administer her the last rites. The ceremony lasted so long that it was time for the children to go to sleep. As Ekgardt, who always slept in Raymond's room, was absent, the countess put the boy to sleep in her room. In short, she managed to occupy everyone in such a way that everyone completely forgot about Eliza's existence.

Raymond also forgot about his little wife, and as soon as he lay down, he fell into a heavy sleep. But when he awoke in the morning, he remembered what had happened and was overcome with horror and pain in his conscience.

What a terrible night Eliza would have spent in that cold, damp room, with no dinner and no light!

He quickly dressed and ran to the north tower, but from a distance he noticed that the door was locked, and the key was gone. Then he was overcome with great despair, which increased even more when Eliza did not answer his call. No matter how much he screamed and knocked on the door, there was no answer.

The boy, as if being chased, left the tower, and ran to his mother's room.

The countess had just returned from the room of Brigitte who had died. Raymond told her in a trembling voice what had happened the day before, that the key was missing and begged her to release Eliza as soon as possible, because he feared she was dead since she did not answer his call.

You naughty boy! What have you done? - exclaimed the countess, enraged. The worthless must have fallen into the cellar in the damned room. Now, there will be many arguments with your father again! Because of my worries about Brigitte, I completely forgot about that horrible girl, who will die so suddenly just to cause us new misfortunes.

[69]

- Maybe she is still alive. I just need to find the key to the door and look for her - Raymond shyly remarked.

The response to those words were slaps and hard blows on the back.

- Shut up, you imbecile! You don't want to awaken the entire castle for this! I will quietly look for the key myself and find the girl's body. Let everyone say that she is lost, and I will punish Marta who was supposed to look for her. I advise you to keep quiet and confirm to your father what I am about to say about Eliza's death. If he learns the truth, he will punish you even more than on your wedding day. I dare not even think about what could happen!

Raymond, frightened, hid in his room. He came out only to have lunch, and then locked himself in again, because they started looking for Eliza. Evidently, the search was fruitless. The countess lectured Martha and declared that perhaps the girl had hidden herself in some nook or cranny and had fallen asleep there. Then, she ordered the young maid to look for the little girl under threat of severe punishment, without alerting the castle, because if the Count knew of her carelessness, he would send her away without forgiveness. She also ordered her to let the others think that Eliza was in her room.

Raymond went to bed early with pain in his heart, and as soon as he was alone, he wept bitterly. Never before had he suffered such a bad conscience. Never before had such sadness gripped the child's heart. The fear instilled in him was replaced by horror. Despite his young age and innocence, the boy realized that the countess wished Eliza dead, and that she lied about the cellar that, even if it existed, the little girl could not open.

Suddenly, the sound of the horn announced the arrival of the owner of the castle and Raymond shuddered. His heart was seized with both joy and fear.

For a few minutes, the boy struggled with himself. Finally, the fear that Eliza was dead, and the acknowledgement that he could be guilty for it, overcame the other feelings. Dressing quickly,

Raymond ran to his father's office. He wanted by all means to confess to him that Eliza was in the castle.

By the door to the Count's chambers, Raymond found Lucien taking the knight's robes.

Seeing the boy's desolate look, he stopped surprised.

- Is my father still awake? - Raymond asked, shaking all over, and, receiving an affirmative answer, entered the room like a hurricane.

The Count was sitting by the table, leafing through a manuscript. The boy threw himself on his neck, pressed himself frightened against his chest, and began the non-stop repeating confession:

- I swear dad, I didn't mean to do that! I just wanted to punish Eliza for not wanting to kiss my hand.

Seeing his dashing, half-dressed, feverishly trembling son, Wolfram thought he had been complaining about some rudeness of his mother's, and at first could understand nothing of the incoherent account, interrupted by convulsive weeping. When the Count finally understood something of his son's words, he was livid.

- What are you telling me? What happened to Eliza? - he asked, startled.

The look and tone of his father's voice startled Raymond to such an extent that he was at first perplexed. Realizing that he would accomplish nothing that way, the Count mastered himself.

- Raymond, it doesn't matter what you've done, but I promise I won't punish you! The fact that you come to me to confess this, already justifies you before me. So, you can speak without fear.

Raymond, calmer, briefly told him everything that had happened.

- How long has Eliza been in the north tower? - asked the Count with a nervous tick.

- Since noon yesterday. The key is gone, otherwise I would have released her this morning.

- All right! Go to your room and I will find Eliza - said the Count, getting up.

He is called Lucien.

A few minutes later, Wolfram, accompanied by two squires and the castellan carrying a bunch of keys, hurried to the north tower.

Inside the cursed room a deadly silence reigned. Seeing that they could not find the right key, Wolfram, furious, raised the acha1 he was carrying and, in a few blows, destroyed the door.

Raising the torches, they entered the gloomy room and soon saw the poor child lying motionless near the wall. The Count lifted the little girl's cold body and clasped her to his chest, ran back to his quarters.

Eliza looked dead. Her little blonde head hung lifeless, and no breath came out of her purplish lips. In terrible desperation, the Count placed her on his bed, began to massage her arms and legs, and then put his ear to her chest. He seemed to pick up very faint beats, and his hope was reborn.

Helped by Lucien, he redoubled his efforts to bring the girl back to life, without even remembering to call the chaplain, so disgusting was everything that was close to his wife since she decided to kill the child in cold blood.

More than an hour passed before his efforts had any result. But finally, a faint sigh escaped Eliza's chest, a tremor ran through her delicate limbs, her eyes opened, and she gave the knight a vague, tired look.

Wolfram, who until that moment was massaging her, terribly pale, breathed a sigh of relief.

- Eliza, my dear child! - he murmured, leaning toward her.

The little girl's lifeless gaze brightened. She recognized the Count, holding out her little hands to him, and exclaimed:

[72]

- I am afraid! I am afraid! Don't leave me!

The Count lovingly lifted the girl and covered her with kisses, while Eliza clung to him with her little arms. Then the girl's excited nerves could not take it, and she had her first attack. Only with affection and promises never to leave her again did the Count manage to calm the screams, the convulsive crying, and the nervous trembling that shook the child's delicate little body.

Eliza ended up falling asleep with her head on her guardian's chest. Laying her down on the bed and carefully covering her, the Count began to walk around the room, wondering how he should act. He did not want to leave Eliza for another day in the castle, where her life was in danger. But where could he leave her? With Mother Vilfrida? It was too far away, and not even Ervin Finsterbach would like that. After thinking for fifteen minutes, the Count decided to leave Eliza temporarily with Giovanna.

There, the girl would recover from the terrible shock she had endured, and he himself would be able to see her more often. What would happen next? Time would tell. Calmer with this decision, Wolfram ordered Lucien to arrange for all the girl's necessary luggage to be packed, because at dawn they would leave with Eliza.

Then he went to see his son. He wanted to question him alone and find out the details of the crime from him.

The boy was not sleeping and was only crying. When his father came in, he stood up agitated.

- And then? Did you find Eliza? Is she alive? - he asked.

Wolfram pulled up a chair and sat down next to the bed.

- Yes, she is alive. God did not allow the death of the innocent child. Now, tell me in detail how it happened.

In a trembling voice, Raymond told her everything, not omitting the scene with his mother, the slaps he had received, and the prohibition against telling his father anything.

Wolfram listened quietly, but inside he felt hatred, contempt, and revulsion stirring for the hateful woman who bore his name. Finally, he pulled Raymond close and kissed him.

- My good boy! You are my true son. Your mother's treacherous and criminal blood couldn't lead you to crime - he murmured.

Feeling that his father's lips were trembling, and a hot tear fell on his forehead, Raymond was stunned. He had never before seen his father cry.

- Don't cry father! I swear that I will never punish Eliza again. Even if she doesn't treat me with respect, I will keep her as my most precious possession - he consoled his father, putting his arms around the Count's neck.

He smiled.

- Thank you, my boy, for the promise, but I cannot leave Eliza here and tomorrow morning I am taking her away. You will only see her when you grow up and are able to protect her. Then you will decide if you really love each other. Do you want to say goodbye to her?

- Of course, I want to! Father, take me away too. I don't want to stay with Mom and the evil Greta, who made me lock Eliza up - Raymond murmured emotionally, in a pleading tone.

A heavy sigh escaped Wolfram's chest. Oh, he would love to take his son away and free him of the criminal mother's evil influence. But how could he install his son of his legitimate wife under the roof of his mistress?

- Unfortunately, that is impossible, my son. But I will be back soon, and woe to your mother if she dares to mistreat you!

Raymond, overcome with emotion, went to his father's room, and leaned over the sleeping Eliza. She was deathly pale and had a very weakened appearance. A heartfelt compassion squeezed the boy's heart. He leaned over silently and carefully kissed the pale little mouth and hand of his tiny wife.

The first rays of the rising sun began to gild the horizon when in the great castle palace Wolfram mounted his horse and placed Eliza in front of the saddle, wrapped in her cape. In Lucien's cell was tied the package with the girl's clothes.

Countess Anna watched her husband's departure from her window and choked with rage. Wolfram did not go to see her, and his departure with Eliza needed no explanation.

She learned of what had happened the night before from the maid. As she concluded that thanks to Raymond her mortal plan had not been carried out and that he was to blame for the new abysm opening between her and her husband, in her soul hatred for her son awoke.

- Stupid and ungrateful creature! You prefer your father, who abandons you for weeks on end, and I, who lives only for him. But you will see! You will pay for this betrayal - she muttered, clenching her fists.

When the creaking of the drawbridge announced the castle master's departure, the countess went to her son's room. Raymond was sitting by the window, crying. His father's departure with Eliza had made him desperate. When his mother entered and locked the door, he was frightened. The anger that appeared on her face aroused in the boy's spirit a feeling of repulsion mixed with terror.

For the first time, he involuntarily compared his handsome and elegant father with that vulgar woman, and then he found her too disgusting, especially because her face was covered with red stains and her thick lips revealed large, blackened teeth.

Raymond felt the approach of one of those unfair storms, which always urged him to be stubborn and to resist. If the Count's affectionate gaze always made him docile, his relationship with his mother sometimes made him show his claws.

Pale, with clenched teeth, Raymond looked resolutely forward to what would come next.

Initially there was a barrage of offenses and curses on Wolfram, and then accusations of ingratitude and treachery began to Raymond.

I will teach you to keep your mouth shut, you filthy brat! Now, tell me what you have told your father - shouted the countess in a hoarse voice.

- I only told him the truth, that is, that Eliza was locked in the tower, that you forbade me to tell anyone about this, and that you lied, saying that there was a cellar there - replied Raymond, who had listened to his mother quietly, turning alternately pale and flushed.

- Did you know that father cried and said to me, "You are really my son! The treacherous and criminal blood of your mother could not induce you to commit a crime."

The countess turned deathly pale and backed away. Then, seized by a fit of rage, she fell on her son and began to beat him with a thick silk cord.

- There you go, there you go! You will learn to respect your mother and never again tell your father lies about me! - she shouted, then paused to take a breath. You will be locked up in this room for three days and you will only have bread and water.

Covering himself with bitter tears, Raymond threw himself on the bed. What misfortune the unpleasant marriage had brought him! If this continued to happen for the rest of his life, then perhaps it would be better if Eliza really had died in the tower. He, at least, did not want to see her anymore.

Chapter 5

Giovanna welcomed Eliza with open arms and treated her late friend's daughter with motherly affection. With that kind treatment, the girl gradually began to recover from the terrible shock to her body and regained her usual joy and carefree manner. For Giovanna, the girl was a joy and a diversion during Wolfram's long absences, caused by business at the Court of the Count of Tyrol. Eliza herself also became fond of her adopted mother.

Giovanna's health continued to worsen. She was melting like wax. The mysterious evil that was growing every day was undermining her health and no one could solve it. Her hands and feet felt as heavy as lead and the slightest effort and emotion made her break into a cold sweat. A dark terror troubled her, making her fall asleep. An inner heat burned in her chest, and from time to time she had prolonged fainting spells, during which she was haunted by horrible visions. Disgusting beings would swarm around her, blowing clouds of black smoke over her and suffocating her, or they would wrap themselves around her like spider webs and suck the life forces out of her.

When Wolfram returned, after a six-week absence, he was startled by the change that had occurred in her appearance. The freshness of her face had changed to a pale-green color, and the eyes deep in her sockets had lost their luster. Her entire figure revealed the somber pattern of weariness and apathy. When Giovanna fainted the moment she saw Wolfram, he had the impression that he was holding a corpse in his arms.

Terribly desperate, the Count racked his brains trying to find a remedy to help the woman he loved. Two of the doctors he called failed to alleviate Giovanna's suffering, and apparently did not know her ailment. Suddenly, the idea came to him to consult Baron Vart. The Count knew that the old scientist had been a doctor and possessed remedies unknown to ordinary doctors. In addition, he was Giovanna's uncle. Even if the Baron did not agree with their union and openly declared his dissatisfaction, he understood human weaknesses and forgave them.

The old man always considered Wolfram as a son, so the Count hoped he would not refuse to treat Giovanna.

The next day he put his plan into execution. He left, telling Giovanna that he was going to see one more doctor whom he trusted more than all the others.

The night after Wolfram's departure, Giovanna felt so bad that she seemed to be dying. A strange weight pressed against her chest, preventing her from breathing, and for the first time she felt a stabbing pain in all her limbs.

A great sadness took hold of her and forced her to get out of bed. Desolate, she barely managed to crawl to the holy image. It seemed that her end was near. The thought of death awakened fear and pain of conscience in her mind.

Wasn't the strange illness a punishment for her criminal liaison with Wolfram? Then she remembered her brother's harsh words, uncle Vart's disapproval, and bitter tears streamed from her eyes. She had not listened to those warnings and had gone away like a scoundrel. In that moment she was deeply sorry for everything that had happened. She felt an uncontrollable urge to see Fulvio, to make up with him and receive his forgiveness before she died.

Then, in the morning, she wrote to her brother about her illness, begging him to forgive her and not to deny her the joy of being able to hold him for the last time, since her end was near. After sending the letter, Giovanna calmed down a little. If Fulvio was in Venice, he would naturally go to see her.

A few days later, the Count arrived and reported that he had gone to visit the Baron to ask for his help. But the scientist

[78]

refused to travel and demanded that the patient be taken to him, because in his castle he had at hand everything he needed for the treatment. So, Wolfram went to get Giovanna and Eliza to take them to his friend's castle.

The Baron was extremely distressed by the state of his niece's health, weakened to the point that she could not even speak. He did everything he could to get her settled comfortably, and then said he needed to observe the symptoms of the ailment before making a diagnosis and prescribing treatment.

The fresh mountain air was probably beneficial for Giovanna, who felt much better. When her uncle was near, she felt a sense of well-being. But the strange thing was that as soon as he moved away the illness manifested itself again.

Fulvio's unexpected arrival thrilled her too much. She suffered one of those long faints and for a few hours lay prostrate as if dead. The letter from his sister frightened and worried the young Venetian too much. All his anger soon vanished, and he was on his way to see her that very night.

When he arrived in the village and learned that Giovanna had been taken to her uncle's house, he immediately followed behind.

Fulvio arrived at the Baron's laboratory, sad and worried.

- What do you think about Giovanna's illness, Uncle Conrad? - he asked. Her condition looks serious to me. You are right! Her state of health is very serious indeed. I have reason to suspect that she was the victim of sorcery. I just do not have precise indications yet of who was guilty of this crime - replied the Baron.

- Oh, that is easy to guess. It must have been Count Reifenstein's wife or one of his mistresses, wanting to get rid of her dangerous rival - Fulvio said.

Then he angrily remarked:

- When will God punish this shameless depraved who mocks the sanctity of marriage and sacrifices to his whims the honor of noble women?

The Baron shook his head.

Don't judge Wolfram so harshly for a simple human attraction, which is excusable considering the family hell to which he was condemned. His father's tyrannical will bound him as an adolescent to that woman, whose soul is even more disgusting than her appearance. Despair drives him away from his own home and pushes his passionate soul into pity-worthy follies. In addition, you need to know that Giovanna needs great care and much peace. If you let her perceive your hostile feelings toward the person she loves, this could have a bad repercussion on her weakened organism.

- I will not treat the Count with hostility. Now, I have only one concern: saving my sister. So, Uncle Conrad, let's get back to the point. There is no longer any doubt that Giovanna was the victim of sorcery. We already have a good idea of who could be the mastermind of the crime and now we just need to find the executioner.

- This has already been established. I have no doubt that the executor of the sorcery is a Jew named Markhodey, a terrible sorcerer who has already caused a lot of harm to people. He lives in the neighboring town. Unfortunately, I learned too late that he cast a spell on poor Paola, who died of the same evil that consumes Giovanna. Now, first of all, we need to know how much the destructive force has undermined her organism. Come, let's go see her!

The Baron took a small box from the closet and went with Fulvio to his niece's room. Giovanna, pale as death, was lying on the bed. Wolfram was sitting by her bedside, and a few steps away from them, Eliza was playing with a doll.

When the Venetian saw the Count, his pale face turned red, and a gloomy flame flickered in his eyes. But, mastering himself, he greeted him with a certain reserve. Then, wishing to dispel the bad feeling that was clearly reflected in his sister's sickly face, he leaned toward Eliza and asked, passing his hand caressingly over her little blond head:

[80]

- Who is this beautiful girl? She reminds too much of poor Paola.

- She is her daughter. Count Wolfram made her married to his only son, and for reasons too long to explain now, was forced to entrust her to me - replied Giovanna.

Eliza raised her eyes and looked at him curiously. She smiled and without any resistance let herself be picked up. Then, wrapping her arms around Fulvio's neck, she said, stroking his cheek:

- I really like your eyes! I have never seen anyone with such beautiful eyes. I would like to stare at them forever.

Everyone laughed and Giovanna complimented Fulvio on his quick achievement. This completely cleared the charged atmosphere and the conversation flowed more amiably.

Then Baron Conrad started the test. Taking out of the box some stones, supposedly precious and not set, he began to place them in sequence and three at a time on Giovanna's palm, observing carefully together with Fulvio if they changed colors. All the stones darkened and one of them turned completely black.

- It seems that we will find the remedy that will restore our health. But we need to discuss with Fulvio which treatment we should follow - said the Baron to Wolfram and Giovanna, who were watching the whole procedure with fear and curiosity.

Being alone in the laboratory, the uncle and nephew discussed at length how to destroy the spell that was undermining Giovanna's health.

- It is a pity that we do not have some girl with mystical strength[13] to serve us as an instrument. It would make our attempt much easier - Fulvio said.

- But we have this instrument, little Eliza. The good spirits protect her, and God has given her enormous power. It seems that

---

[13] Mystical strength – Fluvio probably was referring to "some girl with mediumnship".

Eliza sympathizes with you a lot, and this means that you can influence her. So, try to get her very attached to you and in nine days, after the necessary preparations, we will try to free Giovanna from the deadly spell.

In the days that followed, the scientists spent almost all their time in the laboratory, studying and performing mysterious tests. They appeared only at dinner and spent a few hours in the evening in everyone's company.

Fulvio won Eliza's affection in such a way that she would sleep only on his lap and was so obedient to his every request that she even seemed to guess his thoughts.

Finally, the time has come to begin the important and dangerous experiment, which should decide Giovanna's survival.

Around midnight, Fulvio lifted a heavy curtain that covered the laboratory window. The full moon illuminated the magic circle drawn on the floor. In the center of the circle, on a metal stand, was a mirror, also made of metal, whose polished surface reflected the colors of the rainbow.

Eliza, who spent the whole afternoon playing with her new friend, was sleeping on the bed. Approaching the girl, Fulvio applied a few passes to her, and then extended his hand toward the magic circle. The girl shivered, stood up, and with extraordinary lightness slid off the bed. Following the direction indicated by the Venetian, she entered the magic circle and stopped in front of the mirror.

The child's eyes were closed; her delicate, graceful figure seemed to float without touching the ground.

- Do you see Giovanna sleeping? - asked Fulvio.

- Yes, I see her. She is rolling on the bed, and a black cloud hangs over her, and for a moment envelops her completely - replied Eliza.

The child's voice sounded strange.

- Look closely in the mirror and try to see where this black cloud came from!

- The cloud comes from far away. A red and black cord connects her to that bridge.

- Watch the string and see where it leads!

The child leaned forward and seemed to be intently watching an invisible object, although her eyes remained closed.

- I see it. A black ribbon runs across the mountains. There is a narrow street passing between old houses. The black ribbon disappears into the little house that has a small window with bars...Ouch!

Eliza let out a scream and stepped back.

An imperious gesture from Fulvio made her stop near the line of the circle that she almost went through.

- Stay here and tell me what you see!

- I see a dark room; at the bottom of it sits a monster and between its horns there is a box into which the dark ribbon penetrates. Giovanna is lying in that box and on her chest burns a green flame that consumes her.

- Can you take that box and pass it to me?

- If you command it - murmured the girl in a weak voice.

- Take it! I am ordering you!

Eliza's little hand began to slide across the mirror as if groping for something.

The small town slept; its dark, narrow streets were deserted, and in Markhodey's house silence reigned. At the back of the house, in the room leading to the back garden, protected from prying eyes by a high wall, slept the master of the house; he rested in the oriental manner on a row of pillows covered by a soft carpet. In the adjoining room slept Misael, the sorcerer's son, and helper in his shady dealings.

Suddenly, in that deep silence a mournful moan was heard from Markhodey; shaken and trembling he rose from his bed. For a moment he sat with his eyes wide open, clasping his hands to his heart and panting. Then he got up from the bed, but unable to stand on his weakened legs, he collapsed to the floor.

The old man's thin legs twitched as if in terrible pain, but he soon recovered his usual composure and willpower. Then he crawled into the adjoining room and shouted in a shrill voice:

- Misael! Misael! Quickly! Get up quickly!

The boy, about twenty-five years old, jumped out of bed and helped Markhodey.

- What happened, Dad? Did the Goys[14] attack our house and are they killing our brothers? - he asked, horrified.

- No! By the grace of Jehovah,[15] none of that threatens us, but something terrible has come upon me. Take me quickly to the sanctuary.

Misael lifted his father up like a child and carried him into the sanctuary. But as soon as they crossed the threshold, Markhodey put both hands on his head and a cry of horror escaped his chest. The little coffin with the wax figure was no longer between the horns of the idol.

Markhodey fell to the ground and, clutching his son's arm, muttered:

- Bring me the crystal container with water and light up the black candles...Hurry...Death is coming, and first I want to give you great strength and my power over the invisible beings.

Pale and trembling in his whole body, the young Jew ran to the niche in the wall, hidden by a curtain, took out the crystal

---

[14] Goy - Designation given among the Jews to the individual or people who are not of Jewish origin.

[15] Jehovah - From the Hebrew Jehovah, transliteration of the four letters (IHVH, JHVR, JHWH, YHVH or YHWH) that designate God, whose name was considered very sacred and could not be pronounced aloud. God's name in the Old Testament, Yahweh.

container of water and placed it on the floor in front of his father. He then lit the black candles and sat down opposite his father, on the other side of the container.

It was an amazing and terrible sight!

Both, leaning over the water, were pale as death, and the old man was quickly imparting his wicked sorcerer's secrets to his son. Markhodey's appearance was horrible and disgusting. His face was green, his eyes were popping out of their sockets, and his whole body was writhing in convulsions. With intermittent voicing, as if playing and whistling, he babbled incantations and formulas, looking around him in horror.

Suddenly, from all sides, from the walls, the ceiling and the floor, a black, dense, suffocating vapor began to pour out, filling the room and gradually enveloping the wizard. A mournful crackling was heard, and a gust of wind whistled and roared past. The black candles burned with a greenish flame, and various objects thrown by invisible beings flew thunderously around the room.

Markhodey was seized by a crisis of madness: with roars, groans, and convulsions he rolled on the ground during the storm that raged around him. Then the idol, knocked off its pedestal by an invisible force, crashed down beside the wizard, and one of the monster's horns buried itself in his body.

Markhodey leaped up roaring like a wild animal, but immediately fell to the ground. His desperate screams were answered by the roar of shrill laughter; he resisted furiously, but the cloud of black smoke enveloped and suffocated him. After a few minutes of fighting, Markhodey turned over on his stomach, stretched out his arms, and stood motionless.

Immediately in the room everything was silent. The crackling flame of the candle stump illuminated only the face of the wizard, disfigured, and blackened as if he had been struck by lightning; the idol had fallen, and the vessel cracked in half.

The young Jew, pale, breathing heavily, remained silent and did not move while the execution of the great servant of evil was taking place through the same law that he himself had activated. The destructive force unleashed by Markhodey on the innocent being turned against himself and this backlash eventually killed him.

Misael leaned over Markhodey's corpse and looked with involuntary trembling at the face disfigured by horror. Then he took off his father's left shoe and removed a small object wrapped in a cloth that looked like a cross. He had placed that object in his own shoe, mumbling sacrilegious words.

Giovanna's health had a radical change. She practically came back to life. Her face regained its former freshness, her eyes lit with fire, and her gait became steady and graceful. Only an occasional slight weakness reminded her of the mortal danger she had been in. Eliza was also weak and for about two or three days felt a slight discomfort, but soon recovered.

Reassured about Giovanna's health, Wolfram returned to his castle, driven by the desire to see his son again and also by the need to keep up with business. When he left, he agreed with Giovanna that in a month's time he would return to take her to the village.

The day after the Count's departure, Fulvio went to visit his sister.

- Now that you are completely cured, Giovanna, it is my duty to tell you the cause of your illness and to talk about the future - he said amiably, sitting down next to her.

The girl nodded affirmatively and Fulvio continued:

- The illness that almost killed you was caused by sorcery. Science and the cooperation of an innocent being gifted with an extraordinary power enabled Uncle Conrad and me to save you. The mastermind of the crime was Countess Reifenstein, and the executioner, a Jewish sorcerer who lives on the outskirts, near here.

Giovanna paled and raised her eyes.

- So, what is your conclusion from all this?

- My conclusion is that your life is under constant threat of death. The countess will continue to look for an opportunity to eliminate the rival who stands between her and her husband, usurping her legal rights. Your own conscience, sister, should tell you that immoral liaison with a married man cannot merit divine blessing. You should decide whether your miraculous healing was a sign from Heaven that it is time to retake the true path, the path of duty.

Giovanna put her hands on her head. She remembered the torturous pangs of conscience that had nagged her the night she thought she was going to die and decided to call Fulvio to help her.

- Do you want me to leave Wolfram? - she whispered, and two hot tears rolled down her cheeks. How can I do that now, when he has practically found me again, and when death has returned me to him?

- Are you sure that death has returned you to him and not to a new, honest life worthy of God's commandments? But calm down! Far be it from me to poison your recovery with reprimands and harsh demands. Giovanna, I forgave you long ago and I leave it to you to make the choice. I only wanted to reveal to you the cause of your illness and warn you of the eternal danger you are in because of the hatred of the woman whose husband you drive away from his home and from his obligations. I want you to know: the day you voluntarily return to my house, it will be the happiest day of my life. Let's finish this matter now and may the Lord inspire and direct you! I am leaving tomorrow, as unavoidable commitments await me.

That conversation stayed in Giovanna's mind. However, the attraction for Wolfram was still so strong that when the Count arrived to pick her up, she went with him and Eliza to the village. However, the previous harmony and eternal happiness had been broken.

It is not known whether it was a consequence of the spell or the result of Giovanna's new feelings of fear of God, but the relationship between the lovers was no longer the same:

disagreements and even arguments began. A respectful discretion replaced the former frankness. Once, Wolfram covered Giovanna with reprimands, told her she no longer loved him, and went away for two months to the Count of Tyrol's court. His scandalous affairs, whose fame eventually reached the isolated village, provoked a storm of jealousy in the Venetian's passionate heart.

Giovanna was as beautiful as prideful and vindictive, and the method Wolfram used to express his annoyance displeased her too much.

After maturing thought the young woman decided, with the energy that was particular to her, to end that relationship that was condemned by religion and honor and that no longer brought her so much happiness.

By virtue of this decision, as soon as the Count returned having forgotten his anger, she advised him of the decision she had taken to return to her brother's house.

Wolfram was astonished; but all his efforts and pleas to make Giovanna change her mind were in vain.

- Let's be content with the fact that we were happy and will keep good memories of our beautiful dream of love - she said fondly, but firmly. Anything that is not based on honesty and duty and is poisoned by shame cannot last. We are still friends, Wolfram, this feeling no one can take away from us. Let's say goodbye, without poisoning this separation with reprimands.

Despite the deep sadness that the separation caused him, the Count had to submit to Giovanna's decision. He had long ago predicted that a time would come when pride would overcome love in the Venetian's heart. But the separation was too recent for him to be able to treat Giovanna as a friend.

Wolfram immediately decided to leave with Eliza and decided to leave the girl with Baron Vart for a while. He was afraid to take her with him to the castle, and at that moment he had nowhere to leave her.

Then Giovana told him that Uncle Conrad intended to go and live in Fulvio's house, and that she would go there with him. Then she handed him a letter from the Baron, in which the Baron asked Wolfram to entrust Eliza to him until the time she joined her husband. The Baron promised to take care of the education of the little girl and leave her his possessions. With him, Fulvio and Giovanna, the girl would grow up happy and loved by all. For Eliza it was the best thing to do. After a short inner struggle, Wolfram agreed, although it was difficult for him to leave the girl, he had grown so fond of.

After a cold farewell, the Count left the village in a hurry, and ten days later Giovanna and Eliza also left for Italy under the guardianship of Fulvio, who went in person to pick them up.

Chapter 6

It was a beautiful March day in 1305. The rays of the setting sun played over the surface of the Venetian canals, reflecting the colors gold and purple on the thick gray-green walls of the palaces.

By the bank of one of the canals near the "*Canale Grande*",[16] rose a palace whose freshness and finish indicated that it had been recently restored by its owners.

In a luxuriously furnished room on the first floor, lit by three tall windows, were at that moment three characters we already knew.

Behind a small table, Conrad and Fulvio Faleri were playing chess. Neither of them had changed at all in the ten years that had passed. Mr. Conrad was still a venerable old man with a youthful look, while the prideful, severe, and cold Fulvio looked like a twenty-five-year-old boy.

Near the marble fireplace, in which a high fire was burning, in a carved wooden chair covered with silk, sat a beautiful girl. She wore a white wool dress; the tight-fitting bodice highlighted her elegant, delicate figure, and a thin gold ring held back her beautiful black hair, which flowed in silky locks down to below her knees.

Her face, of perfect features and childlike delicacy, had an amazing pale, opaque color. But the metallic shine of the big blue eyes and the energetic crease of the small pink mouth denoted an authoritative, prideful, and even capricious spirit. A slight wrinkle

---

[16] "*Grande Canale*" - Known as the "most pleasant canal in the world", it is "S" shaped and is the widest and most important canal in Venice, four kilometers long and surrounded by palaces used by the aristocracy.

between her eyebrows and her taciturn gaze, staring at nothing, showed that, at that moment, she was worried about something; her small hand was nervously twisting the silk cord that buckled her waist.

Several times Fulvio glanced toward the fireplace, watching the girl.

- Eliza, you are looking very serious today! What are you thinking about? - he asked.

The girl shuddered and straightened up.

- I keep thinking about Wolfram's arrival and those unpleasant explanations that await me - she replied with a sigh.

Then she got up, approached the small table, and sat down on the armrest of Fulvio's chair.

- Do you intend to fight with the Count? - asked the Venetian with a smile. You used to like him!

- It is true! I like the Count and have the best memories of him, but I do not like his son at all, that mean and rude boy who was always arguing, hitting me and Greta and even dragging her by her braids. I do not want to go back to him for anything in the world!

- You are speaking disrespectfully of your husband. It will not be easy at all to get rid of him! - said Fulvio, with a mischievous smile.

Eliza blew up.

- For nothing in this world will I go back to Castle Reifenstein! To live again next to that disgusting woman who, I am sure, would have been very happy if I had died in the tower where her worthy son locked me up? No, never!

- If Mr. Wolfram wants to force me to do so, then I would rather throw myself into the canal than accompany him.

You could feel the tears in Eliza's voice. Suddenly, she put her arms around Fulvio's neck and squeezed him with her velvety face.

[91]

- Let me stay! I am so happy here with you and Grandpa Conrad. Can't you scientists, possessing so much power, free me of the fate that is so repulsive to me?

Then the girl threw herself into the Baron's arms, and Fulvio's face reddened slightly.

- Calm down, dear! - said the old man, kissing her on the forehead. If marrying Raymond displeases you, then I promise to take all necessary measures to free you from him. Wolfram is very honest and noble and will not force a woman. Fulvio and I are on good terms with the holy priest, which assures us that your marriage to young Count Reifenstein can be broken up.

- Yes, Eliza! I swear that if you do not want to leave us of your own free will, no one will force you to - added Fulvio.

- You just must stay calm, patient and not get worked up - Vart interrupted. Don't forget, Eliza, that you are bound to Raymond by sacred ties and this matter must be handled with extreme care.

On the girl's face appeared an expression of satisfaction and fear.

- I know you are right, Grandpa, and I will follow your advice at face value.

With the information that dinner was served, the girl interrupted the conversation. The three of them went into the dining room and sat down at the table, which sparkled with crystal and silver. Dinner passed in silence, as each was immersed in their own thoughts.

The girl owned rooms that led out to the canal and to a cross street. Fulvio furnished the rooms for his young friend with luxury and comfort.

Eliza pushed the chair up to the window, sat down, and stared thoughtfully at the canal along which *gondolas*[17] were sliding silently.

She was thinking of Raymond. The awaited arrival of Count Wolfram revived her childhood memories. Scenes from her past at Castle Reifenstein, one by one, came back to her: the wedding, the fights, and also the friendly games with her little husband. And in between them always stood the clever, lying, and evil genius Margarita von-Ramets. This went on until the terrible day when, under Greta's influence - Eliza heard and remembered this - Raymond locked her in the abandoned tower.

The memories of what she had suffered there sent an icy shiver through her body. She could still see with sickening clarity the dark room, the bed with the frayed curtains, and the black stains on the floor that according to Raymond were the remains of blood.

The insane horror that had taken over her childish soul rekindled everything again. Her heart beat strongly, as on that occasion, when she sat by the locked door and, she was no longer able to scream and, feeling cold, saw the darkness of the night approaching. Then - she did not know whether it was a vision or just a hallucination of her disturbed senses - she saw how the tower lit up with a greenish light and before her the whole scene of the murder unfolded.

The impression was so strong that even at this moment she could see again before her the pale and deformed face of the young woman, knocked to the ground with a punch from a man in a red suit and a face disfigured by fury. She heard the noise of the struggle, hoarse voices, and a shrill, horrible scream of agony that shook her to the bone. Then she remembered nothing more...

Eliza stood up, walked across the room, and with both hands threw back her long black hair. She did not want to remember that terrible event. She promised herself that she would

---

[17] Gondola- Characteristic boat of the canals of Venice; long, narrow, and flat-bottomed propelled by a single oar.

never return to Castle Reifenstein and that she would stay there, where she was happy and where everyone loved and spoiled her.

The girl lit two wax torches on massive candelabras, sat down at the table, and looked around, full of herself. The expensive and thick fabric of the walls, the inlaid furniture, and the oriental rug that covered the floor, all displayed luxury and comfort that showed the love of whoever had arranged that royal shelter for her.

Yes, Fulvio was kind and magnanimous. From the day she and Giovanna came to live under his roof their lives went on without any problems. The ten years she spent there were times of happiness and peace.

At the time, they did not live in Venice, but on the outskirts of Padua,[18] in a small castle belonging to Fulvio.

Let's stop here with Eliza's memories and tell the readers what happened during the intervening years.

After her separation from Wolfram, Giovanna did not want to return to Venice immediately. No one there knew for sure where she had been, but they naturally suspected that the quarrel with her brother had important motives, although Fulvio had never commented on the matter.

Because of her beauty and wealth, Giovanna was considered one of the queens of Venice, and countless admirers longed for her hand. Among the suitors, the most popular was Oreo Villamarino, a rich, famous, and noble young man. Everyone was waiting for the announcement of their engagement when suddenly the beautiful Venetian disappeared from the city, and no one really knew anything about the real reason for her disappearance. Only Oreo was able to guess the truth. Jealousy helped him catch the

---

[18] Padua - Capital of the province of the same name, located in northwestern Italy, was from the twelfth to the fourteenth century (time of this narrative) an independent commune of great political and economic importance.

Commune - a city that obtained a charter from its liege lord granting it autonomy during the Middle Ages.

suspicious exchange of glances between Giovanna and the German knight. Oreo, who loved her sincerely and deeply became desperate; out of sorrow he entered the service of a Republican galley[19] and for a long time sailed the waters of the Mediterranean.

About a year after Giovanna's reconciliation with her brother, Oreo met Fulvio by chance and then went to visit him. At his house, he found Giovanna at the height of her beauty. The love that never faded in his heart rekindled with new impetus and he asked her to marry him.

Giovanna, honest and proud, was absolutely sincere in revealing to him everything that had happened and adding that she had separated from the Count on her own initiative. She also said that she would like to reward Oreo for his long loyalty by marrying him, if he still considered her worthy to use his name, after all that had happened. Villamarino replied that only God and her conscience could judge the past and that he only demanded her love and fidelity from that moment on. Giovanna, however, insisted that the marriage be postponed for a year. Thus, three years after Wolfram's separation, she married Villamarino.

The engagement was a happy one. Even though she was still in love with the Count, Giovanna respected Oreo, whose love brought her a solid and peaceful happiness.

Deciding to spend the first years of married life away from Venice, Giovanna, at the request of her brother and uncle, left Eliza, whom they adored. The girl grew up lonely, but was happy in the small castle near Padua, where she received a much better education than the noble girls of her time. The Baron together with Fulvio personally taught her sciences and arts.

At that time, it was only three weeks since they had returned to Venice and Giovanna was preparing to present her brother's protégée to society when suddenly the Count's letter unpleasantly reminded her that Eliza was married.

---

[19] Galera - An old warship; a sailing vessel, usually of three round masts with two masts on each.

Wolfram maintained a rare correspondence with Vart; he personally never went to visit him, nor Eliza. The news of Giovanna's marriage made the Count extremely sad, and he avoided meeting her. It is hard to say whether he did not want to disturb her peace or he did not trust his own attitude.

In castle Reifenstein Eliza's name was never mentioned. Even Raymond seemed to have forgotten her. Only Wolfram remembered the young woman, and sometimes, from the bottom of his heart, he regretted having brought together two beings who had so little in common with each other. But the harm was already done! After waiting for Eliza to turn sixteen and Raymond to turn twenty-two, he decided to visit his daughter-in-law and decide with Conrad Vart the best way to unite the young couple.

It was the Count's letter, announcing his arrival in Venice, that disturbed Eliza's mind.

Giovanna was also a little disturbed by the news of Wolfram's arrival. With her usual frankness, she immediately told her husband about it and said that, if he wanted, she could leave Venice for as long as Wolfram stayed there.

- God forbid I should allow you to run away from that man! - replied the Venetian proudly. He belongs to a past that doesn't concern me and I hope he won't represent a danger to the mother of my children. In order not to arouse too much suspicion by avoiding him, we will welcome the Count as a friend of your brother.

The day after that conversation, Giovanna and her husband were having lunch at Fulvio's house. During the meal, the main subject was Eliza's marriage. Count Wolfram was expected for the next day, and the girl was in a fierce state of mind.

After lunch, when everyone moved to the living room, Oreo Villamarino tried to convince Eliza to be obedient and to take on her new life with docility. At that moment, the servant entered to inform them of Count Reifenstein's arrival.

[96]

The Baron and Fulvio got up immediately to welcome the visitor, but they did not have time to get to the door when on the threshold appeared himself. He was still the same handsome and prideful knight, with flaming eyes and disdainful smile. He embraced Vart, shook Fulvio's hand, and then quickly addressed the ladies. He paled slightly when he recognized Giovanna, but Giovanna seemed not to have noticed this, extending a friendly hand to him.

- Welcome Count! I am very happy to see the old friend of so many years again - she said in a calm tone.

Wolfram kissed her hand cordially and thanked her discreetly for the kind welcome. Next, Giovanna introduced her husband to him. Oreo clearly read in his wife's eyes that the Count was nothing more than a memory to her, and affectionately shook his ex-rival's hand.

After that, Wolfram approached Eliza. Eliza stood up, pale and confused. She clearly did not know how to behave with him.

But the Count immediately put an end to her indecision, pulling her to himself and kissing her on the cheek.

- How happy I am to see you, my dear daughter! Don't tell me that you have forgotten me so much that you see me as a stranger!

Eliza was embarrassed and did not react. But when she met that loving gaze, she was again enveloped by the charm he had always had on her since childhood. She forgot all her anger, responded with affection to the Count's kiss and said:

- No Uncle Wolfram, I have never forgotten that you have always been good to me, and I love you as always, but I am just afraid that you will not like what I have to tell you.

- We still have time to talk and discuss the unpleasant things that you intend to tell me. But now, allow me to look at you long enough - said the Count cheerfully.

Then, addressing Giovanna, he added:

[97]

- Don't you think she looks a lot like Paola? Only her eyes and her expression of the mouth there is something different.

- She is different from her mother in taste and character - replied Giovanna with a smile.

Turning to the late friend, she wanted to know where the knight Finsterbach was. The conversation became general, and Wolfram told her that Ervin Finsterbach had been seriously wounded in the last fighting near Jerusalem. After the liberation of Jerusalem and the return of the Templars to the island of Cyprus, he had stayed for a long time with the Grand Magistrate; then he had been assigned as commander for northern Germany. Recently, Ervin had announced that when he traveled to the island of Cyprus, he intended to pass through Venice to meet up again with his daughter, who he had not seen for years.

When the guests had left, Wolfram sat quietly by the fireplace, watching Eliza who was sitting next to him and looking at the fire with an embarrassed and worried air.

"She looks lovely!" thought Wolfram. "I bet Raymond will fall madly in love as soon as he sees her. But I wonder what is going on in her heart that she is afraid to reveal to me? Bloody hell! I wonder if she has fallen in love around here with some Italian. This would be a 'nice' surprise!"

- My child, now we are alone! Tell me, then, the unpleasant things you wanted to talk about - said the Count, going straight to the point as usual.

Eliza turned red and looked at the Count indecisively.

- Maybe I am wrong, imagining that what I have to tell you is unpleasant, Uncle Wolfram. But first, tell me the reason for your visit!

That mischievous question from the innocent daughter of Eve[20] caused a mocking smile to pass across the Count's lips.

---

[20] Daughter of Eve - Metaphorical expression. Eve was the name of the first woman and the "mother of all mankind," according to the Bible.

I came to see you and to thank Uncle Conrad and Mr. Fulvio for the dedication and love with which they have surrounded you - he replied, good-naturedly.

- Just for that? God, how happy I am! - she exclaimed with a sparkle in her eyes.

The Count began to curl his mustache.

- But I must confess that I also came to remind you that you are Countess Reifenstein and that this name imposes certain obligations.

Eliza's face immediately turned grim.

In response, she stated with a decided air that she had decided never to return to Castle Reifenstein and to divorce Raymond. The decision was motivated by the deep dislike she felt for Countess Anna, for Greta, and also for the unpleasant memories she had of Raymond.

- I am sure that Countess Anna will always try to destroy me while Greta will forever sow discord between us. Besides, Raymond has always preferred Miss Ramets and seems to love her sincerely these days. So let them be happy; I want to stay here among the people I love and who love me too. Uncle Wolfram, let me add that, on your part, it was a great sin to unite Raymond to me while we were still children - Eliza concluded, all red.

The Count listened to her without interrupting.

- Maybe you are right - he said after a moment's silence - and I made a mistake in putting you together. But such were the circumstances of the time, I thought I did the right thing. Marriages like yours are common among the nobility. God forbid that I should force you to be my son's wife if this marriage is repugnant to you. Naturally, Raymond will also not oppose the separation if Uncle Conrad gets it from the holy priest. But, my dear, don't you think that before taking this important decision it would be better to get

---

Adam's wife, seduced by the serpent, gathered the forbidden fruit, leading her partner to sin.

to know him and see if you two get along? Only then, after mature reflection, will you be able to cut the sacred ties that bind you together. Eliza, you do not throw away a husband like an old glove, and before making a man pay for his sins as a boy, you must see if he has made amends.

Eliza lowered her head and thought.

- You are right, Uncle Wolfram! Our meeting will not force us to do anything and, moreover, it can have very important consequences. But what will happen if I do not like Raymond, but he likes me? That could happen! Then he will not want to give me the divorce and the law will agree with him.

- My God, your caution is amazing! I cannot deny that he will most likely fall in love with the beautiful woman you are. But this is not yet a reason for divorce; we must find some way out, because in spite of your youth, you must understand that it is not that simple to destroy a union blessed by God.

Eliza did not say a word, lowered her head, and thought again.

Suddenly her eyes sparkled with mischief, and she let out a laugh.

- Uncle, I have an idea! - she said, laughing. If you approve it, then I can see Raymond and he can see me. Does he know where I am now?

- Yes, he knows that you are currently in Venice, but he did not ask me for details, because he knows neither Baron Vart, nor Fulvio, nor Madame Giovanna. So, what is your idea?

- Here's the deal: on your way back home, tell Raymond that I went to visit a sick aunt of Fulvio's. But tell him to come to Venice anyway and to wait for me there so that we can discuss the divorce, which we both want. He can stay at Fulvio's house and find out from Grandpa what needs to be done to separate us soon. While he waits for me, let him enjoy himself in the beautiful and rich city. In the meantime, I moved in with Giovanna. She is awaiting the arrival of a relative of her husband's, Bianca Villamarino, but she

[100]

cannot come soon because her mother is seriously ill. In the meantime, I can freely pretend to be Bianca, because around here almost nobody knows me. Raymond will think he is visiting the Oreo lady. So, I will see him there and it will be easier for me to observe from afar whether he will behave as a married man, aware of his obligations. Then I will arrange a meeting with him myself, so that he will never suspect who I am. In this way we can test whether or not we like each other.

Excited by her own idea, Eliza even clapped her hands.

The Count could not hold back his laughter, listening to the clever trap invented by Eva's imaginative daughter. In fact, Eliza's desire to see her husband and study his character before joining him for good was perfectly fair. Who knows, they really might not match!

- If Mr. Oreo, his wife, Fulvio and Uncle Conrad agree to take part in the plan, then I will do it as well, so that everything happens as you wish. I will bring Raymond here and the rest will be left to God! - replied Wolfram.

Mr. Oreo and his wife gladly agreed to introduce Eliza as their relative. Severe orders ensured the discretion of the servants; Conrad and Fulvio also accepted. It was agreed that Wolfram would warn his friends of the young Count's arrival. For greater certainty, Eliza was to move in immediately to the house of Madame Giovanna under the name of Bianca Villamarino.

When all the details of the trap that had been set for Raymond were settled, Wolfram left immediately.

Despite the affable treatment from Mr. Oreo, his wife and Fulvio, the Count was desolate. The fatal fate, which had separated him from Giovanna and had not allowed him any other sentimental union, was weighing him down more than ever.

[101]

Chapter 7

As the Count returns to his archaic castle, let's see what has happened there in the last ten years.

Wolfram never forgave his wife for her attempt to kill Eliza. He harshly implied to her that he only did not throw her out of the house because he did not want a final breakup. The countess had to keep quiet and pretend to hide from others her deep incompatibility with her husband, who was absent from the house as much as he could.

Raymond was growing up under the harsh control of his mother, who was meaner than ever and had a terrible influence on her son's character.

At twenty-two, Raymond was a handsome, elegant, well-developed boy, and expert in all the knightly arts. By the features of his face, large sparkling eyes, and full, curly hair, he resembled his father; but he lacked the captivating look and smile that made Wolfram so dangerous; also lacked self-confidence and innate politeness that characterized at every meeting singled out the Count, who in the mouths of the envious, acquired the nickname "King of Reifenstein".

Morally Raymond was stubborn and clever and inherited his parents' passionate and enthusiastic character; these tendencies were dormant, for the time being, for lack of opportunity. However, apart from a few weeks at the court of the Count of Tyrol, a few tournaments, and some relations with the neighborhood, Raymond barely knew the society; the hypocritical atmosphere in the castle had taught him to restrain himself.

His relationship with Margarita was strange. Their fiancé relationship was more like a relationship between brother and sister. Greta remembered that the countess had chosen her to be the wife of her son, and she held in the depths of her heart a faint hope of a happy accident that would reestablish her rights. To this end, she missed no opportunity to win Raymond's heart. With cunning, coquettishness, and by force of habit, she made herself necessary to the boy. He thought that he loved her and was very sad, even without showing it openly, when she received a marriage proposal.

For her part, Margarita played the role of victim, and when her fiancé died in a hunting accident, she confessed to Raymond that she considered that death a release, because she only loved him.

Four years have passed since then and no new prospective groom has appeared, much to the disappointment of the countess, who did not want her goddaughter to be the "eternal single lady" and feared that the love match between Greta and her son might end in drama.

The arrival at that time of Arnulf von-Ried, the eldest son from her first marriage, inspired Countess Anna with the idea of marrying him off to her goddaughter.

Arnulf was a taciturn and closed person. Nature had not been fair to him in his appearance: he had the face of his mother. Despite his thirty years and considerable fortune, he did not like the busy life of the nobility of that time. When circumstances allowed, he locked himself in his castle and led a hermit's life, devoting all his time to philanthropy, visiting monasteries and pilgrimages to holy places.

Frozen, reserved, and parsimonious, Arnulf took little interest in his relatives, but showed respect and obedience to his mother and stepfather and a fondness for his younger brother.

Every year, as an obligation, he spent a few weeks at castle Reifenstein. But Wolfram, despite his kindness and attention to his stepson, was not very fond of him and once even told his wife:

[103]

- Such holiness, at Arnulf's age, is not normal! His eyes are not those of a monk! I fear that the devil, whom he avoids so much, is already riding on his yoke and will one day show him his horns.

A few days after the Count's departure for Italy, Arnulf arrived at the castle and at the first opportunity Countess Anna brought up the subject of marriage with him.

- You need to get married, my son! Your lineage needs an heir, and your castle needs a lady. I raised Margarita and I know she will be a good housewife and a kind and loving wife, who will wear your name with dignity at Court feasts - concluded the countess.

Arnulf listened to his mother's arguments with indifference.

- I do not like society and I go to court so little that I do not need a wife to represent me there. Mother, I appreciate your concern for my happiness, but I refuse to marry Margarita. I do not like her; besides, it is not hard to see that she is in love with Raymond. What kind of happiness can a marriage have without mutual love? I imagine you must know this from your own experience.

The countess blew up.

- My life was darkened not by lack of love, but by Wolfram's levity. But, back to our question. Have you forgotten that Raymond is married, and do you see Greta as a sister? I am surprised to hear that that pretty girl is not to your liking. Really, Arnulf, you are a very strange person! You do not have the tastes of a knight, and no woman appeals to you.

In the Countess's voice one could sense a tone of irritation.

Arnulf smiled contemptuously.

- It is true! I think it is more important to win heaven than a prize in a raffle. Besides, this is not a good time for weddings, because I am going to travel to the Holy Land soon. However, you are wrong about one thing, Mother: that I am not capable of falling in love. I am not one to fall in love lightly and I consider women to be dangerous and treacherous beings that reason and religion

[104]

advise me to avoid. However, I once met a woman who was as beautiful as an angel and as intelligent as the devil. I would gladly marry her if it were possible.

- Who was she? Where did you find her? - asked the countess, surprised by the fire of passion that was lit in her son's cold eyes.

- It was Paola Finsterbach, mother of your daughter-in-law. I met her only twice at Ortruda's house. I was nineteen at the time. A little later she died, and since then no other woman has appealed to me. It is quite likely that in time I will join the monastery. So, Mother, please understand that you have chosen a bad time to talk to me about love and marriage, because I am getting ready to visit the Holy Sepulcher.

The Count returned unexpectedly to the castle, long before the scheduled arrival date.

The countess received him with the greatest hostility. She was angry with the world: she was angry with Arnulf for not wanting to marry Greta, angry with the late Paola for daring to please her son, and angry with her husband for marrying Raymond to the disgusting Eliza, whom he, to her enormous disappointment, would soon bring to the castle from Italy.

But the Count paid no attention to the countess's bad mood, and after dinner he called his son to his chambers to play chess.

Raymond, surprised, followed his father.

- Father! - he said, as soon as they were alone. You did not call me here to play, but to tell me the news of your trip to Venice. I have a feeling you will not say anything good - he added bitterly.

- Who knows? Perhaps the news I bring with me will be pleasant to you! - the Count coldly revealed.

He then blurted out that he saw Eliza and talked to Baron Vart.

- I have not hidden from him that this marriage is hateful to you. He replied that he considers it necessary that you should first meet and get to know each other. If, after that, you feel no sympathy for each other, then he will take advantage of his relationship with the holy priest to get the marriage annulled. You will now - he added - have the opportunity to get rid of your wife if she is not to your liking.

- But if I am to her liking and she does not want to leave me? - remarked Raymond worriedly.

Eliza and Raymond's strange fear of liking each other made the Count laugh.

- Dad, what are you laughing at? What is funny about the odds of Eliza feeling attracted to me and her not wanting to stop being Countess Reifenstein? - remarked Raymond, blushing.

- Oh, she does not need admirers! Her two guardians are giving her a very rich dowry. Besides, in my opinion, she is very beautiful.

- Really? Well, if I like her, I will take her with me immediately. But if not, I will divorce her and that is it!

- Not so fast! If Eliza does not want you, then I expect you to behave like my son and a knight and not force her to stay with you and give her back the same freedom you demand for yourself if you do not like her- objected the Count in a so serious and severe tone that Raymond was confused.

- In any case, here is what I propose to you – Wolfram continued. Go to Venice. Now, Eliza is not there. She traveled the same day I left and went to Fulvio Faleri's old sick aunt's house, but she will be back soon. Baron Vart and his friend Fulvio have invited you to stay at their house and await your wife's return. For you, it will be very interesting to visit this beautiful city, full of different amusements. It is a good society, since I will leave you in the care of my friend Oreo Villamarino and his wife Giovana, in whose hospitable home the entire Venetian nobility gathers.

Raymond's eyes sparkled.

- Thank you, Father! What a wonderful plan! I confess that I have long wanted to visit Venice and have fun there.

- I hope you do not forget that you are a married man and therefore have an obligation to be faithful to Eliza until the divorce comes through.

- Not at all! It is necessary first to know if she has the right to be jealous of me! She has been away from my influence for a long time and now she might be interested in some Italian. In that case, I will make her understand that, as long as she uses my name, she has no right to be interested in anyone else - replied Raymond, half angry, half offended.

The news of the young Count's brief departure for Venice angered the two inhabitants of the castle terribly. The countess, who knew nothing of the divorce's plans, because Wolfram had forbidden his son to talk about it, was furious at the thought of having the daughter of that "worthless Italian woman" under her roof again. Eliza was no longer a child, and if she inherited her mother's beauty and charm, she could easily win Raymond's heart and completely destroy the countess's influence.

Greta's irritation was even greater, because she had hoped that the marriage with Eliza, which nobody was talking about, could somehow be annulled. The thought of Raymond going to see his wife and perhaps taking an interest in her aroused her worst feelings.

But Margarita Ramets was the kind of woman who did not give up easily. The next day, in the morning, she arranged to meet Raymond alone and gave a demonstration of such desperation and jealousy of the boy, embarrassed and flattered by so much love, Raymond confessed to her, under promise of absolute secrecy, the secret of the intended divorce. With that news, Margarita's face cleared up and her hopes were strengthened. She had maneuvered the boy's head so well on the eve of his departure that, after a fond farewell, he formally promised to separate from Eliza and marry her as soon as he received his official freedom.

Countess Anna, disguising the anger that tormented her inside, watched the preparations for her son's trip. Besides the disgust that the purpose of the trip caused her, the idea of her not knowing anything of what would happen in Venice made her desperate.

Wolfram would tell her nothing; that was a certainty. The Count treated her with cold contempt and frank distrust, while Raymond could also keep quiet about a lot of things. Besides, as she had already realized, he sometimes omitted the truth.

Suddenly, she had a brilliant idea. Arnulf was going to the Holy Land, and it made absolutely no difference to him whether he boarded a galley in Venice or Genoa. If she asked, he might agree to advance his departure and travel together with his brother.

Then, that same night, she called Arnulf to her chambers and reporting to him her request, he added:

- I am very worried about Raymond's stay in that big city, full of innumerable temptations, especially if he is unattended. He is identical to his father; he is also frivolous, inconsequential and he likes women and pleasures. If I knew that there was someone as serious, correct, and sensible as you, my dear, around him, I would be reassured, because I would be sure that he would have a good example and good advice at his side. Moreover, you could let me know immediately if Raymond gets carried away and does something crazy.

After some reflection, Arnulf agreed to fulfill his mother's wish, for he himself was interested in seeing Venice and had long wanted to visit the queen city of the Adriatic Sea.[21]

Wolfram had nothing against that project. He did not like his stepson very much, but he could not condemn him for anything but discretion and avarice, and these qualities would even be useful on a trip for two. If the Count had known that Eliza's mother had made such a deep impression on the stern boy, he might have opposed that plan. But this circumstance was unknown to him, so he gladly agreed that his older brother should accompany his son.

---

[21] Adriatic Sea - Part of the Mediterranean Sea, between Italy and the Balkan Peninsula.

Thanks to their complete mutual indifference and the absolute difference in tastes and customs, the boys arrived in Venice with the greatest of friendliness and were warmly received by Fulvio. Arnulf expressed the desire to stay in a hotel, but the young Venetian with his innate hospitality replied with a smile that any visitor who stepped foot on his doorstep had the right to settle in his house. Ried quickly agreed to his offer, since he would be very comfortable, and it would cost him nothing.

Raymond was delighted and enjoyed himself so much in the city of the "doges "[22] that he almost forgot the purpose of his trip. So, he showed up at Giovanna's house with his father's letter, where he was very well received and met some of the ladies and gentlemen who were visiting her at the time. But he did not find Eliza. To the acquaintances who asked about her, Giovanna answered that Bianca was ill. Raymond did not even suspect that Bianca and his legitimate wife were the same person, and that she was watching him closely from behind the curtains.

The first evaluation was favorable to Raymond. Eliza found him handsome and kind; but she was serious and intelligent enough to be satisfied with looks alone. As for Arnulf, who accompanied his brother, she found him ugly and extremely unfriendly.

Raymond did not even suspect that he was under secret, but careful surveillance.

This delicate mission was entrusted to Ludovico, Giovanna's old butler who, like a true Venetian, was extremely skilled in this kind of task. Ludovico, who knew Wolfram from the time of his liaison with Giovanna, took an interest in the Count's son. Moreover, he adored Eliza whom he saw grow up. For the time being, despite careful vigilance, Ludovico noticed nothing reprehensible in Raymond's behavior, who was amusing himself within the permitted limits.

---

[22] Doge - Head of the Venetian Republic, who was elected for life.

One morning, during a mass in St. Mark's church, Raymond saw a woman kneeling and was enchanted by her beauty. She was dressed all in black; the black veil further emphasized the opaque pallor of her face and the glow of her black eyes directed skyward.

He could not take his eyes off her; when the lady got up and headed for the exit in the company of an old lady, he stopped by the holy water font to pour her water and watch her more closely. The examination was even more favorable to the stranger. She was tall and elegant, with black hair like a raven's wing and beautiful teeth. The expensive fabric of her clothes indicated that she was wealthy.

It seems that the young knight also made a good impression on the stranger. Her flaming gaze passed fondly over him. Boarding the gondola, she turned toward Raymond and smiled almost imperceptibly.

From that day on, Raymond met the stranger at mass, and they exchanged smoldering glances and expressive smiles. He even knew that the girl's name was Beatrice Salviati, and that she was the wife of an old nobleman who was out of Venice on Republic business at the time.

However, despite his efforts, the Count could not exchange a word with Beatrice. He burned with impatience and passion when once the old lady, passing him whispered:

- Tomorrow, at the afternoon mass in the Madonna-del-Orto church.

Needless to say, Raymond showed up punctually at the meeting place. The Madonna-del-Orto church was an old building that needed major renovation. It was less frequented than the church of St. Mark and other temples are more attractive for their magnificence and beauty.

Kneeling in a corner of the church next to Beatrice, Raymond exchanged his first words of love with her and got the girl to promise to welcome him home. It was agreed that the interlocutor would be Lady Matissa, who would make the knight enter the house through a secret door.

With all the impetus of youth, Raymond plunged into that love intrigue without caring about the danger that threatened him through the jealous old husband; and he completely forgot his obligations to Eliza and also the promise he had made to Greta.

He involuntarily compared Margarita Ramets to the beautiful and demonic Italian woman, and for the first time the stout, blonde German woman with red, plump cheeks and bleached eyes seemed indescribably ordinary to him.

Absorbed in his passion, Raymond became more and more inattentive. He appeared everywhere Beatrice Salviati was, he sang serenades under her balcony, he offered her flowers, at festivities he wore her colors, and if until then no one knew of their intimate relations, now it was no secret to anyone that the German Count was "her knight".

Arnulf, irritated by his brother's behavior, began to scold him severely, but Raymond received this intrusion into his affairs with such hostility that Arnulf shrugged and shut up.

Eliza, who knew all the details of the adventure, was deeply indignant. She had not yet met her husband face to face, which had become an extremely rare visit in the Villamarino palace, but from a closed gondola she saw him singing under Beatrice's balcony; she saw him deposit at Mrs. Salviati's feet the prize he had won in a gondola race and provide the girl with other kindnesses.

Eliza then decided to end the secret surveillance and appear openly in front of her husband. She said she wanted to appear at a big party that Giovanna was going to throw on the occasion of her husband's birthday.

For the occasion Eliza dressed up with special care. She wanted to look beautiful and have admirers, which immediately happened when she appeared at Giovanna's side and began to help her welcome the guests.

[111]

Indeed, the young Countess Reifenstein looked lovely in her rich costume that Fulvio had given her as a gift. She wore a dress embroidered with silver, whose bodice was sown with pearls and rubies. The same stones adorned the belt and the wide headband that held her hair loose.

Raymond looked with surprise and admiration at Eliza standing beside the hostess. The Count was particularly puzzled by the cold, hostile look with which she measured him and responded with a slight, barely perceptible nod to his deep reverence.

As for Arnulf, who went along with his brother, he was crazy about her. This was the vivid image of Paola Finsterbach that had left an indelible impression on his youthful heart: the same elegant, slender figure, the same delicate face with childlike features, the same little purple mouth with a captivating smile. Eliza differed from her mother only by her metallic blue eyes and cold, severe gaze.

Arnulf's heart beat faster and he suddenly had the suspicion that this girl was Paola's daughter. In that case, she would be his brother's wife! This idea made him hate his brother.

But, no! It was impossible! Eliza was not in Venice, and that was Bianca Villamarino he had heard so much about. Calmed by such reasoning, Arnulf never lost sight of the one he thought was Bianca. He kept admiring her, happy with the kind reception the proud and capricious Venetian had given him. Bianca's hostility and contempt stirred Raymond deeply, even more so when he realized that this unwillingness was directed only at himself.

With everyone else she laughed, chattered, and danced! Her joy and intelligence gathered a crowd around her; to Raymond, however, she had only sporadic responses and cold, stern stares. When he joined the crowd of admirers that surrounded the girl, he eventually earned a look of such derision and contempt that it definitely confused him.

Eliza had unconsciously found the best way to interest and attract her unfaithful husband. Indeed, Raymond was already tired of Beatrice's volcanic passion, and her jealousy was sometimes unbearable to him. When he compared his mistress with Eliza, to his own surprise, all the advantages went to the latter. Eliza was more delicate, graceful; in her eyes shone intelligence and not the burning fire of passion for him; her discretion was a pleasant contrast to Beatrice's impetuosity.

In three weeks, this impression increased even more. Raymond's attraction to Eliza grew more and more, and he racked his brains fruitlessly to figure out the reason for her indisposition toward him. He even became jealous of Arnulf, who became a daily visitor to the Villamarino family and with whom Eliza laughed and chatted animatedly. But she replied to Raymond's courtesy with perfidious questioning:

- Has Madame Beatrice left Venice?

Raymond, furious and offended, decided to resolve that situation and openly ask Bianca why she hated, despised, and mocked him.

The opportune moment did not wait. Once, after lunch, when Arnulf happened not to be there and Giovanna was busy with two boys, they were alone at the balcony leading to the Grande Canale. The conversation continued in a relaxed manner, and Raymond offered to sing a song for her. An ironic, contemptuous smile flashed across the girl's face.

- Don't try so hard, Count! Perhaps tonight you still need to sing under some balcony where someone is waiting impatiently for the friendly minstrel.

A dark blush covered Raymond's cool face. Putting the lute aside, he asked unexpectedly:

- Miss Bianca! Why do you hate me? Why, every time you have the opportunity, do you offend me with mockery or harsh and offensive words? What have I done to you?

- Positively nothing! You are mistaken if you imagine that I hate you. You can't hate someone to whom you are completely indifferent. The fact is that I don't accept kindness from married

[113]

men, even more from those who openly have affairs with another lady.

Raymond paled and for a moment was silent and confused; but self-love blew him away that Bianca's words were motivated by jealousy.

- A knight's duty is to be kind to all the ladies he meets. Not even marriage can stand in the way in this case...

- Really? I don't believe that Countess Reifenstein shares your opinion and approves of your affairs in her absence - Eliza ironically interrupted him.

- I care little for my wife and her opinions - Raymond replied with irritation. Our marriage is the kind that doesn't impose obligations and...

He wanted to say, "I want a divorce," but remembered that he should not talk about that intimate subject until the proper time. Knowing what he was implying, Eliza let out a big laugh. Her laughter offended Raymond so much that he got up in a rage and ran away from the counter.

After a few days, anger drove him back to Beatrice again. Never before had he stood out so clamorously with his adventures.

This time he did it to irritate Eliza. Really, the girl was furious; not because she was in love with Raymond, but because her pride had been hurt. She told Giovanna that she had seen enough to have an opinion of her husband and that she was just waiting for the opportunity to put an end to this comedy and expose to Raymond her unshakable decision to divorce him. To do so, she intended to choose an opportunity to hurt him even more.

Meanwhile, Raymond's life was in danger.

In Beatrice's house lived a relative of her husband's, an old and mean spinster who was jealous of the young and beautiful woman who had taken her place, since she had previously been the one to manage Mr. Antonio Salviati's house.

[114]

That person was suspicious of Beatrice and watched her constantly, having foiled several intrigues in her early days, for Beatrice, a voluptuous young woman, was disgusted by her old husband, who she was married to against her will.

Only because of the great malaise of that lady, whose name was Angelica, was it possible for Raymond to meet Beatrice, who fell so madly in love with him that she did not dissimulate her feelings. Angelica soon discovered the lovers' meetings and satisfied, wrote to Mr. Salviati informing him that his honor had been irreparably tarnished. That letter would certainly make the proud nobleman despair.

While the offended husband made every effort to extricate himself as quickly as possible from service duties and return to Venice, the impetuous, passionate, demanding mistress began to think about Raymond more and more heavily. However, Raymond's thoughts were focused on Eliza, whose cold indifference irritated him terribly.

Finally, Raymond decided that he would marry Bianca as soon as he divorced Eliza, no matter what the cost.

Arnulf, for his part, had decided the same, and only the cleverness with which Eliza-Bianca avoided being alone with him prevented him from laying his heart at her feet.

Arnulf's impatience and passion reached its peak when the long-awaited opportunity to propose to the girl suddenly appeared.

Once, upon learning that Giovanna and her husband had left the castle, and expecting to find Bianca alone, he showed up and was welcomed as a daily visitor to the family.

Eliza was sitting in the small room attached to the balcony, embroidering a towel for the altar, when Arnulf entered with a large bouquet of flowers in his hands. Unpleasantly surprised, she tried with lively conversation to prevent any declaration of love, which she already dreaded by noticing the knight's worried appearance and his visible irritation. But Arnulf, absolutely determined not to let that opportunity slip away, interrupted Eliza, who was telling the details of the tour scheduled for the next day, grabbed her hand, and said:

- Sorry to interrupt you, but I can no longer hide what ails my soul and takes away my peace of mind. Bianca, I love you more than life! Accept to be my wife and the rest of my days will be dedicated to making you happy!

Falling to his knees, he pressed Eliza's hand to his lips as she tried to take it away.

- Mr. Arnulf! You are asking me to do the impossible - exclaimed Eliza, getting up, pale and emotional.

- Why? - asked the knight, frowning and also standing up.

- Because I am committed.

- Can you tell me what commitment prevents you from fulfilling my wish?

- If you swear on your knightly honor that you will keep secret what I am about to entrust to you until such time as I find it necessary to reveal it, I will tell you the truth.

- I swear!

Arnulf placed his hand on the hilt of his sword. His voice was hoarse, and his burning gaze overwhelmed the young woman.

Eliza nervously tossed back her black locks and, after a moment's wavering, said in a half voice:

- I am Elizabeth Finsterbach, your brother's wife.

Arnulf let out a deafening scream, recoiled, and slumped helplessly in his armchair. His stern look, full of hate and passion, made Eliza shudder. She understood instinctively that this dark and grim man was dangerous, and that it would be necessary to pour balm on the open wound in his pride and in his heart.

With purely feminine flexibility of mind, she decided in an instant how she should act in that difficult moment. Approaching the knight, she put her hand on his shoulder.

[116]

- Mr. Arnulf! I am desperate to have provoked your passion without ever being able to reward you worthily for this feeling, which flatters and moves me - she said in a deaf voice, in which sounded an even passion. I hope that this difficult moment for both of us will not make you my enemy, and that Raymond's brother will remain my friend.

Arnulf straightened up and measured the girl with a dark look.

- So, my suspicions did not deceive me! The living image of Paola was really her daughter! But why make up this show? Why are you hiding under the name of Bianca?

Eliza, in a few words, told him what motivated her to come up with the plan and added that she had reached her goal by getting to know Raymond's true character.

- But if you get a divorce, which is not impossible, then can I still expect a less harsh response to my proposal? - asked Arnulf in an indecisive tone.

- My freedom is so distant and uncertain that it would be rash to discuss its consequences - replied Eliza evasively. I confess that now I feel no sympathy for Germany, and Raymond's actions makes me feel disgusted by the love and bonds of matrimony. Perhaps, in the future, I will soften from this prejudice and be able to correspond to the love of a serious and noble man, whose honesty and strict morals would serve as a guarantee of my happiness. But I repeat, all this will only happen in the distant future.

- Then, for the time being, allow me to greet you as a sister and to confirm my discretion and dedication - replied Arnulf, with difficulty mastering the storm that was raging in his soul.

After kissing Eliza's hand, he left the room.

Chapter 8

A few days passed. At first, Arnulf locked himself in his room in anger, trying to imagine some way to separate his brother from his wife and prevent their reconciliation. He knew that once Raymond knew that the person, he was in love with was his own wife, he would never agree to a divorce. It was also clear that he would do anything to obtain Eliza's forgiveness, and Eliza was too innocent and pure not to be convinced.

The evil feelings that lurked in Arnulf's soul awakened with great force, clouding in his consciousness the blood ties that bound him to Raymond. All that remained was the wild desire to get rid of him.

But in what way? That was what Arnulf was meditating on. A murder was disgusting to him, and a duel was impossible. Suddenly, he remembered Beatrice: salvation could come from that side. If her husband struck his lover with a dagger, it would be natural and just, for Raymond fully deserved such a punishment for his behavior.

This idea reassured Arnulf, and he first checked all the information about Salviati's character and the inhabitants of his residence. What he learned about Beatrice's husband convinced him that the old man would not quietly endure his wife's affairs. The role of Madame Angelica and her characteristics left him in no doubt that she would not fail to open Antonio's eyes. He learned all these details from lady Matissa in exchange for a few gold coins.

Armed with this information Arnulf began to follow his brother and did so actively that he could not take a step day or night without his brother knowing. He was quietly waiting for the opportunity to kill or embarrass his brother so much that any reconciliation with his wife would be difficult, if not impossible. Then, when Eliza was free, he would hope to overcome her prejudice against Germans and marriage.

ignoring the great jeopardy that threatened his life and his good name as a married man, Raymond continued his unruly life. Although he was tired of Beatrice, he did not end the relationship, fearing some crazy act on her part. The impetuous Italian was so much in love that she seemed to have lost all sense and any sense of caution.

Eliza captivated Raymond's heart more and more. Her hostility, coldness and intelligence excited him; he suffered from jealousy seeing the smiles gifted to others, but the jealousy was very different from the one he felt for Beatrice. He knew that the pure and proud girl was incapable of vulgar attraction, but she might feel serious love for some of the handsome and noble knights that surrounded her. Raymond was jealous of Eliza, even more for not getting equal treatment like the others. The slightest attempt at courtship on the part of the young Count provoked an enigmatic smile on Eliza's face, a mixture of irony and contempt, with poisonous words spilling from her lips.

Eliza, for her part, could clearly see that Raymond was in love. She, however, was still too childish and, at the same time, too much of a woman not to be flattered and somewhat disarmed by that conquest. But she did not trust Raymond, and she did not believe in the solidity of his feelings. The idea of becoming a toy of passing enthusiasm and then being thrown in the same bag along with Greta, Beatrice and many others hurt her pride terribly.

Thus, a week had passed since Arnulf's declaration. At the Villamarino home, on the occasion of the eldest son's birthday, a circle of guests gathered. Raymond, dazzled by Eliza's beauty, could not take his eyes off her. All in white, with pearls on her neck and hair, she was enchanting. To everyone she found a kind word and a warm smile; only young Count Reifenstein seemed not to exist for her.

[119]

Only at the end of the evening did a long-awaited opportunity to talk to Eliza without witnesses finally arise. Eliza, tired from the reception, retired to the small drawing room and, leaning against a large gothic window, thoughtfully inhaled the fresh, aromatic night air.

Absorbed in her thought, she didn't hear Raymond approach and shuddered when the boy leaned over her and said:

- Oh, cruel Bianca, you are finally alone!

- I do not understand why you need to see me alone! "We have no secrets we can trust each other with - said Eliza coldly.

- You are right! The fact that I love you, Bianca, is no secret! But I need to know why you always treat me with such cruelty, contempt, and hostility? What have I done to you? Don't you believe in my feelings, or do you consider me a man unworthy of your love? - Raymond replied impetuously.

- I consider you an entirely noble knight, but with a heart so large that a woman would certainly get lost in it like a pearl in the ocean. At the present moment, a beauty as "massive" as Greta and a sinner as big as Beatrice have so much place in it that I have no desire to share their company.

- Greta? How did you know about Greta? - Raymond exclaimed in amazement.

- Oh! Does that matter to you? Oh, I forgot to mention one more inhabitant of your heart, your wife, who has the right to expel all the others as soon as she is fortunate enough to meet you - Eliza mockingly replied.

- My wife can forbid me to do anything! In my life she plays the role of an unbearable burden that I will let go of at any cost! - exclaimed Raymond.

- What if she doesn't want to give you back your freedom?

- I hope she possesses enough feminine dignity not to cling to a man who doesn't want her. In fact, I will confess all my betrayals to her and accept all conditions, provided she gives me back my freedom.

- I am impressed by your wise decision and begin to believe in the seriousness of your feelings. The confession of your numerous amorous adventures will naturally be the most effective remedy for getting rid of your wife. What would become of her if, after such a confession, she insisted on remaining Countess Reifenstein? - said Eliza laughing.

- Don't laugh, Bianca! It is not frivolity that makes me want to separate, but a deep and sincere love for you. I want to be free to have the right to offer you my hand and my heart. I have even decided not to wait any longer for Eliza's return and to go immediately to Verona to start the divorce proceedings as soon as possible and get rid of the bonds imposed on me since childhood.

- In that case, Raymond, you don't have to travel to Verona. From that moment on, consider yourself free and know that your wife, who is a heavy burden to you, doesn't want you. I am Elizabeth Finsterbach! I wanted to see you so that you would not know who I am; I wanted to meet the man to whom I belong by law before I belong to him by heart. Now I know you well enough and say that I don't want a depraved man without heart or shame, who didn't even think about the orphan who used his name, wanting only to get rid of her like a burden.

Eliza spoke in German. In this language, which Raymond had never heard from her lips, her speech sounded particularly severe and even harsh. Raymond barely had time to recover from his amazement when Eliza turned and left the room. He continued to sit in his armchair, clutching his head in his hands. What he had just learned shook him terribly; his head was working fast, and contradictory thoughts were piling up in his mind, causing an almost physical pain.

From that chaos, only the awareness that Bianca was Eliza, his legitimate wife, his indivisible inheritance that he would naturally never part with, stood out.

[121]

Satisfied and content, he got up in a jolt and ran out of the room. He wanted to find Eliza and whisper to her that now he knew she belonged to him he would love her twice as much and would never part with her. But Eliza disappeared from the drawing room and to Raymond's worried questions, Giovanna replied that she had a headache and had retired to her quarters.

Raymond, furious, said goodbye to his hosts and returned home.

That day, Arnulf did not go to Villamarino and was looking forward to his brother's return. Raymond's visible excitement surprised him, and he suspected that something had happened between Eliza and her husband, perhaps the revelation.

Raymond walked very excitedly around the room, not noticing that his brother was following his every move. He cursed himself for his relations with Beatrice and for the careless words about the divorce, which offended his young wife. But how could he have imagined that the lovely Bianca was Eliza? How could he have imagined that a plot had been planned against him, in which even his father participated? He fell like a duckling into the trap and embarrassed himself in front of everyone. What to do now? How to quickly get rid of Beatrice and win Eliza back? The former was not going to stop grabbing him and making a scandalous scene, while the latter would reject him with contempt even though he had decided not to admit to divorcing for anything in the world.

Raymond turned red at the thought of the insults he would have to hear. But was it worth the love of his wife? Then he remembered his father's advice, once jokingly said: "The more a woman gets angry, the easier it is to calm her down with regret and a show of humility. With women you always have to be prepared and, at the slightest glance, show satisfaction with the sword in hand. Now, with the offenses of a beautiful woman, one can be blind and deaf, without any dishonor to oneself. Even an offensive action on her part should be of no consequence. On the other hand, once you diffuse their anger, magnanimous forgiveness confounds women, and their repentance always brings with itself pleasant consequences and grants us enormous privileges!"

The memory of that useful lesson from his father, a famous conqueror of female hearts, immediately restored Raymond's coolness. The following method would help him: he would let Eliza get angry, but he himself would not be offended and would remain calm, loving, and swear to her that he would become a new person. She would not reach for offensive actions, she was unlike Greta, always ready to use her fists.

Before him, then, there appeared with extraordinary clarity the image of the kind and charming little girl who shared the goodies with him and whom he, at Greta's instigation, had locked in the tower, almost killing her. This was an unpleasant memory that he tried to forget. But the awakened past brought him more and more pictures. He remembered the chapel in the castle, where the old bishop performed the sacred ceremony. Beside him, Eliza was kneeling like a doll in her luxurious wedding costume. A happy smile passed Raymond's lips as he recalled the different feelings that had troubled the eleven-year-old groom's heart, and that Eliza's innocent look and confident smile had disarmed his childish anger.

At the time, he did not understand the charm that dispelled his anger. Now he was falling under this enchantment for the second time and felt an uncontrollable desire to see Eliza, to look into her clear eyes and to silence with a kiss the little mouth that could speak such harsh words. So why leave the conversation until tomorrow? Why should he suffer all night if, as her husband, he had the right to see her at any time?

Let's face it, the time was a bit inappropriate to show up at the front door, as the last guests should have already left. But he knew where Eliza's quarters were, and that there was a balcony there that led off into a small side canal. If there was still light in her windows, he would climb onto the balcony, throw himself at her feet, and one way or another, obtain her forgiveness. Eliza is kind

[123]

and magnanimous. She would not remain deaf to his repentance and pleas.

Without much thought, Raymond took his beret, wrapped himself in his cloak, and left the house through the small side door, the key to which he always carried with him. Below, by the stairs leading down to the canal, there were always a few gondolas of different sizes tied up. Raymond jumped into one of them, took the oars and headed for Giovanna's house.

Nor did he realize that some distance away, another boat was following him. That was Arnulf, surprised by his brother's late escape. Imagining that he was going to see Beatrice, Arnulf wanted to be a witness to what would happen that could make Eliza a widow even that night. By his calculations, Mr. Antonio Salviati had already arrived and, naturally, would not let his wife's lover escape alive if he caught him at home.

Raymond had not been mistaken in his hopes. The window of Eliza's room was lit, and the balcony door was open. However, it was not at all easy to accomplish what he wanted. The balcony was high above the water, so it was impossible to reach it without the help of ropes and ladders. But Raymond was born and raised in the mountains, where during his hunts he had to climb almost all steep rocks or jump courageously over bottomless abysses. After quickly examining the place, he noticed the water trough through which it would be possible to reach the cornice wide enough to hold on and then climb onto the balcony, despite the risk of falling into the canal.

Without the slightest flinch, Raymond tied up the gondola, quickly climbed the cornice, and in an instant was on the balcony. Sneaking up to the door, he looked in curiously. In front of him was Eliza's room: two candles on the table, illuminated with flickering light the heavy cloth covering the walls, the baldachin bed, covered with green velvet, and high-backed, carved wooden armchairs. Eliza was sprawled in one of the armchairs, lost in her thoughts.

[124]

She was wearing a white woolen robe whose sleeves opened almost to her shoulders, revealing bare arms. Her fair hair was braided for the night in two thick braids.

Raymond's heart, then, beat faster. In the relaxed pose, in simple clothes, Eliza looked even more stunning to him than in the luxurious outfits. "Oh, I hope she'll forgive me," he thought.

Raymond slipped into the room on tiptoe. He intended to take her by surprise, squeeze her in his arms, and humbly ask her forgiveness.

Eliza was so entertained that she paid no attention to the slight noise on the balcony, but the creaking of the parquet forced her to shudder and turn around. Seeing a man, she let out a deafened cry, jumped up the armchair, and wanted to flee to the next room; but, recognizing Raymond, she stopped. Her cheeks turned red, and she exclaimed, angrily:

- You, brazen! How dare you show up here?

- Me, brazen? I am the husband who has every right to enter his wife's room whenever he wants, even if it is through the window when the door is locked - objected Raymond, furious at the bad reception and the fact that he could not catch Eliza off guard and disarm her with affection.

- A husband should enter through the door and not through the window like a thief or a lover. You probably made a mistake and intended to enter Beatrice's room - said Eliza scornfully.

- You have no right to be so arrogant with your husband, whom you have an obligation to love and must obey - Raymond replied, trying to restrain himself.

- You have done nothing yet to deserve my respect. I have no obligation to love and even less to obey a husband who wanted to kill me in the damned tower. Why did you come here? Do you want explanations? Then come tomorrow in the morning as a decent man would do. But if you are in a hurry to get my consent for the divorce, then I repeat that you are free, and I do not want to have a husband like you either. Now, get out! Go out the same way

[125]

you came here, or I will call the servants and order them to take you away by force!

The contemptuous tone of that reply and the proud gesture with which she pointed at the door and put Raymond off and her father's wise advice and his own decision to hold back and be humble to the end were forgotten.

Furious at the flaming look of indignation Raymond threw his beret on the floor, sat down in the armchair in which Eliza had previously sat and, crossing his legs, said:

- I am staying to see which devil is going to get me out of here! I am your husband, and I will leave only when I want to. Do you understand me?

- Well done then! I am the one who leaves then.

Eliza ran to the door, but Raymond caught up with her and grabbed her by the arm.

- Eliza! Listen to what I have to say! Don't be so cruel.

- But first, let me go! Have you come to Venice just to betray and offend me? - asked the young woman, pulling her hand away.

- No! I came here to tell you that I will never leave you and that you must love me.

The girl stepped back and said with debauchery:

- Really? Do you command me to love you? Don't tell me you think love can be forced?

Raymond lowered his head. He understood that Eliza was right and that he had chosen the wrong path.

- You are right, Eliza! True love cannot be commanded; it rises from the heart like sunlight - he said, after a moment's silence. Only anger could make me speak foolish words that offended you. But God is a witness! I have come to beg your forgiveness and to say that I want to deserve your love, starting from this moment on a new life. I recognize that I am deeply guilty before you. But, Eliza, be as fair as you are beautiful and before you condemn me mercilessly examine the circumstances that made me guilty. Did our union have any solid basis? Were we children whom the will of our parents united; did we have any understanding of the duty and obligations they placed upon our future? You were taken away at a very young age and I never saw you again; nor was your name ever spoken in the castle. How could I, without knowing you, be unquestionably faithful to you? I knew I was bound to you by law, but my heart was silent and the woman who used my name was far away. I confess that these shackles weighed heavily on me, and I came here to break them. But you won my love, even when I did not even know you! What else do you need? A few hours ago, when you revealed the truth to me, you knew that I longed to get a divorce from Eliza to marry Bianca. Was I not punished enough by the strange whim of fate that threw me at the feet of the woman whom I, in my own blindness, wanted to get rid of?

As he spoke, he approached Eliza, knelt, took her hand, and pressed it passionately to his own lips.

- Eliza! My beloved! Don't be cruel! Don't turn your back on me! Forget the past, forgive me and believe in the future!

Eliza listened to Raymond with embarrassment. What he was saying was mostly true, and the sacred bonds that bound them together urged her to patronize him. But what guarantee of future happiness could that fickle heart gives her?

- You are right! I cannot condemn you for the past. You are young and you were enjoying life -Eliza replied quietly and indecisively. But I have no confidence in the future. My absence cannot be an excuse for your amorous intrigues with married women. I also barely remembered you and had no lack of admirers, but I did not forget that I was engaged. I felt it was my duty to keep the name your father imposed on me immaculate, without trying to justify any infidelity by the fact that we were married when I was only five years old.

- Eliza, you are a woman. Moreover, man's sin does not carry with it such terrible and shameful consequences.

- You really do not miss sophistry. It is just that, for me, they are unconvincing. However forgivable men's sins may be in your eyes, I do not want to sacrifice my peace. I do not want to be a passing amusement for you, and if I agree to forgive you...

- You will never regret this, Eliza! I agree in advance with all your conditions.

Standing up quickly, Raymond pulled Eliza into his arms and covered her with burning kisses. But Eliza, of a nervous and impressionable nature, feared a show of passion involuntarily, and agitated feelings provoked disgust in her. She paled and broke free of his embrace.

- Don't do that...do not do that...Raymond - she said in an indecisive tone. You have to give me some time to get used to you. I will tell you frankly: I like you, but I do not love you yet. I cannot love a person who before my eyes was dating someone else and wanted to break up with me. I also warn you that in the future I will not put up with any betrayal.

- For the future I will answer, but for the present I must submit and be patient, for it is all my fault - Raymond replied in a mixture of laughter and irritation.

- If I believe you and try to love you, do you swear I will never regret it? - murmured Eliza nervously and with tears in her eyes.

Raymond took a solemn oath to become an exemplary husband. Then, to soothe Eliza's emotion, he went on to talk about the past. They then sat down on the bench covered with cushions. The memories of some funny childhood scenes made them laugh heartily.

After talking for about an hour, Raymond got up.

- It is time for me to go out the same way I came in, as you demanded - he said cheerfully. But tomorrow I will enter through the main entrance.

- But, no! I will show you another way, otherwise you might break your neck climbing up the walls like a cat - replied Eliza, laughing.

[128]

The young couple exchanged friendly farewell kisses. Then, passing through a long, narrow corridor, they descended a staircase, under which was a small door, the heavy latch of which Raymond opened in his companion's direction.

- Are you armed? You will have to walk about fifteen minutes until you reach the canal - said Eliza, handing her husband some topographical indications.

- Fear not! I have got the sword and dagger - Raymond replied, kissing Eliza's hand.

A moment later, the door closed behind him, and he found himself in one of those narrow inner alleys so plentiful in Venice. Passing through the alley, Raymond thought about everything that had happened. He was indescribably happy about his reconciliation with his wife. His heart was full of plans for the future.

Suddenly he remembered that Beatrice had arranged a date for that evening, and a feeling of disgust came over him. He needed, as quickly as possible, to break up with her and endure the imminent and unpleasant scene that awaited him. Why not take the opportunity to tell Beatrice that it was over between them? Of course, the appointed time had long since passed, but that did not mean anything; that crazy woman was undoubtedly still waiting for him! In any case, it would be better to go soon, or else she would be able to hang around Fulvio's house during the day, as she had done the other times when he did not show up on time.

Making such a decision, Raymond changed direction and quickly headed for the Salviati house that was closer on foot than by the canals.

The small door leading out into the alley was open, which proved that they were waiting for him. Raymond quickly climbed the stairs and entered the room where Beatrice usually received him.

Pale, her face covered with spots and her gaze flaming, the young woman walked around the room. Seeing her lover, she ran to him and grabbed him by the hand.

Why did it take so long? Why this sloppiness? - she exclaimed, choking. They are already saying that you are dating Bianca Villamarino. Be careful! I will not tolerate any cheating on your part.

Raymond pulled her hand away and measured her with a cold, unsatisfied gaze. The harsh severity of a man who wishes to get rid of the woman he has grown tired of sounded in his voice when he replied:

- I came here to talk to you and tell you that our fleeting dream of love is over. Let's forget it all and remain friends...

Beatrice let out a deafened cry and looked at him in confusion.

- Raymond, are you rejecting me? Do you want me to forget our love? And you dare propose this to me? - she babbled.

- Have you gone mad?

- Not at all! I am simply reminding you of your duty as a married woman, which you should not forget. In addition, I found out that Bianca Villamarino was actually my lawful wedded wife, whom I feared so much. We made up. She forgave my past and I swore to be faithful to her in the future. I want to keep my word and correct my mistakes. Now, Beatrice, you must understand that our relationship is broken.

No, no, and no! All I know is that I cannot live without you, because I love you madly, and that I will kill the wretch who dared to steal you from me! - cried Beatrice, throwing herself on Raymond's neck.

The latter stood still, stunned. Suddenly he pushed her away with force and exclaimed, red with rage:

- If you touch Eliza, you will pay dearly for it, you vicious, shameless woman! Have you no shame in clinging to a man who is kindly letting you know that he does not want you anymore?

Beatrice thudded, took a few steps back, and leaned back in her chair. Pale and breathless, she stood motionless for a moment, clasping her hands on her forehead. Suddenly she straightened up. Her teeth were clenched, and her face distorted into a crazed expression of rage.

- You miserable, contemptible thief of my heart and honor! You coarse German who dared to offend a noble woman only because she loves you! Wait for me! I'll pay you back for your treachery! - she exclaimed in a hissing voice.

With lightning speed, she pulled something from her belt and threw it on Raymond, who had time to see that in her hand gleamed a stiletto. He grabbed Beatrice by the arm, disarmed her, and when she fell, he ran out of the room. He hurried down the stairs like a hurricane and opened the door to the street with force. That sudden movement was his salvation, for he knocked to the ground a short, gray-bearded man who was waiting for him, concealing a dagger under his cloak. Probably the man expected the night visitor to leave quietly, taking every precaution. But, thrown aside by Raymond's unexpected blow, he stood up as two masked men emerged from the darkness, who jumped on the Count. The latter managed to cross to the other side of the street and leaned against the wall.

Raymond immediately understood that he was being attacked by Beatrice's husband, who intended to kill him, and decided to sell his life dearly. With a dagger in one hand and a sword in the other one, he waited for the attackers. A silent but fierce combat began. However uneven the balance of forces was, Raymond defended himself bravely, thanks to his Herculean strength and incredible agility. When the old man slipped and opened his guard, he buried the dagger in his chest.

The wounded man opened his arms and, letting out a scream, fell to the ground. One of the masked men was wounded

[131]

in the arm and dropped his sword, while the other left the battlefield and got lost in the darkness of the night.

Raymond hurriedly left the fateful place and, more instinctively than by reasoning, headed back to the Villamarino palace.

In the heat of battle, Raymond did not notice that he had received two blows, but the warm blood trickling down his arm, the weakness that came over him, and the sharp pain in his wounds made him realize the situation he was in.

Barely able to stand, Raymond, in a last effort, reached Giovanna's house and with the hilt of his sword slammed the door. A few minutes later, the castellan's irritated voice asked who dared to make so much noise at such an inappropriate hour.

- Open up quickly, Giacomo! It is me, Count Reifenstein - Raymond replied in a weakened voice.

Extremely surprised, the old man opened the door. Seeing the Count bloodied, without further question he took him to the guest room, put him to bed, and with the experience of an ex-soldier gave him first aid.

Raymond, who was given first aid by Giacomo, lost consciousness due to the hemorrhaging, so Giacomo went to tell his lords about the event. Half an hour later, Oreo and Giovanna, as surprised as the castellan, appeared at Raymond's bedside. Since at that time bloody disputes and night raids were frequent, this event did not cause much of a stir. After sending for the surgeon, Oreo said:

- He probably started some new love intrigue and was discovered by the brother or the mistress's husband. The fight must have happened somewhere nearby, otherwise this disgusting bum would not have come to hide in our house.

Leaving her husband with the wounded man, Giovanna went to Eliza's room, who was still sleeping. She woke up the girl and told her about the incident with her husband.

- Good heavens! Are the injuries serious? I need to see him right away - Eliza exclaimed in fright, jumping out of bed.

- Their injuries are not fatal if there are no unforeseeable complications. He just lost a lot of blood - replied Giovanna.

Then she added with a slight smile:

- I am surprised that you are sympathizing so much with the injured. You had decided to divorce him!

Eliza looked confused, red, and then, continuing to dress, told Giovanna about Raymond's evening visit and their reconciliation.

- I may have made a fool of myself by giving in to his pleas and condoning his behavior, but Raymond vowed to redeem himself. Before, he was always good to me, except for the tower story - Eliza said, visibly embarrassed.

- Why do you seem to be apologizing for forgiving your husband? You just did your duty. Who, besides Raymond, has more right to your condescension? But, come on! Since he loves you so much, your presence will ease his pain - replied Giovanna, kissing the girl.

When the two women entered the wounded man's room, he had already been medicated by the surgeon. The pain from the stitches made Raymond regain his senses, but a fever had set in. Eliza leaned, worried, over Raymond. His eyes were open, but he did not recognize her.

His face burned, his breathing was heavy and irregular, and his lips were dry, ajar. However, the sight of the girl awakened in the patient's mind a vague recollection of the night scenes. He tried to stand up, his eyes sparkled, and before the stupefied ladies his dialogue with Beatrice took place, except for the replies.

- He swore to me that he would redeem himself and imagine that he went to Beatrice to cut ties with her - murmured Eliza visibly moved, sitting down at the wounded man's bedside.

[133]

Chapter 9

Arnulf saw with surprise and sadness that his brother was headed not to the Salviati house, where he knew Beatrice was waiting for him, but to the Villamarino palace. When Raymond climbed on the balcony and disappeared into the girl's room, Arnulf was seized with such fury that, disregarding any precautions, he wanted to follow him, but fortunately common sense managed to hold him back. Raymond was Eliza's husband, and that nighttime invasion could even be part of his rights. In that case, Arnulf would only be considered an impertinent trespasser, but... he still clenched the dagger hilt convulsively. If Eliza screamed or was outraged by Raymond's violence, then the knightly duty would give him the right to enter the room and bury his weapon in his rival's heart.

But all was quiet. Sometimes the sound of voices reached the knight's attentive ear, but the conversation was apparently quiet. Suddenly, a burst of double laughter startled Arnulf on the boat. What did it mean? Had the young couple come to an agreement between themselves, then reconciled? In that case, why had Raymond climbed the walls, risking breaking his neck, when he could quietly enter through the main door? But if Eliza was taking him as her lover, then everything was even more confusing.

Impatience, jealousy, and anger simply drove Arnulf crazy. In feverish excitement, he decided, despite the risk, to climb up on the balcony and see what was happening in the room. But at that moment, the balcony door closed, the curtains were lowered, and a few minutes later, the last light through the curtain went out.

Confused, Arnulf waited another half hour. His anger and jealousy were so great that if Raymond appeared at that moment, he would stab him to death and throw his body into the canal. But no one appeared, and all around reigned the silence of night.

Arnulf returned home in terrible despair. He could not sleep. Raymond did not return, and he racked his brains trying to find an explanation for all these strings.

Nervous and worried, Arnulf paced the room, deciding to seek information at the Salviati house as soon as dawn came. In any case, he could, through Lady Matissa, show Beatrice the place where Raymond had spent the night while she waited for him.

This time, despite the agreed upon signal, Arnulf had to wait a long time for his informant. Finally, she arrived visibly emotional and worried, and told him that Raymond had shown up late at night, had a heated conversation with Beatrice, and had therefore left. Then shouting and the clanging of guns were heard. As she went downstairs to lock the small door, a man shouted at her:

- Take your master inside if you do not want him to die in the street!

So, she called one of the servants and they found Monsieur Antonio with a dagger embedded in his chest. The old woman supposed that her master had learned of his wife's adventures and had laid in wait to catch the Count and kill him. What really happened and where Raymond had gone, she did not know. Monsieur Antonio was in agony. As for Beatrice, she was so strange and indifferent to everything that had happened that she, Matissa, could not understand why.

Arnulf heard the account only halfway through and concluded that Eliza had shown her husband another way out. Raymond then ran to Beatrice. But something had happened to Raymond, and it could be that at that very moment he was no longer among the living, and Eliza had been widowed!

Full of hope, Arnulf returned home. There, he received news that a messenger had arrived from Oreo Villamarino informing him that his wounded brother was in his house.

Arnulf was seized by a furious disappointment, but he was too reserved to expose his feelings and decided to visit Raymond. He was unable to tell his hosts, since Fulvio had been away on a trip for two days, while Baron Conrad was locked in his laboratory, where no one dared to disturb him.

When Arnulf arrived at the palace, the sick man was asleep, and he was greeted by Eliza. The conversation, naturally, was about the accident with Raymond. The girl naively said that thieves must have plowed the Count.

Arnulf shook his head and looked with such commiseration at Eliza that she was stunned.

- Do you know anything? Be honest with me! - she said with a mixture of concern and curiosity.

Arnulf shrugged.

- I know nothing, my dear sister! Only, by a strange coincidence, that same night Madame Beatrice's husband was found in the street, dying with a dagger in his chest.

Eliza turned red and embarrassed. Raymond's dagger was missing. Was it possible that, after meeting with her, Raymond had gone to that woman and, to top it all, had killed her husband?

Giovanna's arrival interrupted the conversation and Arnulf left, promising to return later.

- What did that phony tell you? You look so worried! - said Giovanna as soon as they were alone.

The girl then told what she had heard from Arnulf and exposed her own assumption that Raymond, after all that had happened between them, still went to visit his mistress at night.

- You have nothing to worry about! What the Count keeps talking about in his ravings clearly explains the purpose of his visit to Beatrice. It would be more interesting to ask that hypocrite how he knows what happened to Salviati and what relations he has with that house - replied Giovanna with contempt.

The young woman managed to convince Eliza so well that Eliza calmed down completely and decided to help Raymond to get back on his feet more quickly.

- So, do you consider yourself a better surgeon than Mr. Ricardo? Or, instead of the ointments, do you want to treat him with kisses? - asked Giovanna, laughing.

- Neither this nor that! It turns out that Fulvio and Grandpa taught me how to treat some diseases in their absence. Fulvio traveled to Padua for a week while Grandpa, as Knight Ried says, locked himself in the laboratory. Sometimes he stays there for two or three days. So, I intend to appeal to the remedy they taught me to relieve Raymond's pain if the fever does not cease. Here is the water over which I will apply some passes. Then I will offer it to the patient and lay hands on him.

- How interesting! You never told me that you know how to treat the sick.

A day passed and there was no change in the sick man's health. He remained immersed in a listless stupor and seemed to see and recognize no one. At night, his health worsened. Raymond became agitated, groaned, and began to rave.

- It is time to apply my medicine. I only ask that you keep the other people away - whispered Eliza in Giovanna's ear.

The latter dismissed the housekeeper who was helping them. Then Eliza leaned over the bed and placed both hands on Raymond's head. A few minutes later, he visibly calmed down. The convulsive movements stopped, the feverish redness reduced, the lips closed, and the wheezing, intermittent breathing changed to normal. Eliza sat on the edge of the bed, took the wounded man's hand, and said:

- Look! He sleeps and his pains are gone. Now, my dear Giovanna, I will prepare fluid water for him.

She picked up a crystal vat, filled it with water, and held her hands over it. Gradually, her fingertips began to light up and the water took on a bluish reflection.

[137]

- It is ready! Now let's treat our patient with this remedy.

Eliza took a towel, dipped it in water and approached the bed.

- You'll wake him up with that wet towel! - said Giovanna.

- It does not matter! He will sleep better later. Now, my dear, light the candles.

Eliza leaned over the bed and began to rub the wet towel over the patient's face and hands. Raymond shivered and opened his eyes. He was fully conscious. When he saw Eliza, an expression of joy and gratitude lit up his face.

- Eliza, are you taking care of me? How kind you are! Don't believe anything bad they will talk about me. Circumstances are against me, but I swear I just wanted to end things with Beatrice - he babbled.

- I believe you, although you might have chosen a more appropriate time to do so. But the harm is done, and your injuries are punishment enough for this levity, which I hope will be the last I have to forgive. Now, drink this!

Eliza held out the glass of fluidized water to him.

Raymond took it all in eagerly.

- What did you give me to drink, Eliza? I have never tasted such a drink. What an aroma! What freshness! I feel like I am coming back to life, and even my wounds do not burn like before.

- It is a remedy that Grandpa Conrad and Fulvio taught me to prepare. It will help you to recover quickly. In the morning, when the surgeon comes to change your dressings, have him wash them with the water from that container and impregnate the dressings with it.

- All right! I will see to it that your prescriptions are followed to the letter, my guardian angel. If you want to make me fully happy, then give me a kiss.

- How insatiable you are!

Eliza leaned over and, blushing, kissed him.

- You do not deserve it but if I give you a kiss it is exclusively because you are sick. But enough chatter! Go to sleep!

Raymond obediently closed his eyes. A deep well-being filled his whole being, and soon the deep, quiet breathing announced that he was sleeping an invigorating sleep.

A few days passed. Raymond's health was improving rapidly. His wounds closed, his fever disappeared, and Eliza's presence kept him in the best of spirits. A few days passed. Raymond's health was improving rapidly. His wounds closed, his fever disappeared, and Eliza's presence kept him in the best of spirits. A friendly harmony was established between the young couple. They talked, laughed, remembered the past and talked about the future. Eliza said she did not want to live with her husband in Castle Reifenstein, which left her with sad memories. Besides, she had no desire to meet Countess Anna every day. So, she suggested that they go and live in her father's castle, which she owns.

Raymond, who was more in love every day, agreed with everything and tried by all means to win the trust and love of his young wife.

The presence of Arnulf, who came every other day to visit his brother, disturbed the couple's good mood; especially Eliza, who felt bad when she saw the knight's gloomy eyes. That look weighed on her; on the other hand, Conrad's and Fulvio's visits were a real feast for her.

The sixth day of Raymond's illness was the eve of a big holiday and Eliza went to the afternoon mass with Giovanna in a nearby church. At the end of the celebration, they returned talking in the gondola without noticing that from the church they were being followed by a woman in dark clothes, wrapped in a thick veil that hid her face. She was walking faster than them and in the same direction as the ramp where there were numerous gondolas.

Suddenly, Eliza felt someone grab her by the hand. She turned around in surprise and saw a masked woman, who leaned over her and with lightning speed buried in her flank a small

[139]

stiletto that she kept under the long veil that covered her from head to toe. Eliza stood still for a moment with wide-open eyes, and then fell to the ground without letting out a single scream.

The crime happened so quickly and with such precision that neither Giovanna, who was a few steps ahead, nor the two pageboys noticed anything, even more so when the large crowd was crowding the steps.

The noise only started when Eliza fell. Giovanna and one of the pageboys ran towards her, lifted her up and carried her to the gondola.

Giovanna, beside herself with horror and sorrow, was placing the wounded girl on the pillows when suddenly, from the neighboring alleys, shouts were heard. The second page had seen the veiled woman approach Eliza and then slip into the crowd, trying to reach the narrow, little-visited alley. Thinking, with some reason, that this might be the murderer, he began to pursue her. Realizing that she had been discovered, the woman ran, but the page caught up with her and screamed to a halt:

- No!... You will not get away from me... you wretch!

A brawl would have broken out if some passersby had not held the pageboy back. The fugitive, who was struggling like crazy, was arrested and her veil was removed.

The woman was Beatrice Salviati. The surprise of the mob was great when the wife of a rich and respected patrician was accused of murder. Since the girl had the air of a madwoman, they decided to take her home and keep her locked up until further action by the authorities.

One can imagine the horror and concern in the Villamarino's home when Giovanna arrived, carrying Eliza prostrate as if dead. In a few minutes, the whole house was on its feet. Oreo also came to their rescue. He himself helped transport the wounded young woman to the lobby where they hurriedly improvised a stretcher to take her to her quarters.

[140]

Eliza had already been placed on the stretcher and Oreo had made a temporary dressing of the wound, from which blood was pouring out, when Conrad Vart appeared in the hallway who had gone to visit Raymond.

The Baron quickly understood the situation, rushed to Eliza's stretcher, cut her belt with the knife, loosened her dress, and discovered the bleeding. Then, taking a ruby ring from his finger, he passed it around the wound, muttering some incomprehensible words. The blood stopped gushing almost immediately, and Eliza, who until then had shown no signs of life, moaned faintly.

- Cover her with a cloak and put the stretcher on my gondola! I am taking the patient to my home - said the Baron to those present.

- Is she alive, Uncle Conrad? Will you be able to save her? - asked Giovanna, covered in tears.

- For now, she is alive, but the injury is serious, and I cannot say anything yet. But at home I have the necessary medicines at hand.

- That despicable Beatrice! I hope they punish her with all the rigor of the law - exclaimed Giovanna, furious.

- No doubt, this woman is unworthy, but if Raymond did not have that criminal connection with her, she would not have committed this crime - replied Baron Vart, boarding the gondola.

The noise of the commotion that the attempt on Eliza's life caused reached the room where Raymond was lying.

Hearing screams and the commotion in the nearby hallway, he sent the maid to find out what had happened.

A few minutes later, she returned so pale and frightened that Raymond exclaimed worriedly:

- Carlotta! Has some misfortune happened? Tell me! I am ordering you!

- Yes, sir! A terrible misfortune has happened: Mrs. Beatrice Salviati has stabbed the countess, your wife - murmured Carlotta.

Raymond collapsed on the pillows as if he had received a blow. But this weakness quickly changed to mad excitement. Forgetting his own illness and injuries, he jumped out of bed, grabbed the cloak that lay on the chair, and ran out into the gallery. Then his strength gave out and he, with a deafening groan, collapsed.

- Carlotta! Get someone to help me walk. I need to see Eliza! - he screamed out of his head.

- Calm down Count and do not move while I'll get someone to put you back to bed! - exclaimed Carlotta, frightened. You are not allowed to see the countess. Baron Vart took her to his house and did not allow anyone to accompany him, not even Madame Giovanna, who wanted to look after her friend. I heard it with my own ears. As I entered the lobby, the stretcher with the countess was already in the Baron's gondola.

While two servants were carrying Raymond to his bed, Oreo and his wife arrived. Seeing the feverish state of the patient, they told him everything that had happened.

It is difficult to describe Raymond's state of mind. He berated himself bitterly for his liaison with Beatrice, for whom he now felt only a merciless hatred. The thought of losing Eliza on the threshold of happiness and even more through her fault tore at his heart like red-hot iron. At night, the fever returned; his wounds opened and caused him terrible pain. Yet he remained fully conscious, and sleep did not ease his excitement even for an instant.

Then Arnulf arrived and stayed to watch over his brother for the night. The news of the attempt provoked mixed feelings in the Ried knight's dark spirit. He grieved for Eliza, and at the same time he would rather see her dead than belong to Raymond. The night passed in long and weary worry. There was no news of Baron Conrad and Raymond positively burned with sorrow and pangs of conscience. The waiting was driving him mad.

[142]

- Calm down and resign yourself to the ordeal you have brought upon yourself! - Arnulf remarked. Instead of tossing and turning like mad, it is time to pray to God! That way, you only harm yourself to no avail. As long as you do not receive news of your wife's death, you can hope for divine mercy.

Raymond shuddered and tried to lift his body. His eyes glowed feverishly, and his lips trembled nervously.

- You are right, Arnulf! We must appeal to the Savior's mercy. Give me that ivory crucifix on the table there.

Raymond grasped the crucifix with an impatient hand and pressed it to his lips. Then, lifting it aloft, he exclaimed in a burst of faith and enthusiasm:

- Our Lord Jesus Christ, Savior of the world and comfort of all sufferers! Answer my prayer! Save Eliza! Don't let an innocent woman die because of my sins! If you answer my prayer, I promise that I will go to Jerusalem, go around the Holy Sepulcher on my knees three times, and offer You a silver lamp. Accept my promise, Lord, and also you, Virgin Mary, the consolation of all those who are bitter.

Calmer and apparently comforted by the prayer and the promise, Raymond placed the crucifix on the table and extended his hand to Arnulf saying:

- If Jesus accepts my promise, I will go with you to Jerusalem, brother! I hope you will wait for me while I recover enough strength to be in condition to undertake that trip.

- Of course! - replied the knight, in an indecisive tone. The pilgrimage party will not leave for Yafa[23] for another three weeks; maybe even later. So, you will have plenty of time to regain your strength and undertake this journey if it is the Lord's will.

---

[23] Jafa (Yafa) - Part of the city of Tel Aviv in Israel. It was originally a Phoenician city known for having one of the eight gates of Jerusalem.

With equal impatience, but moved by different feelings, the two brothers awaited news of Eliza's fate. Raymond prayed, while Arnulf reasoned how much his brother's pilgrimage would coincide with his plans if his wife survived.

And indeed, it seems that God heard the Count's earnest prayer. At dawn, Fulvio's servant arrived with a note from the Baron, in which he informed Giovanna and Raymond that Eliza was alive and that he had hopes of saving her.

Chapter 10

The news that he would not have to reproach himself for Eliza's death acted beneficially on Raymond's state of mind, and the medicine applied by Fulvio healed his wounds extraordinarily quickly.

Within a week the patient got up and began preparations for the trip by writing a letter to his father, confessing everything that had happened and asking him to send him a sum of money needed for the trip. He also informed him that he was going with Arnulf and that from Jerusalem he intended to return directly to Venice to pick up his wife and go, as she wished, to Castle Zapnenstein in the Tyrol.

The same messenger also carried a letter addressed to Margarita Ramets. In it, Raymond frankly confesses that he has reconciled with Eliza, whose beauty and kindness have definitely won his heart.

"Forgive me, dear Greta, for not keeping the promise I so lightly made you. Before God and men only my obligation to Eliza has any meaning. I cannot and will not separate myself from my wife, whom I adore. The feeling I have for Eliza has made me realize that I have a brotherly love for you. Once again forgive me, dear childhood friend, and remain sister and friend to your devoted Raymond," he concluded the letter.

When the messenger left, Raymond sighed with relief. How could he be such an imbecile as to prefer Greta, with her coarse physiognomy and huge bust, to Eliza, the true embodiment of grace and elegance?

In Castle Reifenstein, Raymond's letters caused different reactions. Only Wolfram felt indescribably happy about the reconciliation of the young couple. He was certain that Eliza would bring happiness to his son, the only being who held him to life and who illuminated with a radiant light the impenetrable darkness of his married life.

A mischievous smile lit up the Count's kindly face when, among the impetuous and enthusiastic praise for Eliza, he read the following sentence:

"How I bless you, father, for the beating you gave the fool I was on our wedding day and who has made me happy now. Were it not for the ties that bind us, I might not have been able to win the heart of the lovely woman, whose possession I owe to fatherly wisdom and foresight."

- That's my son! I knew there would come a time when he would prefer the rose to the piece of cheese - Wolfram murmured happily. "The fact that he almost lost Eliza because of his behavior isn't bad either. At least in the future he will be more cautious and will value the treasure that fate has gifted him," he added in thought.

The countess received a letter from Arnulf that related what had happened in his own way. He superficially highlighted all of his brother's mistakes and his liaison with a married woman, which had caused a series of events and misfortunes and burdened his conscience with grave responsibility, in addition to the attempt that had almost cost Eliza's life and his own wounds, he had been the cause of Mr. Antonio Salviati's death and his wife's madness, whom the relatives had locked up in a monastery. At the end of the letter, Arnulf hoped that the pilgrimage to the Holy Sepulcher would help Raymond to redeem himself from these sins.

While the Count rejoiced and the countess worried about the fate of her son, a terrible storm was raging in Margarita's head.

She then locked herself in her room to read Raymond's letter secretly delivered to her by messenger. As she read the words that crumbled her illusions and hopes and destroyed the results of her clever tricks with which, despite the obstacles, she hoped to reach her goal, the strong blush on her cheeks acquired a deadly pallor. Crumpling the letter, he threw it into the fireplace and, like a tiger in a cage, began to walk around the room.

If Margarita did not have strong nerves, she would have fainted because of the unexpected disappointment. In her vanity, she was sure of Raymond's love and victory over Eliza, whom she hated even more than she loved her childhood friend. But Greta was the kind of person with a stubborn and limited nature like a mule; so, the blows and her convincing made her even more stubborn. Lady Anna had chosen her to be the countess Reifenstein, wealthy owner of the castle and wife of the handsome young Count; therefore, she wanted to become Countess Reifenstein anyway.

In fact, she was intelligent enough to understand that Raymond's love for his young wife and their reconciliation created an insurmountable obstacle to her plans. This conviction, when it fell into her narrow and jealous soul, provoked a mad rage that ended in a river of tears and musings.

Claiming a severe headache, the girl did not show up for dinner and called her maid Marta to help her undress. She was the milk sister of Margarita's mother and went to live together with her in castle Reifenstein. Marta loved Greta blindly and was both servant and confidant to the girl. Clever and wicked, she was hated by all the castle's servants and was absolutely trusted only by Countess Anna for her gossip and spying.

Undressing her young mistress, Martha asked the reason for her sadness. Margarita told her, without hesitation, everything that had happened.

Martha thought hard and then said

- Wipe away those tears, poor child! Did the wretched wretch betray you and not understand you? Well, Marta tells you that you will be Countess Reifenstein!

Seeing the girl's surprise and mistrust, Marta told her that a terrible wizard lived nearby who could eliminate uncomfortable

[147]

people and sold drinks that provoked passion and revived cold feelings.

- Who told you this? - asked Greta, in a tremble of hope.

- Ortruda Finsterbach's maid. She said that her mistress sometimes calls on the services of this sorcerer. He is Jewish and lives in Brixen.[24] You only have to invent a reason to go there, and everything will be arranged according to your wishes.

Martha's advice fell on fertile ground. With her innate cleverness and tenacity, Greta invented as a reason to go to Brixen the need to visit an old relative who lived nearby, whom she had never been interested in before. The Count and his wife were so busy preparing everything their son might need for his trip to Palestine that they paid no attention to the girl's request. Countess Anna authorized her departure with the understanding that the young couple's reconciliation was a severe blow to Greta and that she needed distraction.

One night, about ten days after Raymond's letter arrived, two women wrapped in cloaks secretly knocked on the door of a half-ruined house that had been visited by Countess Anna and her friend Ortruda eleven years ago.

With the same precautions as before, both were ushered into the house and found themselves in the wizard's room furnished in the Asian style and adjoining the laboratory.

The sorcerer was Misael who continued the criminal profession of his father Markhodey. He was now thirty-six years old. His face was distinguished by his rigidly Semitic forms and sickly pallor. His black eyes glowed like dark fire and his being exuded an indescribable expression of cruelty and bitterness.

---

[24] Brixen (Brixen or Bressanone in Italian) - Italian city located at the confluence of the rivers Isarco and Rienza. Brixen and the surrounding territories were ruled by prince-bishops from the 11th century. In 1803, the bishopric became part of Austria, belonging to the province of Tyrol; but it returned to Italy in 1919. Its population is mixed, German, and Italian.

- Kindly, ladies, lift your veil and explain clearly what you want from me. I become a tomb and forget the secrets entrusted to me as soon as my visitors leave this room. Total trust is the first condition for success - said Misael, in his clear, calm voice, looking intently at Greta's pale face as she removed her veil.

As if overwhelmed by the Jew's dark eyes, Greta told him in a few words everything that had happened and expressed her desire to provoke in Raymond's heart a passion so great that he would eventually separate from Eliza and marry her.

As Greta spoke, a deadly pallor began to cover the Jew's face and, in his eyes, a savage hatred was kindled.

- Are we talking about Count Reifenstein? - he asked in a hoarse voice.

When Margarita nodded in the affirmative, Misael became somber and thoughtful.

After a prolonged silence, which seemed like an eternity to Greta, the Jew stood up and said:

- Follow me, madam, I will see what I can do.

The wizard's shrine had not changed in appearance. The magic mirror and the idol remained in the same place. Misael approached the mirror and seemed to immerse himself in contemplation of what it reflected.

Finally, he turned to Greta, who was waiting fearfully, and said in a mournful tone.

- Almost insurmountable obstacles stand in the way of your happiness, noble lady! Your rival is beautiful, clever, and her power over her husband is so great that it drives away any outside influences, even more so because she receives help and tutelage from a very powerful old magician.

- So, you are saying that you cannot help me, and I won't be able to take revenge? That is how powerful you are? - asked Margarita, angrily.

The Jew shook his head.

[149]

- Noble lady, we have not yet touched on the subject of revenge, and in that sense, nothing prevents your wishes. I am speaking only of love for the lady, which the Count opposes under the influence of his passion for his wife and the will of the old wizard. Besides, the Count is a frivolous person and never had any real feelings for you, lady: his oaths were empty words. If you could hear what the Count thinks about you, you would naturally want revenge, not his love.

- I want to know what he thinks! Tell me!

Misael shook his head.

- I dare not repeat to such a beautiful and noble lady as yourself the unworthy and unjust thoughts of the Count!

- I want to know! Tell me!

- Well! He compares you to his wife, a thin, pale, beautiful woman, and laughs at your exuberant beauty, the freshness of your face, and your golden hair, all of which he considers vulgar attributes of a peasant girl.

Greta let out a scream and slumped helplessly in the armchair; but the momentary weakness changed to a mad rage.

- Vengeance! Avenge me, Misael! Make him miserable and despised, and I will pay dearly for every suffering of Raymond! - she exclaimed, stamping her feet.

Having said this, she collapsed in a fit of nerves on the cushions that served as a divan. Martha and the Jew supported her; then the sorcerer brought a cup and forced the girl to drink the contents.

Margarita then calmed down. Only the scattered red patches on her face and the disheveled hair showed how nervous she was.

- I can avenge you and cover the Count in disgrace and misfortune. His peace will be destroyed, his heart will be torn apart, and happiness will flee from him like a deceptive mirage in the desert that draws a cool spring in front of the thirsty man. But to do this, I must have some object that belonged to Count Reifenstein.

Margarita took a medallion from her bodice and handed it to the sorcerer.

- Take it! This medallion has the traitor's portrait and a lock of hair. He gave it to me before he traveled. Is it enough?

- Definitely! Tomorrow night I will recite the incantations that will cover the Count in disgrace.

- Take this on account of my gratitude.

Greta placed a heavy wallet in the Jew's hand and then left the house.

That night, Misael forbade the attendance of new visitors and locked himself in his room. Sitting at the table, he opened the medallion, removed the lock of curly, silky hair, and began to examine the fresh, pleasant face that smiled at him in the golden frame. At that instant, the Jew's face expressed a pure hellish rage, his eyes flamed, and his thin lips uncovered white, sharp teeth like those of a wolf. He looked horrible and disgusting.

- Damned goy! At last Jehovah puts you in my hands! Maybe you will pay at the stake for the crime you committed against Rebecca and me - he hissed, clenching his fists.

Under the influence of furious emotion, Misael leaned his head against the back of the armchair and closed his eyes. All the details of the event of two years ago appeared in his memory with a sickening clarity, opening again the wound that had never healed.

It was a beautiful September afternoon. He was traveling to Brixen with the young wife he had just married. They were riding through the forest when they were suddenly overtaken by a group of knights consisting of a few noble lads accompanied by squires and pageboys, who were probably warmed by the wine.

Misael and his wife respectfully stepped aside and hurried off their mules to greet them. One of the handsome, arrogant-

[151]

looking boys halted his horse and, laughing, uncovered Rebecca's veil.

When he saw the beautiful and frightened Jewish girl's face, his eyes shone. Grabbing the girl by the clothes, he lifted her up like a child and wanted to kiss her, but Misael, forgetting everything in anger and jealousy, rushed to his wife's aid, snatched her from the aggressor's hands and applied a furious blow to the horse's abdomen. The horse reared up and almost threw its rider to the ground.

The fury of the hunters was indescribable. The squires immediately grabbed Misael, stripped him of his clothes and flogged him mercilessly.

As the cruel reprisal, accompanied by booing and jeering, Rebecca's desperate cries indicated that she was also being abused.

Remembering that moment, Misael writhed in groans in his armchair. Finally, he mastered the storm raging in his soul, and taking a sheet of parchment from the drawer, he began to write a long letter to Eliazar, a rich Venetian jeweler.

Raymond recovered quickly. He was already up, his wounds had closed, and then he began to walk. His strength increased every day, and he regained the old freshness of his face. He had not seen Eliza yet. Fulvio told him that she was out of danger, but very weak and in need of absolute rest.

Such a situation left the Count extremely disgusted, even more because the day of his departure was approaching. He received a very affectionate reply from his father and a sum of money enough to guarantee him luxurious independence during the trip.

Finally, with ten or twelve days to go, Baron Vart authorized the boy to visit Eliza. Seeing her, pale and emaciated, a bitter regret gripped Raymond's heart. It was his fault she had almost died!

Kneeling in front of the armchair, he pressed his young wife to his chest and began to whisper words of love to her, begging her to forgive him for all the suffering she had endured for his sake.

Eliza returned his kiss with a kind smile. The young couple kept talking, but she seemed sad. When Raymond went on to talk about his pilgrimage to the Holy Sepulcher, Eliza watched with a sigh:

- I know that you made a promise if God helped me recover. I am deeply grateful for the love that has been instilled in you by the idea of traveling to Palestine, but I am being tortured by an ill omen that the trip will be fateful for you and will bring us misfortune.

- What is this, Eliza? What doom do you sense for us? - murmured Raymond, desolate and emotional.

- I do not know... I cannot say anything concrete. I keep trying to convince myself that it is nonsense, but I cannot rid myself of an incomprehensible weight when I think about this trip.

- In that case, instead of Jerusalem, I will go to Rome! - exclaimed Raymond with his usual impetuosity.

- Oh no! It is a great sin not to keep the promise given. Go to Jerusalem, say a prayer at the Holy Sepulcher and God will protect us from any danger! Besides, who knows if all these feelings are just a result of my weakness and nervous breakdowns? - concluded Eliza, trying to smile.

From that day on, Raymond spent all his free time with Eliza, surrounding her with all his attention and love. He was happy to see that Eliza became more and more fond and accustomed to him, and deeply regretted that he had to leave on a trip. Were it not for the fear of breaking his promise, he would gladly stay, since it was very difficult for him to part from Eliza at the moment of their blossoming happiness.

The day before the departure, Raymond went to see his wife, sad and thoughtful. The conversation, usually so animated, this time did not get off the ground. Finally, after a long silence, Eliza said:

- My dark thoughts have infected you, Raymond, and I reproach myself for hindering your holy journey that love for me has instilled in you. But follow bravely on to Jerusalem! I will pray for you and hope that my memory will deter you from any fatal distraction.

- Yes Eliza. You give me such a warm and pure feeling that I have never felt before. Despite the criminal levity, which I frankly admit, I hope never to repeat my old sins. For me it is enough to remember your innocent look to be immune to any vulgar temptation. Your pure image, my beloved Eliza, will be my shield! Only you reign in my heart!

Eliza directed her pure, confident gaze at her husband. With a timid gesture, in childlike affection, she ran her tiny, emaciated little hand over her husband's black hair, then drew him close to her and kissed him.

- I trust you Raymond, and hope that on your return the Lord will give us a happy and peaceful life.

Before saying goodbye to Raymond, Eliza told him with visible embarrassment:

- Listen! Between us there can be no secrets, and I want to tell you something that may be useful to you.

- Of course, dear! There can be no secrets between us. You can speak frankly - replied Raymond curiously.

- Don't trust Arnulf! I cannot accuse him of open animosity toward you, but he has a special ability to explain your every act in the worst possible way. Besides, he is in love with me...

- Arnulf? That stump of wood, that hypocrite, who since he was born has never dated a woman, is in love with you? - Raymond laughed cheerfully.

- You are very beautiful and dangerous to the male hearts. But this time, dear Eliza, you are wrong!

- I wish I were wrong and then I would be reassured, but I have too much clear evidence of his feelings. I swear to you that when he declared his love to Bianca Villamarino and asked for her hand in marriage, he got rejected.

Seeing that a strong blush covered Raymond's face and his eyes sparkled with jealousy, Eliza laughed happily.

- Why were you worried? Do you fear Arnulf's competition? - she asked, mocking and coquettish.

- No - replied Raymond, embarrassed and repressing a fit of jealousy. Thank God I do not fear his competition! I respect you too much to be jealous of him. Besides, I will make sure that this gentleman does not admire you too much. I am not afraid for you, but we should not trust hypocrites like my brother.

Chapter 11

At that time, a pilgrimage to the Holy Land was an extremely rare event. Jerusalem had again fallen into the hands of the Saracens.[25] The dangers that threatened Christians in a country where no one protected them discouraged the faithful and turned into a mere stream that bustling torrent of faith that once flowed to Palestine.

The pilgrims who were driven by devotion and courage to undertake that journey, despite all the dangers, usually gathered in Venice, often waiting for weeks on end for the ship that was heading to the East. People of different nationalities would settle in special hostels, and when they were large enough in number, they would rent a private galley.

Raymond and Arnulf were lucky. A significant number of German pilgrims gathered in Venice, and they would then go to Jafa exclusively in the company of compatriots.

The day of departure was always a kind of solemnity. All the pilgrims prayed in church and then went to the pier.

Villamarino, Fulvio, Conrad Vart and even Elizá, who was leaving the house for the first time since the attack, accompanied the two brothers. Eliza was again overcome by dark omens. When Raymond kissed her goodbye, tears rolled down her face and she babbled in a trembling voice:

- May God protect you from the dangers of this long journey and bring you home safe and sound!

---

[25] Saracens - Pre-Islamic nomadic people who inhabited deserts situated between Syria and Arabia; Moorish, Arab.

Raymond, moved, pressed her against his chest.

- I have faith in the Savior's mercy and in your prayers! In order not to show his own emotion, the boy quickly turned around and jumped into the boat that would take him to the galley.

On the ship were hoisted the pilgrims' flags with the red cross, the banner of St. Mark, and the Pope's banner. As they were lifting anchor, everyone on deck fell to their knees. The singing of the prayer imploring God for a happy crossing was heard.

For the first few days of the trip, Raymond was very sad, but gradually his usual nonchalance returned due to his lively and agile nature.

At first, he was interested in his new surroundings, but then he began to get bored for lack of company. He could not count on Arnulf, who was quiet and not very sociable: the captain of the galley, an old "sea wolf," was stern and also quiet, while most of the pilgrims were ignorant people. Raymond was almost bored to death when a new pilgrim appeared on deck who had been ill since the day of departure. His appearance and manner showed that he was from a good background.

They then quickly got to know each other, and the young Count learned that his interlocutor's name was Beovulf Sharfenshneid and that he was the son of a wealthy merchant from Augsburg.[26] His father had a trade in Asian goods, but he himself, both out of devotion and business, was going to Jerusalem for the third time.

The boys soon became friends. Beovulf provided the Count with much valuable information concerning the journey and the stay in the holy city.

---

[26] Augsburg - City located in southern Germany, capital of Swabia; it is considered the largest industrial center of the Lech River, including the production of fabrics, engines, vehicles, and airplanes. Important commercial and banking center of the fifteenth and sixteenth centuries and meeting point of German science and art.

Under different circumstances, Raymond might have felt a certain distrust of his new friend, for Beovulf's whole being exuded cleverness and dishonesty. His grayish eyes never stared at his interlocutor; his exaggerated faith was suspicious, and the earthy pallor, dark circles under his eyes, early wrinkles, and a large, fleshy, sensual mouth, suggested that his past had been full of numerous "exaggerations".

But Raymond, young, frivolous, and inexperienced like all the people whose lives passed happily and smoothly, paid no attention to these external signs. He enjoyed the conversations, for Beovulf was a great storyteller and knew how to deftly address the most different and daring topics.

The young merchant was particularly interested in getting Raymond settled in the holy city. His stories were full of details about the repressions the Muslims used against the Christians, forcing them to pay fees even for the right to leave the tents on the sand where they settled, and creating numerous difficulties for them when it came time to visit the Holy Sepulcher and other traditionally consecrated sites.

Once, when the conversation touched on this subject again, Beovulf advised the Count not to settle in the hostel intended for pilgrims, but in the house of a Jew known to him.

- Not that one! - said Raymond in disgust. I do not want to get dirty entering the house of a filthy Jew! Especially not in Jerusalem, where they killed our Savior! You do not know what you are talking about, my friend Beovulf!

He smiled.

You do not know the living conditions in Jerusalem. Old Abdias, where I intend to install you, that is, if he agrees, does not look like our German Jews. He is a wise physician, whose science is respected by Christians and Muslims alike. During my last stay there, he cured the pasha[27] of Jerusalem of a mortal illness, and thus

---

[27] Pasha - High title among the Turks, which corresponded to "excellency" in the West.

[158]

acquired such a predisposition from the Saracen that, thanks to his protection, I was able to visit all the holy places without any problems. Besides, in his house there is the comfort that you will not find in the dirty hostel where pilgrims stay.

From that day on, the Jewish man Abdias became the main topic of conversation for the boys. Everything Beovulf told was so strange and curious that Raymond took a lively interest in the Jewish sage.

In this spirit, Raymond disembarked in Yafa and made his way to the holy city. But, it seemed, bad luck was pursuing him.

Still at sea, his galley barely managed to escape the pirates; on dry land, his caravan was attacked by Arabs. The pilgrims managed to repel the attack of the evildoers, who eventually escaped, but part of their luggage was stolen, and Raymond lost the package with the gold and silver lamp he was taking to Jerusalem to fulfill his promise. In addition, the Count was slightly wounded during the battle. Although the wound presented no danger, the heat and the grueling journey took a toll on his health, and he came to Jerusalem sick and weak.

Beovulf was right about the difficulties he would have to face in the unfortunate inn where the crowds of pilgrims stayed and where Saracen warriors lived who watched over the hateful gavurs.[28]

Arnulf, completely absorbed in his prayers, paid no attention to his brother. Once, when Raymond was feeling very ill and was extremely irritable, Beovulf went to visit him. He listened with sympathy to the Count's complaints and again repeated his advice to stay in the house of Abdias, who would take care of him with a doctor and, in addition, protect him from the boldness of the soldiers and from the demands of the Muslim authorities, who

---

[28] Gavur- Name given by Islam to all non-Muslims, especially in the Middle Ages.

were extremely irritated by the rumors coming from Europe about a new Crusade[29] being prepared.

Raymond was so tired and upset that, despite his disgust for the Jews, he decided to stay at Abdias' house and consult him about his unhealing wound.

Beovulf led his friend to the block near Solomon's Temple,[30] where King Baldwin[31] had built a palace, now half-destroyed by the Saracens. At the end of a narrow alley was an inconspicuous house, on whose door Beovulf knocked gently. The door opened immediately, and a young man ushered the visitors into a small, well-painted room modestly furnished with low divans.

Exchanging a few words with the boy in the Arabic language, Beovulf told his companion that the owner of the house would soon receive them. Indeed, a few minutes later the door opened and, on the threshold, appeared a man wearing a long, wide black coat and a white gauze turban on his head. For a moment, his attentive gaze was fixed on Raymond with a strange expression.

---

[29] Crusade - The Crusades were expeditions organized by inspiration of the church in the 11th century, composed of European nobility, with the objective of liberating the Holy Land (Palestine) from the infidels (Arabs and Turks) who expanded throughout the Near and Middle East and the Mediterranean Basin, from the 7th century on, including Jerusalem. There were eight Crusades, the first in 1095 and the last in 1270.

[30] Solomon's Temple - Solomon was a king of the Hebrews (970 B.C. to 930 B.C.), son and successor of King David. His reign was marked by foreign alliances, especially with Egypt and Phoenicia, and the expansion of Israel's territory. His temple was built in the tenth year of his reign and reproduced the plan of the tabernacle, but in larger dimensions. The building was 60 cubits long, 20 wide and 30 high. One cubit = 66 centimeters.

[31] King Baldwin - Baldwin II, Latin king of Jerusalem (1118 - 1131), Count of Edessa (1100 - 1131), cousin and successor of Baldwin I. He accompanied Godfroy de Bouillon (Godfrey of Bouillon) on the First Crusade and was captured by the Muslims in 1104 and released in 1108. He spent most of his reign warring with the Turks in northern Syria.

The man approached and greeted the visitors with the respectful eastern friendliness, without any of the humiliation or servility that the young Count had grown accustomed to finding in European Jews.

Raymond looked with mild surprise at the newcomer. He was a handsome man of about thirty. His pale white face bore the Semitic features, but without that rigidity of features that made them unpleasant. His hooked nose was slightly curved, the small mouth well outlined, and the large, velvety black eyes resembled those of birds of prey. A silky, bluish-black beard framed his face.

From the conversation held in the Frankish language,[32] Raymond learned that Abdias was not at home; he had been summoned to attend to a sick person, and that his interlocutor, Uriel, was the doctor's son. The young man immediately offered to accommodate the Count if he could find suitable quarters.

Through a small inner door and gallery, Uriel led the visitors to a small enclosure that consisted of two rooms: one large and luxuriously furnished in the Asian style; the other intended for the Count's squire.

There everything pleased Raymond. But what had really attracted him was the garden, where the larger room led off. It was not large, but the palm trees and the countless rose bushes and jasmine trees made it a small paradise, shady and fragrant. Moreover, the rent was so advantageous that Raymond did not hesitate. It was agreed that he would move there that same night, and the next day Abdias would examine his wound, as he would be returning very late.

At first, Arnulf did not approve of his brother's decision to stay at the Jew's house, but upon learning of the advantages Raymond would have, he stopped protesting.

After the dingy, cramped room, which he occupied with Arnulf at the inn, Raymond felt like he was in paradise in the large

---

[32] Frankish language - Germanic language spoken by the invaders of Gaul.

[161]

room filled with fresh air and the scent of flowers that permeated through the window and door. After strolling through the garden, and feeling tired, he lay down on the soft divan that served as his bed, and soon fell into a deep sleep.

Raymond could not tell how long he slept for. He woke up with a strong sensation of pain. Something heavy and cold squeezed his chest, his tempers pulsed, and a pleasant but suffocating aroma gave him a strong tachycardia and dizziness.

Choking and barely able to breathe, Raymond opened his eyes and saw with surprise that a woman was leaning over him and unashamedly examining him with curiosity. Despite the room being lit only by the night lamp, Raymond could tell that the stranger was a very young and slender girl. The simple white tunic highlighted her lovely forms, leaving her neck and lightly tanned arms bare. A ring of golden stars adorned with precious stones held a large veil, from which hung long, thick black braids. Countless strands of pearls attached to the golden hoop at the temples framed the girl's face, reflecting in assorted colors and sparkling on her neck and chest. The young woman's face was perfect and stood out for its fine features. Her large almond eyes sparkled, and her purple mouth revealed teeth of blinding white. She was pure oriental beauty, provocative and sensual. The suffocating aroma was coming from her. But what seemed incomprehensible to Raymond was that the stranger held in her outstretched hand a round, glowing object emitting rays that struck his forehead and caused him a terrible pain in his brain.

Worried and surprised, he wanted to get up, but his limbs did not obey and seemed paralyzed.

"Who could be this woman? What does she want from me?" - he wondered.

But his thoughts worked with difficulty and his dimmed eyes closed. He watched when the stranger stepped back and disappeared into the wall, like in a dream. Then he lost consciousness.

In the morning, he woke up late feeling extremely exhausted. His head was too heavy. All that remained of the night vision was a vague memory. He then convinced himself that it had been a dream.

A little later, Abdias arrived, a venerable old man with a long gray beard, with a piercing gaze and respectful treatment. He greeted Raymond kindly, examined him, and bandaged his wound. Then he told him that the ointment he had applied, and a few days of rest would make him fully recover.

The days passed quietly. Raymond rested as prescribed; he slept, dreamed in the garden, and in the evenings, he amused himself admiring the miniature portrait of Eliza, which had almost been taken from Giovanna by force.

Arnulf also visited his brother, praised his quarters, and talked to Abdias, who arrived just at that hour to change the dressings. The knight looked worried and said that something extremely sad had happened: one of the pilgrims had a disagreement with a Muslim; during the fight he had killed him, and as a result the Saracens had taken up a threatening position.

- This is very unpleasant! You should leave the Pilgrims' lodge, because it might be attacked by people who are irritated by rumors of a new Crusade, despite the agreements signed during the surrender of Jerusalem - said the Jew.

- In that case, wise Abdias, could I stay with you until the time we are allowed to return to Yafa? - asked Arnulf.

- Sir, I am afraid I cannot host you here at home, as I already have two Christian guests. However, I will try to find you a safe haven in the house of one of my relatives. I will have my son Uriel inform them tonight.

The next day, Arnulf also stayed at the house of a Jew. But the city remained quiet, and, except for a deafening hostility, nobody messed with the Christians who wisely avoided appearing in the streets.

[163]

A few days later, Beovulf invited Raymond to his house for lunch.

During lunch, the boys chatted happily and drank heavily. The wine was excellent. After lunch, Raymond felt a bit excited. The blood burned in his veins, a tremor ran through his skin, and he was overcome with a thirst for fun, some great excitement; in short: some crazy adventure.

- Damn it to hell! How boring everything here is! Isn't there a place around here where I can have some fun? - complained Raymond.

Beovulf smiled.

- What kind of fun do you want? - he asked.

- How will I know? For example, seeing dances that I have never seen.

- I can fulfill your request and take you to a place of entertainment. There, we can play games and enjoy beautiful dances - said Beovulf. Of course, I did not mean it, because you, Count, are a married man and came here for religious reasons only.

- What's that got to do with it? Married men and Christians are not forbidden to play board game or enjoy dancing - Raymond impatiently replied.

- If it does not weigh on your conscience, then let's go! I will take you. We just have to wait until evening and change into our costumes. As a knight, you cannot show up in that gambling house, whose owner, I do not know if he is Greek or Jewish, has a bad reputation.

Extremely interested, Raymond waited impatiently for nightfall. He and his companion dressed in the half-Eastern costumes worn by Greeks and Armenians, and Beovulf led him through the dark and deserted streets, arriving at a garden gate, which he knocked on several times at agreed intervals.

Raymond was strongly tempted to experience all the thrills of gambling. He took a seat at the table where the owner of the

[164]

gambling house took him, a short-colored man with a hooked nose and small black evil eyes.

Raymond liked to gamble. His father usually diverted him from this fun with other, less dangerous pleasures, but now there was nothing to hold him back, and he wanted to play more and more despite the bad luck that dogged him insistently. He had lost the last coin when shouts and applause caught his attention. Irritated and dissatisfied, he stood up and muted in admiration. At the back of the room a curtain rose. A woman slowly came out on stage, accompanied by two others, with tambourines in her hands and stopped in the center of the carpet stretched by her companions.

Never before had Raymond seen such stunning beauty as that of the daughter of the East, elegant and slender as a cat with big flaming eyes and a huge mane of loose black hair that came down to below her knees.

The dancer wore a striped silk skirt with a silver belt. Her naked torso was half-covered with a purple scarf, fastened around her neck with a golden brooch. They sat down with their musical instruments and began a mournful, monotonous song, accompanied by tambourines. The dancer began her act. The slow dance consisted mainly of gentle arm and hip movements. Her whole being breathed something indescribably exciting with sensual languor. Her eyes, as dark and deep as the night, seemed to smile exclusively at him. The young Count's cheeks burned, and his eyes flamed. In that instant, he completely forgot about Eliza and surrendered himself headlong to the enchantment that the dancer provoked in his aroused senses.

Beovulf was standing next to Raymond. When the dance was over, he blew in the young Count's ear.

- This is Guella, the tavern keeper's daughter! Do you agree that she is beautiful as a dream? But she is extremely severe. Now she will make us pay for the pleasure of admiring her and offer each of us a glass of wine.

- But I swear I just lost all the money I had, and I do not have a penny in my pocket! - murmured Raymond, irritated.

[165]

- How much do you need? - asked Beovulf, handing him a few coins.

Raymond grabbed the gold coin. At that moment, the dancer approached him and, with a mischievous look in her sparkling eyes, offered him a glass of wine. The Count dropped the coin on the small tray and in a single gulp emptied the cup. Ten minutes later, Guella disappeared behind the curtains and the boys left the gambling house.

From that day on, Raymond became restless and nervous. As soon as night fell, he definitely could not find a place for himself, and the demon of gambling lured him into the lair, where an unusual gambling misfortune and Guella's provocative smile awaited him, who, each day, showed more and more openly that she liked him, and that it was enough for her to make him happy.

In the morning, awakening from a heavy and almost lethargic sleep, Raymond thought, horrified, about his own situation, and vowed never to set foot in that accursed lair. But as soon as it was dark, his willpower and his wise decisions disappeared, and an uncontrollable force took him to the fateful place.

Raymond spent all his money so quickly that he had to take out a loan with Arnulf. Arnulf handed him the requested amount without question, but his cold, watchful, suspicious gaze forced Raymond to blush. Arnulf then advised his brother to spend less, since his stay in Jerusalem could be prolonged for a long time. There were rumors that the roads were full of highwaymen. And when the pilgrims appealed to the pasha, he advised them to wait for the detachment of soldiers who were to leave for Jaffa. Then the caravan reached the port, taking advantage of its guard. Furthermore, there were worrying rumors circulating in the city. It was said that Sultan Malekh-Naer had personally gone to Jerusalem and that the least of his reprisals would be the expulsion of all the Christians as well as some monks who served at the Holy Sepulcher, since he was offended by the cowardice of the Christians who, disregarding all agreements, were preparing a new Crusade.

[166]

Despite such serious circumstances, Raymond continued with his nightly madness, and each morning he was horrified at what might ultimately happen to him. He was penniless. He did not want to ask Arnulf for another loan; it was almost impossible to contact his father, and if he did, it would be months before he received any answer.

In this difficult situation, the boy appealed to Beovulf, who had become his close friend. The latter lent him a small sum of money, claiming that he had also lost a lot, but that both could easily get out of the difficulty with Abdias willingly lending money to his guests.

Indeed, the deal went through without any difficulty; the Count handed the Jew a promissory note for a large sum. But bad luck continued to visibly pursue him; the next day, in a completely absurd way, he was robbed of a large part of that money.

Gloomy and desperate, Raymond returned to his quarters. For the first time, despite the agitation that tormented him, he did not go to the gambling house, and he started walking around the room like a tiger in a cage. Sad thoughts plagued him. How had he gotten himself into this? How would he get out of it? How would he appear before his father after those shameful adventures? About this, he did not even dare to think. Finally, in terrible despair, he threw himself down on the couch.

A hand touched his shoulder, causing him to shiver and turn around quickly. In front of him, he saw with surprise Abdias who was looking at him intently with his fox eyes.

- Count, I noticed that you came back today extremely worried. You live under my roof and my age gives me the right to consider you as a child. I have come to ask you if you need anything. Although you Christians despise the children of Israel, the law of Jehovah tells us to regard everyone who steps on our doorstep, even if he is an enemy, as a brother. So, speak frankly and, if possible, I will help you!

Raymond's hatred and contempt for the Jewish race had diminished considerably since he had stayed at Abdias' house. At that moment, seeing the venerable face of the old man, he almost forgot he was standing in front of him and, under the pressure of the need to get things off his chest, confessed to him all his problems, basing them mainly on the difficulty of getting help from his father.

An enigmatic smile passed across the Jew's lips.

- So, the problem is gold? You see, gold is a very capricious gentleman. To those who know how to master it, it is given without difficulty, but it brings disgrace and humiliation to those who grovel for it.

- So, is it possible to master gold? - murmured Raymond, confused.

The Jew stared into the young Count's eyes.

- Yes, by learning how to create it, and by penetrating the temple of the secret knowledge that subdues the forces of nature to its adepts and makes them masters of the blind and ignorant mob. My son, do you wish to penetrate the sanctuary of knowledge and be the lord of gold? If you like, I can introduce you to it.

- Of course, I do! - Raymond exclaimed impetuously.

At that instant, he screamed as he felt a terrible pain in his finger. The boy looked at the ring, Baron Vart's magical gift, and noticed that the emerald had darkened and seemed to be covered in a dark mist.

Raymond paled and stepped back, giving Abdias a suspicious look. Abdias laughed disdainfully.

- Sir Count, your ring warns but does not help. In fact, I am far from the idea of influencing you. If you wish, continue in your ignorance, and do not slam the door of the temple if you have doubts. To become a servant of the great god "Science", you must give yourself to it and serve yourself without arguing, love what it loves and hate everything it despises. In return, it will give you all the goods of the earth, countless pieces of gold, and power over living beings and inanimate objects. But I tell you frankly, if you are

[168]

afraid and doubtful, then you had better forget everything I have told you.

In addition to distrust, pride and curiosity were fighting in Raymond's spirit.

- For me there is no such word as "fear", but my distrust is fair! Who can prove to me that you, a Jew, are not deceiving me, and that, as you say, it is really science that makes you so rich, and not the loan sharking your people like so much, or your medical knowledge? - asked Raymond, measuring Abdias with a dark and arrogant look.

The latter seemed not to be offended by such words.

- The mistrust of Christians towards Jews is totally natural; but between the master and the disciple there must be total trust. What interest do I have in causing you harm? None whatsoever! If you like, I can show you what kind of treasure can be obtained by dedicating yourself to the science I told you about. You will only need to go blindfolded and leave your weapons here. But I repeat: do not be afraid of anything.

- What if you kill me to drink my blood as is the custom of your coreligionists?

The Jew's face turned deadly pale.

- I will not even try to answer this false and disgusting accusation. By the way, Christians accuse us of killing children, but you are already a grown man. Your disappearance would be noticed immediately, and if your brother complained to the pasha, the pasha would take the opportunity to suppress the entire Jewish colony. So, make up your mind!

A thousand contradictory ideas swirled in Raymond's head. An inner voice whispered to him that the Jew's compassion was very suspicious, but natural boldness urged him to take a chance on this extraordinary adventure erasing his suspicions.

- All right! Show me the treasures and then I will decide how to act - he said in a resolute tone, taking off the sword from his belt and placing it on the table.

Abdias took a silk handkerchief from his pocket, folded it, and tightly sealed the Count's eyes. Then he took him by the hand. They both left the room and went down to the terrace. The suffocating scent of lilies and roses showed Raymond that they were headed to the garden. But soon he lost all sense of the direction they were going. He suspected that the path was being purposely lengthened. Then they descended an endless staircase and passed through a narrow corridor, as he could lean against both walls. Finally, Raymond's guide stopped and removed the blindfold from his eyes. Raymond looked around and from his lips came a cry of surprise. He was in a large room or an underground cave, brightly lit by countless tall bronze candelabras of ancient form. Everywhere his dazzled gaze glittered with gold and sparkled with precious stones. On the floor were piles of gold and silver ingots; chests were completely filled with gold coins and precious stones. On the large table in the center of the cave were two large, deep gold containers, one of which was filled with pearls of the most diverse sizes, and the other with diamonds that sparkled with the colors of the rainbow.

Never before had Raymond felt what he felt at that moment. He was overcome by an avid urge to possess similar riches and the uncontrollable desire to dip his hands into those mounds of gold and precious stones, to feel how the cascades of pearls flowed through his fingers, and to admire the sparkle of diamonds in the palm of his hand. He took a step toward the table, but the Jew's hand immediately landed on his shoulder.

- You cannot touch anything here until you are one of us and an adept of secret science! Then you can take whatever you want from here until such time as you can create for yourself, with your knowledge and will, fabulous wealth.

- I want to be one of you! I want to learn this wonderful science that can create so many treasures - replied Raymond with his voice hoarse and his face burning.

- All right! From tomorrow Uriel will be your master, but before you leave the room, swear on what is dearest to you in the world, on your father's life and on your honor, that you will never report to anyone, not with a single word or insinuation, what you have seen here and what they are teaching you.

Raymond took the required oath without the slightest wince. Then he let the Jew blindfold him and they walked out of the underground.

Chapter 12

From the next day on, Uriel gave Raymond lessons every night. He was a skillful teacher who knew how to interest his pupil and maintain his will to learn. Raymond was too ignorant and inexperienced to realize that he was being deceived, and that under the false name of alchemy, cabala and other pompous names, his soul was slowly being impregnated with unholy heresy, a material and immoral cult of contempt for everything he had hitherto loved.

Now Raymond had learned that Abdias and his son were members of a secret society, into which he was being groomed for acceptance. Twice he had been to the old Jew's quarters and had seen his second son and his niece Maakha there. To his great surprise, he seemed to recognize in Maakha the woman he had seen in a dream on the first night of his stay in that house.

Raymond's prejudice against the Jews disappeared completely and with it also disappeared his simple and pure faith, his views on sin, goodness, and duty.

Once, answering Raymond's impatient question about when, at last, he would be initiated, Uriel replied that the next day, in the evening, there would be a meeting of the adepts and that, taking advantage of the opportunity, he would be introduced to the Brotherhood and admitted taking the oath.

Raymond spent the day agitated and nervous. As the appointed time approached, he was overcome by a deafening dread and a growing sadness for no apparent reason. This depressive state reached its peak when Uriel entered his room and looked intently and wryly into his pale and desolate face.

- Are you afraid? Are you under the influence of fairy tales again? - he asked scornfully.

- No! I am not afraid of anything, and I am ready to follow you! - replied the Count, trying to master his unhealthy emotion.

This time, it seemed to Raymond that they were leading him down a different path. He heard a door close behind him, and then the blindfold was removed. Raymond then saw that they were going through a narrow underground gallery, lit by torches stuck in the wall. The gallery snaked downward and widened into circular rooms.

The construction of that labyrinth had probably been carried out in archaic times, judging by the dimensions of the Cyclopean rocks used in the work and the signs that appeared occasionally on the walls, painted with red paint, or carved in relief on the stones, which Raymond thought to be Hebrew letters.

Finally, they stopped before an iron door beside which stood a metal figure in the shape of a winged bull with a human face.

Raymond, who had no knowledge of all Assyrian buildings and the monsters that were placed at the palace gates, looked at the statue with supernatural terror. In fact, he did not even have much time to think, because the door opened noiselessly, and they entered the treasure room he already knew. But this time, the room had its appearance somewhat altered. The two containers with pearls and diamonds had disappeared, and the table was covered with a golden tablecloth, richly embroidered with precious stones. On the table was a tray with two goblets; one of them, made of gold and glitter, was half-filled with a purple liquid; the other was simple, made of ebony, in whose contents shone a liquid that looked like melted gold.

On the other side of the table was a man in white robes and covered face.

- Come closer, neophyte! Choose one of the goblets and drink - said the stranger in a deaf voice. One of them will give you

[173]

pleasure and life, the other, work and death. Take it and may everything happen according to your choice!

Raymond faltered for a moment, then grabbed the gold cup and emptied it in a gulp.

You have chosen wisely between pleasure and life - said the stranger. The black cup represents the earth from whose bowel's gold can only be obtained with the sweat of the face. But when the man finally holds the tempting liquid in his hands and is ready to bring it to his lips, death freezes his tired arm, and the cup falls from his hands before his lips can touch its contents.

A nervous tremor ran through Raymond's limbs. The liquid he took ran like a torrent of fire through his veins, filling him with energy and awakening in him a wild desire for pleasures and emotions never felt before.

- And now - said Uriel - you must go your own way. You will find me in the sanctuary next to the statue of the great god.

Uriel tied Raymond's hands in such a way that he could move only one of them with difficulty, and then opened a door so well camouflaged in the wall that it was impossible to even suspect its existence.

Raymond entered a small, dimly lit vaulted hallway, at the end of which a purple curtain could be seen. Behind the curtain she entered a rounded, well-lit room. There were piles of gold and precious stones everywhere. This time, the knight's gaze passed indifferently past the treasures and fixed on the large door that was on the other side of the room.

On the doorstep, on purple pillows was a woman lying down. Only a light gauze covered her wonderful body shape. Loose hair covered her like a silky cape; on her forehead was a string of pearls, and a veil hid her face.

When Raymond approached, the woman raised her body on her elbow and offered him a bowl filled with a steaming liquid that emitted a strong aroma. At the same time, he noticed that in her other hand she held a long stiletto with a glistening blade.

After a moment's hesitation, Raymond pushed the cup away and wanted to step over the obstacle that was preventing him from moving forward, but the woman threateningly raised her stiletto.

- No one passes through this door without first drinking from the cup or dying here - she said with a shrill tone, looking at Raymond with hostility.

The Count wanted to take the cup, but the woman pushed his hand away, and said with a cynical smile:

- You must buy the wine. Give me your sweater! Raymond almost mechanically let them take off his silk sweater and drank his glass.

Then the woman let him pass, lifting the heavy curtain lowered behind her.

He entered a second large, round cave, filled with the same treasures as the first cave. Besides gold and precious stones, there were also valuable weapons, silverware with gold and precious stones of a richness never seen before. Next to the new door was another woman with a cup and a sword in her hands. She also offered the drink and demanded payment.

In this way, Raymond then passed through seven rooms filled with fabulous riches. And when he stepped on the threshold of the last room, he had nothing left that he could give in payment. But that did not bother him. His body burned like fire. The glitter of gold, the strong lighting and the suffocating aromas that filled the caverns made him dizzy. He staggered drunkenly out of the last cave and found himself in a room twice as big as the previous ones and also very well lit. At the back of that new room was a throne on some steps. Some people came out to meet him, in costumes as brief as his; they only had red cloaks over their shoulders and their heads were swathed in black scarves.

They surrounded Raymond and began to decorate him. They put a wide necklace around his neck, a shiny belt around his waist, and golden sandals on his feet. Then they threw over his shoulders a purple cloak and a crown on his head. The ropes that bound him were removed.

At that instant, out of the side gallery came a gaggle of women adorned with jewels. Their faces were covered by veils, and they held tambourines over their heads. Four of them carried a large golden sedan chair, which they placed on the floor in front of Raymond. The men forced the boy into the sedan chair, then lifted him up and put him over their shoulders. The women surrounded him, started a wild dance, and sang in chorus:

- Glory! Glory to You, King Solomon! Your five hundred wives salute you and lead you to the Queen of Sheba,[33] who has come to admire your power and together with you offer a sacrifice to the true King of the Universe, the dark angel, named Lucifer.

The procession proceeded through the gallery and into a colossal underground, lit by countless torches. In front of the entrance, on a rise of several steps was a black stone pedestal, above which rose the figure of an idol, half human, half animal, of gigantic dimensions.

The statue had a female torso, goat's head, and feet, and behind its shoulders were huge wings. A lighted torch was fixed between the monster's horns, and a reddish flame burned in its eye sockets.

At the idol's feet was a semi-dead woman, covered by a transparent, silver gauze. On her head she was wearing a crown identical to the one they had placed on Raymond. Her elegant and wonderful shapes stood out in relief against the black background.

On the ground at the foot of the steps, on one of which a man in a white suit was standing, was a large ebony crucifix. On

---

[33] Queen of Sheba - queen of the Kingdom of Sheba, according to Jewish and Islamic traditions; a region located south of Arabia, at the extreme east of the Red Sea, in the present-day region of Yemen. Legend has it that the Queen of Sheba - Makeda - knowing King Solomon's fame, decided to pay him a visit, but sent him gifts in advance, in order to impress him. She had a son with him named Menelik, who founded the Kingdom of Ethiopia.

either side of the idol stood men in red or black cloaks, adorned with jewelry.

The sedan chair was lowered a few steps from the idol and Raymond was led to the priest.

Come closer! - he said. Bring an offering and worship the great god Lucifer, the firstborn of Heaven, creator of visible matter and merciful ruler of the Earth! He commands you to enjoy yourself, frees you from all vain prejudices, allows you to consider all earthly pleasures as your inalienable property, and authorizes you to obtain them by any means. Evil is only a fiction; any punishment is an injustice, since everything that can serve to give pleasure to man belongs legitimately to him. To get pleasure from the flesh means to worship Lucifer; to hoard gold and, with its help, to subject to their own feet the imbeciles with their childish pangs of conscience means to glorify his power. Swear allegiance to Lucifer and disown Him Whom the weaklings worship and whose symbol is the cross!

Pale and barely able to breathe, Raymond listened to this sacrilegious speech. He already knew the tenor of those shy theories from Uriel's lessons, but for the first time he heard the poison in its purest and most summarized form, as did the priest of Lucifer.

Then he realized the abyss into which he was about to fall. Although he felt strange and excited, in Raymond's darkened mind came the memory of Eliza, his father, and the pure and holy faith of his past life.

Seeing that the Count had remained silent, the priest said, after a moment's silence:

- Do you hesitate to worship Lucifer? Come forward, spit three times on that symbol, break once and for all with your stupid past, and all the pleasures of love and wealth will be your reward!

But instead of moving closer Raymond stepped back and put his hands on his head. For the last time, reason, faith, and love for his wife fought inside him.

[177]

- No! - he shouted in a hoarse voice. I do not want to perform this disgusting sacrilege! I want neither your company nor your god! What you profess and demand can only be done by the servants of hell!

Raymond turned to run away from that room but was caught. Through the ranks of those present ran a low, malevolent chuckle.

- You stupid, blind, crazy man! - said the priest. Don't tell me you think you can get this far and then back out? Then you must know that you will only leave this room dead or as Lucifer's servant!

- I would rather die!

- It is up to you to become a victim of your own stupidity.

At the same instant, the black curtain that concealed part of the room pulled aside showing a cross surrounded by twelve men. They fell upon Raymond, and in an instant, he was tied up, his cloak and crown were torn off, and a shower of blows fell upon his bare back, then, despite his desperate cries, they dragged him to the cross to crucify him.

With extraordinary effort Raymond managed to escape from the hands of his executioners. Blood dripped all over his body. The powerful instinct for survival overcame at that instant all other senses. Driven mad by pain and horror, he ran to the cross, spat furiously on it, and collapsed helplessly to the ground.

Immediately, the woman lying at the idol's feet jumped up from her seat and, with the help of some dancers, lifted Raymond and brought to his lips a vial whose contents acted on the Count like a galvanic shock. The pain passed instantly, and he stood up as if in fever. Life seemed to have deserted him, but his brain, meanwhile, retained a sickly clarity.

To the sound of songs and tambourines, they again put on his cape and crown, and together with the woman, whom they called the Queen of Sheba, they led him to the throne that was in the adjoining room.

All the people present greeted them. Then a banquet began, which soon turned into an orgy so crazy that Raymond had never seen it even in his dreams, and which immediately made him forget everything.

Exhausted and broken in body and soul, Raymond lost consciousness and did not see how the members of that wicked sect silently left the banquet hall. Soon, next to the fainting Count were only Abdias, Uriel and Maakha.

- Tomorrow I will notify Misael that his order has been carried out and that the proud Count was paid in the same coin - said Uriel, looking mockingly at Raimond's pale and battered body.

- Not so much! He must still pay for the offense to Rebecca who washes herself only with blood - Abdias remarked, and a purely diabolical expression distorted the always tranquil and venerable face of the old man.

Maakha, leaning against the table, listened quietly to the men's conversation. Those last words made her straighten up and put her hand on Raymond's shoulder.

- Stop! I protest against the murder of this man. He belongs to me, and I will keep him!

- Maakha is right! If she wants to keep him for herself, we have no rights over him. Evidently, he himself will try everything to make Maakha get tired of him and fall definitively into our hands. Now, my son, call the servants and order them to bring the Count to my laboratory.

When Raymond came to his senses, he was lying on his bed. He felt weak and tired, but not in any pain, and at first, he could not remember anything. His lifeless gaze wandered distractedly around the room. Suddenly he saw a woman wrapped in a veil at the table. She was preparing a drink from a goblet, talking in a half-voiced voice to a visibly worried old man, Squire Ekgardt. The woman was trying to convince Ekgardt that the attempt on his master's life would not have fatal consequences, that her uncle was responsible for his life, and that he had charged her with giving that medicine to the patient until his return from the pasha's palace.

Finally, he suggested that the squire go to the knight Ried, who was very worried about his brother.

As he spoke, the memory came back to Raymond, awakening in his soul the most contradictory feelings.

The sacrilege instilled fear and horror in him. But the hurricane of inordinate pleasures and carnal satisfaction he endured made him view his past life as pale, poor, and paltry. Eliza, with her innocent look, with her grace and virginal shyness, seemed to him now only a weak shadow of life in comparison with the skanky woman who shared with him her ephemeral glory.

In his memory were the orgy scenes, in which he played the role of the King, vividly resurfaced, and his sparkling gaze fixed on the woman who approached him with the cup in her hands. Yes, that must have been the Queen of Sheba herself! Those classically contoured hands, that smooth gait and passionate, demonic gaze, everything indicated that it was her. That same full, silky hair that covered her like a royal cape as she lay at the idol's feet.

Raymond obediently drank the invigorating liquid and then, seeing that Ekgardt was not in the room, he pulled the Jewess close to him and with a brave gesture uncovered her veil. It was Maakha! Succumbing again to her devilish beauty, Raymond pressed her against his chest and kissed her passionately. She offered no resistance, and in turn kissed him back. Suddenly, a double scream was heard. The Jewess escaped from the boy's arms and ran away, leaving Raymond face to face with Arnulf and Ekgardt, who looked at him with indignation.

Making a sign for Ekgardt to leave the room, Arnulf approached the bed, crossed his arms, and said sternly:

- Check it out! You, on a pilgrimage and only a few steps away from the Holy Sepulcher, indulge in depravity and get dirty through contact with a filthy Jewess? Have you no shame, Raymond? How dare you kiss your innocent wife with those tainted lips? Where have you been all day and all night? We have been looking everywhere for you. The Jew told us he found you unconscious in the street in the morning. You were naked and all your belongings were gone. Confess, what happened to you?

- I was in a nightclub, playing craps, and I do not remember anything that happened afterwards. In fact, I do not need to account to anyone for my actions - Raymond concluded with irritation.

Arnulf measured him with a cold, contemptuous look.

- Far be it from me to demand from you a report of the unworthy secrets you have surrounded yourself with, or to interfere in your amorous adventures. I came to tell you that three days ago the pasha of Jerusalem informed the pilgrims that tomorrow a detachment of soldiers will leave for Yafa, under whose protection we can safely reach the port. If you want to go with us, be at the inn at dawn.

Without waiting for an answer, Arnulf turned and left the room.

It is difficult to describe Raymond's state of mind after his brother's departure. The news of the pilgrims' departure the next morning was totally unexpected for him. With his physical condition and the pain, he felt at the slightest movement, it would be difficult to undertake such a difficult walk, and at the same time, the idea of being alone in that faraway country horrified him, but he had to leave anyway. But would they let him go after all that had happened? He had given himself body and soul to the Satanic Brotherhood, and he could no longer dispose of itself. In that difficult moment, he had no one to turn to, no one with whom to share his misfortune. With bitterness and despair, he remembered his father. What I would not give at this very moment was to fall into his arms and confess everything to him! Hot tears gushed from his eyes, and he fell into convulsive weeping, covering his head with the pillows.

Suddenly, Raymond shuddered and straightened up.

[181]

He remembered that at the Lucifer worshipers' banquet he had seen Beovulf. Obviously, he was also a member of that disgusting society. With him he could speak openly. He needed to know if he was allowed to leave the next day; he needed to ask his advice. Raymond already wanted to call Ekgardt and send for Beovulf when the latter, seeming to guess his wish, appeared alone.

Beovulf's appearance was terrible. The deep dark circles under his eyes and his pale-green face clearly showed the traces of the diabolical banquet.

- I really need to talk to you! God himself sent you here, Beovulf! - exclaimed Raymond excitedly.

- Or was it the devil, who cares? But tell me, what do you want from me? - asked Beovulf, sitting down next to the Count.

Raymond told him how worried he was about his brother leaving. Then he asked if Beovulf would also leave Jerusalem and asked his opinion on what to do.

He thought for a moment.

- I am going to stay here a little longer; but you, even if you wanted to, could not leave. Your foolish stubbornness has earned you such a beating that you will not recover for another two weeks. Besides, the time of the Brotherhood's annual solemnities is approaching, and they will not let you leave before the two particularly important and interesting festivities. After that, I and some other Christian members will leave Jerusalem and you can join us. We are not in any danger like the other pilgrims, because the Brotherhood will protect us. So, if you want to listen to my advice, then tell your brother that you owe Abdias so much that he is holding you hostage here. Also, ask through him that your father send you money to Yafa on behalf of a rich Saracen merchant, who has business with our trading house. This merchant will bring the money to Jerusalem, and only then can you return to your fatherly and conjugal roof. Enough of this, stop looking so downcast! Our Brotherhood also has its good side. The Lucifer cult is comfortable, and King Solomon's wives are beautiful, not to mention the Queen of Sheba, who is simply enchanting.

[182]

And Beovulf let out a loud, mocking laugh.

Raymond, with pain in his heart, followed his advice without paying attention to old Ekgardt's despair when he learned that his master would be staying in Jerusalem.

At dawn, bravely overcoming the pain that bothered him, Raymond went to the pilgrims' inn. The caravan was ready and only awaited the signal from the detachment commander to leave. Arnulf listened coldly to his brother's explanation, slightly embarrassed. Then he jumped in the saddle and said, making a farewell sign with his hand:

- So, see you later! If it is God's will, I will give your letter to Mr. Wolfram. But what will I tell Eliza when I pass through Venice?

- Don't say anything! I will talk to her myself when I get home - replied Raymond, bowing his head.

At that moment, the bugle sounded. The caravan set off and soon disappeared around the bend in the road. A bitter feeling of loneliness gripped Raymond's heart, causing him physical pain. He felt the ties that bound him to his homeland had been cut, and that he was now like a rudderless boat tossed in the middle of the stormy sea.

Gloomy and sad, Raymond returned home where Uriel was waiting for him. The young Jew tried to distract the Count with jokes and then gave him a drink that made him fall into a deep sleep.

Chapter 13

A few weeks went by. Raymond recovered completely and regained the healthy color of his face, but he no longer possessed the former animation and joy. Worried and apathetic, he lay on the couch for days on end, thinking about the past and the future that seemed equally bleak to him.

Uriel continued to give him lessons in astrology and magic, but he could no longer brag about the evolution of his disciple. Raymond did not have enough patience for long, tenacious work. The only things that kept him interested were the prospect of learning to make gold and the company of Beovulf. He stopped gambling and also visiting the gambling house as well. He wanted to be free as soon as he received the money, he asked his father for. Also, his attraction to gambling suddenly disappeared.

Raymond did not attend the meeting of the Lucifer worshipers, but as a souvenir of that memorable evening he was left with the love of Maakha, which flattered his ego. Raymond was too young and impulsive to ignore the possession of a woman as beautiful as the young Jewish woman. Only her jealousy and pretensions irritated him at times. There were times when Maakha's overwhelming passion became disgusting to him. At such times, before him rose the pure image of Eliza as a shining vision of tranquil happiness.

One evening, a couple of months after Arnulf's departure, Raymond and Uriel were studying the occult sciences as usual. The Jew explained to his disciple the possibility of invoking anyone and hinted that his power in this respect was unlimited, and that if the Count wished, he could invoke any of the great men of both past and present centuries. But Raymond was too ignorant and

[184]

superstitious for his time to take advantage of this proposal. He did not even dare to protest, for it seemed to him that a deep chasm had opened between him and Jesus Christ ever since his denial. The Count flatly rejected any invocation, saying innocently that he feared the dead and had no interest in people buried centuries ago.

- But - he added, "I would be very grateful if you could tell me what a certain very dear person does and thinks.

- That's very easy! - replied Uriel, who was amused by the Count's answer. - I can even fulfill your wish right now.

He went to his room and brought out a box, from which he took out a metal circle and a flask containing a dark, dense liquid. He then told Raymond to hold the flask, think about the person he would like to invoke, and then pour the liquid into the circle. When the Count had done as he was told, the Jew leaned over the disk and began to examine the threads of liquid that were spreading randomly across the surface.

- You thought of a woman who is very close to you.

- Yes, my wife. Does she think about me?

A mocking smile momentarily crossed Uriel's face.

- Your wife? Then, Count, I must inform you that there is someone between you who can replace you in the countess's heart. In any case, I see that she is in danger of a fatal love.

A strong blush covered Raymond's face.

- What are you telling me? Would Eliza have the courage to love someone else? Who is the miserable one?

- This I do not know. I see only facts, not faces.

- But if you have the power to summon people who have been dead for hundreds of years, how come you cannot see what a living person is doing at this very moment? - Raymond observed in a dissatisfied tone.

- I see what the countess is doing now, but not what she thinks.

- So, take a closer look! I want to know what happens there!

[185]

- Right! Do you have any of her objects?

Raymond brought the locket with the portrait and a lock of Eliza's hair.

As he looked at the portrait, Uriel shuddered, and his pale face was covered with feverish blush.

Then he took a crystal vat out of the box, filled it with water, threw in a pinch of a white powder and squeezed it with both hands, then he leaned over the container.

He looked longingly at the water, which took on a bluish coloration, became agitated and sparkling; this observation absorbed him so much that he seemed to have forgotten the Count. Raymond, moved, did not notice the passionate expression that flashed in Uriel's dark eyes.

Finally, the Jew gave him a full description of Eliza's room in the Faleri house and added:

- The countess is embroidering a silk towel and next to her is a very pretty lady in a green brocade dress. Both are happy and laughing.

"That must be Giovanna," Raymond thought.

He asked Uriel to keep looking, but to no avail. The Jew said he was tired and left.

From that day on, a strange change took place in the relation between the Count and Uriel. Raymond felt fear and respect for the Jew's knowledge, while the Jew secretly hated him. Uriel became more and more gloomy and circumspect; for days on end, he would not come out of his room and began to miss classes. Such a circumstance did not bother Raymond at all, whose mind was occupied with entirely different things. The fear of losing Eliza's love haunted him like a nightmare, and he took as a bad sign the strange disappearance of the locket with her portrait. At first, he was suspicious of Maakha, who was becoming more capricious, jealous, and demanding every day; but finally, he was convinced of her innocence.

Raymond waited feverishly impatiently for his father's answer, firmly resolved to leave as soon as he paid his debt to Abdias.

In this state of mind, he learned in a mixture of terror and satisfaction that one of the festivities, at which his presence was required, would be held in the next few days. All the horrors that would undoubtedly take place there were repulsive to him. However, a feeling that he would see something unusual and experience new and unknown sensations appealed to his avid nature for strong emotions.

On the appointed day, Uriel went to get him and with the usual precautions took him underground, where he forced him into a small room lit only by a torch. There, Beovulf was waiting for him.

- I leave your compatriot in your care. Instruct him and take care of him - said Uriel, leaving the room immediately.

Beovulf opened a wooden chest and took out several objects that he placed on the table. Then, turning to Raymond, he said:

- Undress quickly and then put on this red cloak, the metallic belt, the sandals, and put this horned hoop on your head.

Raymond obeyed quietly. But as he began to tie his sandals, he noticed that a red cross was drawn on the soles of his sandals.

- What does it mean? - he asked, furrowing his brow, and showing Beovulf his sandals.

- It means that we have overcome all prejudices - replied the latter calmly, tucking the golden ring adorned on his forehead by two curved horns into his thinning blond hair.

A strong blush covered Raymond's face.

- Why didn't you warn me of the trap, the abyss into which I fell so blindly? The silence was positively unworthy.

Beovulf laughed loudly.

- A refined depravity is also a kind of science...

- Yes, the science of decay! - interrupted the Count.

- Maybe! But you cannot deny that you have experienced such intensity of sensations and strong emotions, that after that ordinary life seems bleak. Today's evening festival is preparing many surprises for you, since you have not yet seen how they invoke our lord.

- What Sir?

- Satan, of course!

Raymond took a step back.

- Are you kidding or mocking me? Is it possible that Satan himself will appear?

- In person! In fact, you will see for yourself.

- In that case, I will not go!

- Take my advice, be prudent if you want to avoid trouble. You already know that no one is fooling around here. So, let's get going! The people are already gathering.

Without waiting for an answer, Beovulf hurriedly dragged him along.

They entered the wide underground, where Solomon's throne was last time. Now, in that place was a lavishly served table, bowing under the weight of precious silverware, and surrounded by large silver candelabras still unlit.

The huge adjoining cave was already crowded with people. On either side of the idol stretched long rows of men in costumes identical to Raymond's. Mixed in with the men were women in short, striped skirts. Heavy bracelets adorned his arms and feet. Their hair was loose, on their heads they wore flower crowns, and in their hands, they held tambourines.

Raymond and his companion stood in front of him. The Count did not even have time to get situated when Maakha approached him and grabbed him by the hand.

Suddenly, in the deep silence that reigned in the room, strong fanfare sounds resounded, the black curtain, which last time concealed a cross, opened, and from the door at the bottom of the

[188]

underground, which the Count had not noticed the previous time, came a strange procession.

Blowing the horns loudly, there appeared in pairs small, repulsive, monstrous beings with hair-covered limbs, huge heads, and disfigured faces. Behind them followed a group of old women, most of them completely naked, with wrinkled, repulsive, and disgusting faces, in which all the animal passions were reflected. In one hand they held bundles of quince sticks in the shape of brooms, and in the other they waved a certain sack.

- Who are these beings? - murmured Raymond, leaning his back from Maakha to Beovulf.

- They are witches! - he also answered softly.

Raymond felt a cold sweat appear on his forehead and his hair shiver in horror. Mute with fear, he looked at the disgusting procession parading in front of him. Then, slowly, a huge black goat rode by a woman wrapped in a red cloak. She held a black rooster in her hands. After the goat followed repulsive old men, holding in their hands something resembling drums. Again, monsters and defectives closed the procession. However, terror sealed Raymond's mouth when a repulsive old woman approached him and began to smear him with a smelly ointment. Feeling the contact of those cold, bony hands, Raymond closed his eyes and murmured:

- Almighty God! Save me!

The witch recoiled backward in one leap as if she had been bitten; a repulsive tick disfigured her wrinkled face. Then, clutching her broom, she delivered several furious blows at Raymond, repeating:

- That's for your prayer! That is for your God!

The deafened groan that the Count let escape was muffled by the noise that rose from one of the last rows. A male voice shouted angrily:

- You've smeared me wrong, you damned witch! I cannot feel the ointment. You did not prepare it properly.

The witch justified herself in a shrill voice. Opinions differed and a fight was already brewing when the monsters interfered. They grabbed the witch and covered her with beatings for her lack of effectiveness at preparing the ointment. The complainant was smeared again, and peace was restored.

Raymond's body burned as if on fire...Painful pangs passed through his skin; his breathing became heavy. It even seemed as if his hair crackled and stood on end. The boy looked around, worried. The faces of everyone present were on fire, and one could clearly read in them the unbridled animal passions. He really was in a cluster of demons! The disgusting stench, mixed with the odor of sulfur and something else he could not figure out, now filled the cave.

Suddenly, a new vision absorbed all his attention.

Through the same door from which the procession left, entered a man led by two witches. He was totally naked and only a black hood over his head concealed his face. Everyone bowed to his passage. He stopped in front of the idol, in the same place wet with the goat's blood that had been occupied by a cauldron and where a heap of ashes was still there.

Raising both hands, the stranger began to spin with incredible speed in the center of the circle, formed by the witches who sat around him. In that instant, all the fires were extinguished, except for the torch that burned between the idol's horns. The reddish light of the torch caused bloody reflections on the white, slender body of the stranger, who kept turning, snaking like a lizard to the rhythm of the strange chanting of those present. From time to time the women would beat the tambourines, and these beats would be accompanied by the shrill sound of a bell coming from somewhere else. Something indescribably evil hung in the air and made him hold his breath.

Raymond stared as if hypnotized by the stranger. When he noticed that, as he turned, the man's white body began to darken, he thought he was going mad. At the same time, a high-pitched whistle was heard, strong gusts of wind rushed through the cave, the walls shook, and strange black shadows fluttered in the air, flapping their wings heavily like gigantic birds.

Suddenly, the strange dancer stopped his mad dance, jumped up on the idol's lap and, grabbing the rope, started to ring a bell, supposedly hidden behind the monster's back.

Deep, trembling sounds flooded the underground. At the same time, the singing became louder and louder, the tambourines resounded, the eardrums rumbled, and the horns sounded.

All that infernal noise made Raymond a little dizzy, and he might even have fallen over if his neighbors and Maakha had not held him up. When the weakness dissipated and Raymond regained his sight, he saw that a strange and terrible being was standing on the idol's lap and kept ringing the bell.

The Count had no doubt that this was the devil himself, into which the hooded man had probably transformed. Something like a black, shiny fuzz covered his entire body. His head was now uncovered, and a totally black face of evil beauty could be seen. From his forehead rose two curved, black, phosphorescent horns.

In addition, the crowd had been enlarged with new people that Raymond had not seen before, that is, evil-looking men and women who came out of the dark corners of the underground and advanced slowly. The crowd opened up before them, giving them a wide passage.

More gliding than walking, they passed through the crowd casting right and left watchful glances. Suddenly, one of the women broke away from the group and stopped in front of Raymond. She was a beautiful creature, thin and slender like a snake. Her whole body had a greenish pallor, and only her blood-red lips proved that she was alive. Under the gaze of strange enchantment, Raymond felt as if paralyzed. Such must be the feeling of the bird hypnotized by the serpent.

A deadly chill ran through the Count's veins, and he could not resist when the woman grabbed him by the hand and stood

[191]

beside him, taking the place of Maakha who, terribly pale, stepped back trembling with her whole body.

Confused and stunned, Raymond watched as the devil or his representant jumped from the idol's lap to the floor, letting out a high-pitched scream that shook the air and the nerves of the onlookers, and putting his arm around the waist of the woman in a red cloak, led her into the room.

Everyone followed him.

Of everything that happened next, including the hellish orgy that went on into the early hours of the morning, Raymond had only a vague recollection.

The woman who chose him caused him disgust mixed with mad terror. Her look and her touch seemed to take his life. Despite the steaming wine they served him in profusion, an icy cold began to grip his limbs, and a sharp pain nagged at him. Finally, it seemed to him that as he fled from the terrible gaze of the green pupils, he fell into a black abyss. Then Raymond fainted.

When he came to his senses, he was lying on the sofa in his room. Abdias, leaning over him, was massaging his arms and temples with an aromatic essence.

You will soon get well! But if you care about life, keep quiet! - whispered Abdias in Raymond's ear.

Then, offering him a glass of warm and very aromatic wine, he left while the Count fell into a deep and invigorating sleep.

He awoke in the night. Peace and silence reigned around him. Only old Ekgardt, sitting by his bed, sad and worried, read his prayers in a half-voice.

Seeing that Raymond opened his eyes, the old man leaned over him and respectfully kissed his hand.

Finally, my lord, I see that you have recovered your usual look! Holy Mother of God! How frightened I was when I came in to see you yesterday morning! You were terribly pale and lying as if dead. I started screaming so much that Abdias himself came to help

[192]

me. He ordered them to give you a bath. Then they massaged you with something and you opened your eyes. But your eyes were so vacant that I thought you had gone crazy. The Jew gave you a few drops of medicine and you fell asleep. Oh, Sir Raymond! Let's get out of here! My heart tells me that God has turned his back on you and that you are in danger as long as you remain in Jerusalem.

- You are right, Ekgardt! It is not good to hang around here. I swear that if I recover from this faintness, which reason it is still unknown to me, we will leave Jerusalem. I will not stay here even if I have to walk!

Then he squeezed the old man's hand tightly and his oath seemed to calm him down completely.

Raymond, meanwhile, was very slowly recovering from the terrible shock his body had suffered. He was pale, and his face, once always fresh, had become yellowish like wax. In addition, he began to suffer from terrible hallucinations. Sometimes, at night, it seemed as if the disgusting woman who had possessed him on the night of the "Sabbath"[34] appeared in the window aperture or at his bedside. He saw how she glided towards him, leaked out with her terrible gaze, and grasped his hand with her icy fingers. He would then start to scream, struggle, want to run away, and only a deep faint would interrupt the terrible crises.

After such hallucinations, Raymond would spend several days nervous, agitated, shivering at the slightest noise, and suffering from insomnia.

Beovulf visited Raymond regularly, but they never talked about that nightly "sabbath". Anyway, once Raymond asked him if they had really seen the devil.

---

[34] "Sabbath" (Shabbat) - In this plot, Rochester refers to the "sabbath" as a board of "wizards and witches" who, according to medieval superstition, gathered on Saturday at midnight under the devil's presidency to perform orgies. Originally, however, "Shabat" means the sacred rest that, according to the Law of Moises, Jews must rest on the seventh day of the week: the Jewish Sabbath. This Jewish day of rest is counted from sunset on Friday until sunset on Saturday.

[193]

- Who can say that for sure? - Beovulf replied questioningly and shrugged his shoulders. - I only know that each time they bring a man as white as you and me. This man starts spinning like a real demon, turns black and takes on that terrible satanic appearance you saw. But it is hard to tell if the transformation really happens or if it is just a hallucination of the excited senses of those present. In general, in these meetings such extraordinary and incredible things happen that I have given up researching them.

- These great mysteries quickly annihilate the person. Happy are those who do not even suspect their existence! - Raymond remarked bitterly.

- You are right! But perhaps this limited life will give you more complete and extraordinary sensations than a long and discolored existence. To be honest, I thought you were tougher! You looked much tougher. You probably did not get used to these meetings.

Finally, Raymond went to Abdias' quarters one morning and offered him a document leaving him a guarantee of the debt, a property that he had personally received as an inheritance from a distant relative.

The Jew looked at him long and hard.

- Then leave! - he said, after a short silence. - I am not holding you back, Count! In three days, there is a caravan leaving with which you can get to Jafa. I do not need your paper and you do not owe me anything. Look! I am tearing up your receipt. The amount you refer to was not lent by me, but by the Brotherhood, which is too rich to demand from its members the return of the gold taken. Besides, you have already paid your debt to your body and soul. So, keep your gold! Now that we have settled this business, let me add this: remain silent as a grave about what you have seen here. Treason is punishable by death, and no force in the world can save the traitorous and informer. Don't forget also that the Brotherhood has eyes, ears, and arms all over the world, and that you are obliged always and everywhere to answer its call.

[194]

Raymond listened to everything in silence. The thought of remaining a slave, and perhaps finding himself dependent on some Jew, briefly provoked an uncontrollable anger in the proud boy's mind. But he had learned to control himself. Besides, he wanted more than anything in the world to leave Jerusalem. When he returned to his country and began to live a normal life again, he would think about how to act.

Three days later, he left Jerusalem. In Yafa, an unexpected joy awaited him. On the same day of his arrival, a ship docked, bringing on board his father's messenger, the faithful Lucien with the money requested and a letter from the Count, containing the following laconic words:

- "Come back immediately if you want me to still consider you as my son."

Chapter 14

Arnulf left the Holy Land and sailed to Venice very pleased with what happened to his brother. Raymond's behavior gave him new hope. He thought it impossible that the proud Eliza could quietly endure such cruel offenses as her husband's scandalous adventures with the Jewess, all the more so when it all happened during the pilgrimage to the Holy Sepulcher undertaken, so to speak, in order to thank God for saving her life from an attempt on her life caused by Raymond's own fault. Then Arnulf decided to take on the task of informing Eliza of all her brother's misdeeds.

Fate, however, seemed to test the patience of the Ried knight. The crossing took place under the worst conditions. A terrible storm nearly destroyed the ship. Finally, Arnulf landed in Venice completely ill and delayed by almost three weeks. He did not want to stay at Fulvio's house, as he counted on staying in Venice only to rest and recover from the wear and tear of the trip. Besides, it would be difficult for him to live under the same roof as Eliza. Therefore, Arnulf opted for an inn.

Now luck was smiling on him. A couple of days after his arrival, Arnulf saw Eliza and Giovanna. They passed by in an open gondola. The countess was pale and had a tired appearance. A sullen and sad expression appeared clearly on her lovely face.

Arnulf's heart filled with terrible jealousy. If Eliza was so sad and worried about Raymond's absence, then he, Arnulf, would radically cure her of her amorous dreams.

He almost guessed the truth. Eliza really was concerned about Raymond, but not in the sense that the knight imagined. In Eliza's virginal and childishly pure soul, passion was not yet born. The feeling she had for Raymond, during his recovery, was

[196]

brotherly: a mixture of childhood memories, duty obligations and deep sympathy for the handsome and repentant boy who loved her. But there was no doubt that Raymond's departure had curbed the development of this feeling, and as a result it prevented it from turning into true affection.

Loving and gullible, Eliza was quietly awaiting her husband's return, when suddenly a series of terrible nightmares and visions confused her peace and instilled dark forebodings about Raymond's fate. She, however, told no one. The first of these strange phenomena was revealed in the portrait of Raymond that hung in Eliza's dormitory and had been painted shortly before the Count's departure by a young painter, Giovanna's protégé, and stood out for its amazing resemblance to the original.

The girl ordered the portrait to be hung in front of her bed, and before she fell asleep, she used to stare at the image of her husband.

One night, after her usual prayer, Eliza lay in bed, unable to sleep, and, as usual, began to look at Raymond's portrait. The lamp lit in front of the image of Our Lady illuminated the painting so well that it was possible to distinguish, besides the features of the face, all the details of the costume.

Without even knowing why Eliza felt a certain nervousness and worry. Her head felt heavy, she felt a pressure in her chest, and a cold shiver seemed to run through her skin, freezing her hands and feet.

Trying to overcome the sick feeling, Eliza curled up in her blanket and, as sleep really was not coming, began to think about the future and about her new life with Raymond at Castle Zapnenstein in Tyrol, where not even the evil Countess Anna and the disgusting Greta could sow discord between them. As she began to imagine the wonderful horse rides they would take in the surroundings of the castle, her gaze suddenly fell unexpectedly on Raymond's portrait. She saw with deep surprise that a black shadow covered the boy's forehead, then descended to his eyes, and finally covered his whole face like a black hood.

[197]

Eliza, curious, sat up in bed and tried to understand what could cause this strange optical effect. Suddenly, the portrait screen lit up with a blood-red light, the black shadow disappeared, and Raymond's figure drew itself with such relief and vivacity that it seemed to rise out of the frame. The boy's pleasant face had undergone a terrible transformation: He was deathly pale and deformed by convulsions; the veins on his forehead bulged, his eyes injected with blood, and a savage expression appeared on his lips. His torso appeared bare and was half-covered by a purple cloak. In his full, disheveled hair was a crown.

Mute with fear and horror, Eliza stared at that vision: she had been the disciple of two scientists who taught her to control her feelings and nervousness.

Quickly shaking off her stupor, she jumped out of bed and approached the portrait, but there was nothing unusual about it close: Raymond was, as usual, wearing a velvet shirt, and smiling peacefully with his hand on his dagger hilt. Eliza, calmed down, crossed herself and went back to bed, murmuring:

- Thank God! It was just an optical illusion!

But as soon as she lay down, a tremor of dread shook her. The vision appeared again; only this time Raymond was not alone. Next to his disfigured face appeared the physiognomy of an Asian type of woman, also with a crown on her head.

Eliza felt as if she were paralyzed. The feeling of horror and disgust that invaded her was so great that she covered her head with the blanket and started reciting prayers to the Virgin. Even so, she only managed to fall asleep at dawn.

The daylight dispelled the horrors of the night, and she became convinced that she was the victim of a simple nightmare. The strange thing was that since that night vision, Eliza felt an enormous anger for Raymond, lost the will to see him, and avoided looking at the portrait.

This inexplicable state of mind, which she carefully concealed from her relatives, was already beginning to dissipate little by little when one night the vision was repeated. This time, the background of the painting presented a black cliff onto which Raymond was falling, pushed by a woman and a man whose face, illuminated by a greenish light, breathed a purely diabolical rage.

Then Eliza was so distraught that she decided to tell her friends everything. She called Loretta and ordered her to help her get dressed. The faithful maid, startled by her pale appearance, asked if she was ill. Eliza took a glass of warm milk to recover her color and went straight to Fulvio's room.

The young Venetian was sitting by the window in his study, immersed in reading an archaic manuscript. As his protégée entered, the young man left the scroll and held out his hand friendly.

- Sit down Eliza and tell me what made you come to see me so early? Are you feeling ill? You look very sick - he added.

- I can't understand whether I am sick or not! But one thing is certain: my state is very strange and incomprehensible. Things are happening to me that are so extraordinary that I decided to consult you. Maybe even I was wrong to keep quiet for so long.

In a voice broken by emotion, Eliza told him about her strange visions and added:

- I have no doubt that Raymond's life is in danger and that misfortune has befallen him. Tell me Fulvio, I beg you, what do you think about this?

The boy became thoughtful.

- It is true! Your husband is following a very bad path and I predict much misfortune for him in the future.

- Is there a woman involved in this case?! He is cheating on me again, after he swore, he loved only me! - exclaimed Eliza, her face on fire.

- No! I do not need him. I want to divorce that depraved man who in the holy city, near the Holy Sepulcher, delights in criminal love! I am sure that the feeling of repulsion and contempt

[199]

I have been feeling, as soon as I start thinking about him, is provoked by his affairs- she added, throwing back her black locks in a nervous gesture.

Fulvio looked at her thoughtfully.

- You should pity your husband and pray for him instead of condemning him. Any sin, any transgression of the divine laws brings punishment in itself. But remember that terrible temptations suddenly appear in people's lives. Woe to him who gives in and allows himself to be overwhelmed by his own passions. He will pay dearly for it. Sometimes, a lifetime is nothing more than a prelude to such a decisive moment that forces us to prove the strength of resistance to the evil we have managed to accumulate in our soul. No person is free from that terrible moment of trial. Be assured, Eliza, that for you as for everyone else there will come this moment of struggle, and only the future can tell whether you will be victorious! I tell you this to prove that our duty is to be lenient with others.

Eliza, moved, listened to him with an indecisive air.

- Do you want me to understand that I am virtuous only because I have not fallen into temptation yet, and that in time I will indulge in the same foolishness as Raymond?

Fulvio laughed and brought Eliza close to him and kissed her on the forehead.

- No, no, my dear! God forbid that I should suppose things like that! I hope that our disciple will emerge victorious from all the trials that the future holds for her. One of them, no doubt, is Raymond. I only meant that, up to now, your life has gone on clearly and smoothly, and that the feeling that the Count provokes in you is still too weak to serve as a shield in case you meet someone else who attracts you and arouses in you one of those passions whose power and danger you don't even suspect. Pray, my dear, that God will deliver you from such an ordeal, or give you strength and an unshakable sense of duty, to bear it worthily. But now, be kind, condescending, and patient. The duty of a healthy person is to clean and treat the wounds of the sick person, and she should do so with compassion and never with disgust.

- Fulvio, you know so well how to point out the path of duty and describe the pleasure that comes from the consciousness of duty done - said the girl, her eyes shining with enthusiasm. - I want to be indulgent with Raymond, however guilty he may be before me! I will implore the forces of good to support me! But Fulvio, do you really think that prayer is so powerful that it can keep temptations out of our way?

- No, my dear! Prayer does not ward off temptations, only the danger of giving yourself over to them. This is because prayer extracts from the depths of the soul the pure light that strengthens the body and clears the mind. And if the concentration of thought is strong enough to make a person forget his own body, his own needs, and his physical and moral pain, then he really gets rid of the mortal body. Then, on wings of ecstasy, in a single bound, he soars up to the source of the heavenly light and absorbs from it the forces he needs.

Liza listened to him quietly and emotionally.

Fulvio took a bottle from the drawer, put a few drops in the glass and gave it to her.

- Drink up, my dear, and then go rest! A few hours of sleep will restore your energy. We will have time to talk about the rest.

When Eliza left the room, Fulvio leaned against the table and stood thoughtfully. On his face appeared an expression of sadness and bitterness, presenting a violent contrast to his usual slightly careless tranquility. Finally, getting rid of his thoughts, Fulvio stood up, took a horoscope from the locker, and, returning to the table, studied it for a long time. But probably what he read in the book of the future was not at all pleasant, for, putting the horoscope away in a sudden gesture, he plunged into deep thought again.

He was so absorbed that he did not notice when the curtain rose at the back of the room and Baron Vart entered the office.

[201]

Stopping a few steps from the table, he began to examine his friend's somber face attentively.

- What are you thinking about so much? - he asked.

Fulvio shuddered and straightened up.

- Were you, by any chance, thinking about Eliza, her unhappy marriage, and the dark, emotion-filled future that awaits her? - insisted the Baron with a sigh.

The boy then spoke in a few words about the girl's visions.

- Despite all my efforts, I could not protect the unfortunate man from the trap he fell into and which I had foreseen, although I could not determine exactly what kind it would be. In any case, it will be a heavy blow for his father - said Baron Conrad with a sigh. - I see you are studying Eliza's horoscope. What does it say? - asked Vart.

- Nothing good. It predicts that Eliza will soon find in her life a man marked by fatality, who will awaken in her heart a great passion, and that this love, in fact reciprocated, will be the source of great misfortune for her.

- Will Raymond stop them from uniting?

- Not only him! An insurmountable obstacle will probably arise between them. In general, Eliza's future is always covered by a strange penumbra.

- And you cannot see through this penumbra, right? - observed Vart.

Then, leaning toward the boy, he added softly:

- Between us, we never talk about the feeling you have for Eliza. You have always hidden it carefully, but no one will be able to give her more happiness than you!

A strong blush covered Fulvio's face.

- Why open the wound that should close by itself? - he asked after a moment of silence. - You are omniscient, and a famous astrologer and you must know that fate is against me, and it separates me from Eliza!

- Right! But, sometimes, a quick and firm decision deviates the path marked out by destiny in the direction that the human will desire.

- I know this, but I also know the dangers to which anyone who goes against the astral flows is subjected. I do not feel knowledgeable enough, nor powerful enough to fight them. Eliza loves me like a brother. Why should I confuse the poor child's soul and take away from her the firm support of her friendly shoulder, replacing it with an unfortunate in love and a despised suitor for her hand? Not this! This role is unbearable to my pride and my conscience. I want to dedicate my life to science! I will sacrifice all my earthly passions for science, and it will help me overcome the flesh and become spiritually superior!

Fulvio sighed. His big black eyes shone with energy and enthusiasm. In that instant, he did not look anything like the cold and measured man he usually was.

Baron Vart, who was watching him, held out his hand and said:

- You are right! Your victory over the most powerful feeling that disturbs the human soul will serve as a guarantee that you will reach the pinnacle of science. And if fate deprives Eliza of the best of husbands, it leaves her the most faithful and magnanimous of friends.

- Yes, I wish to be a faithful friend in the moments of heavy trials that await her - said Fulvio, locking Eliza's horoscope and changing the subject.

A few days after this episode, Loretta, helping her lady get dressed, informed her that a ship from the Holy Land had arrived in the port three days ago. The brother of one of the maids who served the sergeant in the port administration had told him that on the ship, among other passengers, there was a German knight, who seemed very ill, he even had not been able to get off the ship without the help of others.

Eliza was very excited, but if the knight was Raymond, why then had he not gone directly to Villamarino, especially if he was ill?

She immediately wanted to inform her friends of the news and ask them to investigate, but to her great disappointment Fulvio was receiving visitors and Baron Vart had traveled to visit a sick friend.

After some thought, Eliza decided to go and talk to Giovanna, who in turn suggested that she go to the port immediately and find out for herself if Raymond had come back. But her inquiries only resulted in the description of a German knight who looked nothing like Raymond.

Arnulf saw them just as they were returning from the port. As the Ried knight had almost recovered from the exhausting sea journey, he decided the next day to visit his sister-in-law.

Sad, emotional and worried, Eliza was embroidering a rug when she was informed that the knight Ried wished to see her.

Eliza shuddered. So, the German knight who had arrived from Palestine was Arnulf! But why did he return alone? The girl hurried to the drawing room. The knight who was waiting for her greeted her respectfully.

- Welcome, Mr. Arnulf! Why have you returned alone? - Eliza asked, holding out her hand.

She did not notice the evil, ironic look that shone from behind the knight's lowered eyebrows at her question.

- Why didn't Raymond come along with you? Where is he? - she repeated impatiently.

- My brother stayed in Jerusalem indefinitely.

- Why did he stay? Did he get sick?

- No, he is fine. As for the reason for his stay in the holy city, he said he will explain it personally - Arnulf replied schemingly, and a double-edged smile instantly flashed across his lips.

Eliza turned red and closed her face.

[204]

Seeing that she was silent and thoughtful, the knight, after a moment's silence, said:

- I did not want to leave Venice without seeing you, dear sister, and to make sure that you are in good health, but I also came to say goodbye, because tomorrow at dawn I leave the city. Do you have a message for Mr. Wolfram? I would be happy to take it.

Eliza raised her head and said, giving him a beaming look:

- You called me sister. Therefore, I am asking you to tell me the truth about the reasons why Raymond was imprisoned in the Holy Land. Tell me everything, without leaving anything out! I have the right to know what he is doing.

Arnulf was visibly embarrassed and indecisive.

- Your question puts me in an extremely difficult situation. I do not want to harm my brother and I cannot lie to justify it. I beg you to release me from this answer and wait for Raymond's own explanations.

- I do not want to wait to hear a pack of lies, and I demand, Arnulf, that you tell me the whole truth right now! - exclaimed Eliza angrily. - In fact, I even suspect that a woman is involved in this case - she said more calmly.

After such a statement, Arnulf did not let himself beg and told her everything he knew about Raymond's misdemeanors from his gambling losses to the affectionate scene with the Jewish girl he happened to witness when he visited his sick brother.

Despite the apparent silence and condescension with which he seemed to try to justify Raymond, his account presented the Count in such a repulsive manner that Eliza, who was listening to him with her face on fire, exclaimed:

- What you are telling me is too disgusting to be true! So, Raymond is leaving me for some impure Jewess? And all this after the solemn oaths of fidelity?! That does not seem to be a passing fling, but a serious connection since it is keeping him so long in Jerusalem. After that, for me he became a dishonorable person.

[205]

- The Jewess is beautiful as the embodiment of temptation! By the way, old Ekgardt also saw her in Raymond's arms, and the people in my procession can confirm that my brother lives in the Jewish Abdias' house. I understand the feelings that trouble you, Eliza, since they are legitimate. But you must not treat me so unfairly! I told you all this at your insistent demand, and I would never profane my lips that have kissed the Holy Sepulcher with slanders about my brother.

- Forgive me, Mr. Arnulf! Anger made me lose my head - Eliza justified, holding herself back with difficulty.

Arnulf was pleased to see the effect his words had had. Now Raymond could return and would be received as he indeed deserved. Moreover, after such adventures it was difficult for him to oppose a divorce.

In order not to cool Eliza's anger, Arnulf said a quick goodbye, declined the lunch invitation, claiming he needed to prepare for the trip, and left.

Returning to her dormitory, she threw herself on her bed and cried with rage. The thought of having been exchanged for a despicable Jewish woman outraged her to such an extent that she forgot everything Fulvio had told her about indulgence and patience. Never had the ties that bound her to Raymond weighed so heavily on her as they did at that moment. Her husband became a hateful being to her, and then she made the unwavering decision to separate from him.

Chapter 15

While in Palestine and Venice the events described in the previous chapter were taking place, life in Castle Reifenstein was going on with sober and heavy monotony.

Since the departure of his son, Count Wolfram had avoided his castle much more, living for weeks on end at the court of the Count of Tyrol, at some of his castles, at the homes of friends, or even on distant hunting trips. During her husband's long absences, Countess Anna indulged in an exaggerated religiosity. She spent whole hours praying in her oratory or talking to the chaplain. But such devotion, besides not softening her temper, seemed to make her even harsher. All the time she had left from prayers and spiritual conversations, the countess devoted herself to the persecution and punishment of the servants for the slightest fault. She would even personally flog little page boys for stealing sweets or for being too curious.

Therefore, everyone in the castle hated the countess. Since it was no secret that the Count's cold disgust for his wife was an eternally open wound for her, the servants were pleased with the contempt Lord Wolfram treated Anna. With the Count's arrival everyone was excited, from the kitchen to the storerooms, because his presence put a stop to Countess Anna's mischief and mistreatment.

The relations between the Countess and Greta, once so affectionate, had also cooled off recently. Because of her cleverness and her coarse tastes, Margarita Ramets resembled her godmother. No one knew how to win the countess's consent better than she did. But since the arrival of the letter announcing Raymond's reconciliation with his wife, the girl had become gloomy, angry, silent, always seeking to isolate herself.

Greta's jealousy and hatred could not calm down. With the characteristic of foolish people, she clung to the idea that, despite everything, she would succeed in becoming Countess Reifenstein. All that was needed was to find a way to get rid of Eliza, and Raymond's fickle and frivolous heart would undoubtedly return to her.

Once, when Wolfram was away, Ortruda arrived to visit her friend. Ortruda had changed a lot in the twelve years that had passed. There was no sign of her former beauty. Her elegance had turned to thinness, the color of her face had taken on a dark yellow hue, her hair had turned gray, and deep wrinkles had cut into her forehead and face. But her change was not only physical. A terrible nervousness made her run from side to side, and in her bleached, deep gaze shone something agitated and sinister.

Ortruda seemed to treat Countess Anna less kindly than before. On the other hand, she began to treat Greta with unexpected attention and managed to entice the girl so much that she traveled with her to Finsterbach Castle and spent a few weeks there. From then on, Greta became such a regular visitor to Ortruda that she only stayed with her godmother for short periods.

Had the Countess led a less reclusive life and not stayed locked up in the castle, she might have put a limit on her goddaughter's strange friendship with a woman old enough to be her mother and about whom there were unflattering rumors.

Finsterbach Castle has become suspicious. It was said that unknown people visited it and that secret meetings of people from different social classes took place there. In those days, such meetings raised suspicions that repulsive sects were gathering to perform their satanic orgies in the dead of night.

Most probably such a sacrilegious sect had its beginnings in Palestine, a sandy territory that Christians and Muslims fought over with great ferocity. That country teemed with adventurers attracted to the Holy Land more for greed, thirst for plunder, and the warlike disposition of the time than for virtue. For such people, the comfortable ideology that professed that all vices and passions were just requirements of human nature, and that freed its adherents from the restraints imposed by duty, was a real find.

Every society of this kind is surrounded by secrets, and so it is difficult to say whether they gave themselves over to the cult of Lucifer from the beginning; moreover, this sect had many branches and acquired more and more followers. In the 12th century it was brought to Europe and began to spread like a plague, encompassing Austria, Styria,[35] Tyrol, Bohemia[36] and finally the whole of Germany, from where it had already spread to France.

Therefore, Ortruda was suspected of belonging to that criminal society and of placing the castle underground at the disposal of the sect; but these rumors spread quietly among the ordinary people. No one dared to openly accuse the rich and noble lady. As for the neighboring nobility, they gladly attended the luxurious banquets that Baroness Finsterbach promoted from time to time, despite her apparent eternal illness, with which she explained her isolated life.

Ortruda took Greta with her under the pretext of amusing her a little. In reality, she had a very different goal, that is, she wanted to introduce her to the satanic sect, to which she herself belonged and which always needed girls for its sacrileges and bloody rites.

But before she could reveal her dangerous secret to Greta, Ortruda wanted to acquire her complete trust so that she could dominate her completely.

One evening, when Margarita Ramets was visiting Finsterbach Castle for the first time, Ortruda started talking about Raymond and conducted the conversation so deftly that Greta, longing to unburden her galled heart to someone, told her

---

[35] Styria (Estiria) - Austrian province that in 1180 became a duchy.

[36] Bohemia - Former kingdom and historical region that was incorporated into the Czech Republic.

everything that simmered in her breast against her childhood friend.

- Poor child! I really understand the feelings that afflict you! - said Ortruda, listening with ostentatious sympathy to her visitor's confession. - But Margarita dear, in this case it is not Raymond's fault. Men are often fickle, frivolous, and easily led astray. If Eliza has inherited some fraction of the art of seduction that her mother possessed, then it is no wonder that, because of her, Raymond has forgotten all his obligations to you.

- Oh, no doubt that wretch did everything possible to seduce Raymond and force him to betray his oath. But that is not the case! An honest man does not become a perjurer at the first temptation and does not pay with forgetfulness and contempt for a love like mine. I am not the kind of woman who forgives such offenses! I took revenge and threw a disgrace on him! - said Greta, her face on fire and her gaze flashing.

- Whoa! Do you, Greta, have the power over people's happiness and misfortune? - asked Ortruda with a slight laugh.

- Not me, but a man who knows about a secret science. I think he is a terrible sorcerer. He is a Jew named Misael, from Brixen, replied the girl in a low voice and leaning towards Ortruda.

She shuddered.

- Do you know Misael? Oh! So, woe to Raymond! Mishael will send the spirits of darkness upon him.

Greta told her new friend all the details of the enchantment.

- Oh, now I have no more doubt that misfortune will befall Raymond's head. But, my child, wouldn't it be wiser to harness the power of the sorcerer to bring the traitor to your feet and bring about a break between him and Eliza?

- Probably the sorcerer who protects Eliza is stronger than Misael, and the Jew was not able to help me in this case - said Greta, lamenting.

- He, unable? No, my child, for Misael there is no such word as "impossible". If I can bring him to your side, because we are old acquaintances, then you can be sure that you will become Countess Reifenstein. But for that you must let me be free to act - Ortruda added with a mysterious air.

Encouraged by the new hope, Greta agreed to everything that Ortruda thought necessary to undertake on her behalf. From that moment on, a close friendship began between the two women of such different ages.

A few days after the conversation, Ortruda retired early to her quarters, claiming indisposition. She ordered her maids to undress her and then dismissed them, forbidding them to disturb her under any pretext.

Two hours passed. Gradually, silence reigned in the castle, and everything fell into a deep sleep. When the old clock struck ten, Ortruda rose from her bed, dressed quietly, and, like a shadow, went to the small room that served as the castle's library and archive. There, she pressed a hidden lever and immediately a part of the wall with bookshelves opened, revealing a small door leading to a corridor carved into the thick wall.

Ortruda passed through the corridor, down a long staircase, and then emerged into a wide underground gallery that ended in a large circular room lit by two torches fixed to the wall. The reddish, flickering light of the torches faintly illuminated the furniture of the room, which probably had a special purpose, for on one side, in a niche, was an altar, and opposite the entrance was a stone bench on a three-step rise.

A man who was pacing impatiently around the room, on seeing Ortruda stopped and, inclining his head slightly, said in a broken and stern voice:

- The lady sets the day and then makes me wait! What do you want from me?

- I want to talk to you about the business of the Brotherhood, Misael. I hope you will accept as a new member a person who is

[211]

very hard to get - replied Ortruda, not offended by the tone directed at her by the Jew who, when he met her by day, treated her with the docility of a servant.

But underground, Misael no longer looked like the humble and fearful Jew that the inhabitants of Brixen knew. There, he was the lord who directed and gave orders to the proud owner of the castle. Even his appearance changed the moment he exchanged his long Asian garb for the citizen suit, which highlighted his tall, slim figure.

They both sat down at the table and engaged in a lively conversation. They talked about Greta. At first Misael seemed unwilling to accept her into his satanic gang, but after wiser reasoning he said he agreed, and gave Ortruda detailed instructions, which she promised to follow carefully.

From that day on, the main topic of conversation between Ortruda and Greta was Misael and his amazing hidden power. When the young girl was sufficiently prepared, Ortruda told her that there was a society of "initiates" who studied the secret sciences that gave their adepts infinite power over people and nature.

- If you were accepted into the Brotherhood, you could then, by yourself, command Raymond's heart and make him feel so repulsed by Eliza that he would immediately get rid of her.

Pretending to accept Greta's pleas, Ortruda promised to try to introduce her into society and confessed that she herself was studying magic and already possessed a certain power.

One night, after taking a solemn oath to be silent about everything she saw, Margarita Ramets descended into the underground, where Misael received her as a disciple.

The Jew was a very skillful tutor and managed to interest his lazy, limited pupil by teaching her a few empty magic passes, among which were those that provoked and removed toothache.

Foolish and vain, Greta imagined herself a great sorcerer, and when she managed to give a maid, the chaplain, and even

Countess Anna herself a toothache during her stay at Castle Reifenstein her pride knew no bounds. She assumed a mysterious and concentrated posture, which caught Count Wolfram's attention.

This last circumstance did not bode well for the friendship and Margarita's endless visits to Finsterbach castle. Some unpleasant rumors about Ortruda reached the ears of the Count, but knowing from experience that any remark from him would only provoke a fight, he decided to keep an eye on everything personally, hoping that with his perspicacity he would easily discover the mystery that surrounded Margarita. But in the meantime, there was an event that gave a completely opposite direction to his plans and even forced him to forget about Margarita's existence.

Arnulf returned from Palestine and the news he brought about Raymond was of the kind that caused enormous concern in his father's mind. Moreover, the need to send Raymond a significant sum of money immediately gave Count Wolfram a lot of trouble.

In that distant time, the wealth of the nobility consisted mainly of real estate. Money was very rare and concentrated mainly in the hands of merchants and Jews.

Although the Count was very wealthy, he did not have the considerable sum of money requested by Raymond. But Wolfram took the necessary steps, and within a week of Arnulf's arrival, a procurator with the money was already on his way to the Holy Land.

Fear and worry tortured Wolfram's heart. Raymond had never shown an attraction to gambling, and how then was he to reveal this addiction in Jerusalem? How could he, forgetting his obligation to Eliza, enter into a criminal relationship with a Jewish woman? Perhaps he was even led astray by her, causing him to join one of her secret sects! Many Templars had been accused of belonging to Satanism. The danger for a young, inexperienced, and frivolous person like Raymond was great.

[213]

Besides the fear that tortured Wolfram's paternal heart, the news brought by Arnulf provoked constant quarrels between the Count and his wife, as Countess Anna insisted on blaming Eliza for her son's unfortunate pilgrimage. Taking advantage of this argument, she covered her husband with reproaches about the cursed marriage with which he had united the children, just to spite her, and which had become the ruin of their only son, because the daughter of the "Italian adventuress", who had a "bad death", could only bring misfortune.

Irritated, the Count appealed to his usual means of getting out of marital squabbles, in other words, he traveled to the court of the Count of Tyrol, determined not to return until the time of Raymond's probable arrival.

While all this was going on at Reifenstein Castle, Greta settled almost permanently in Ortruda Finsterbach's castle. The news that Raymond had not returned with her brother did not worry her one bit. She already considered herself master of his fate. If she had time to acquire a little more knowledge and power until Raymond arrived, all the better.

Misael continued to administer the pseudo magic classes to Greta. In fact, he organized a meeting in her honor, at which she was solemnly admitted to the circle of "initiates". Only at this meeting were there no orgies or sacrileges. They sang only hymns praising the sciences; then, on the altar, a hooded figure appeared and handed Greta an emblem of the society, a golden triangle on a purple ribbon, and everyone present greeted her loudly. Mishael placed a laurel wreath on her head and made her sit on the stone throne as the Queen of the meeting.

Ortruda was confused by the strange comedy she could not understand. To her restrained questions, Misael answered with half-ironic and mysterious smiles, and ultimately told her that she would soon know the reasons for such a change in the usual "initiation" ritual. Ortruda, despite her anger, had to be content with these promises.

A few weeks after the "initiation" ceremony, which filled Greta's heart with happiness and pride, Misael summoned Ortruda to a secret meeting underground. There he informed her that two important members of the Brotherhood would soon be arriving from Palestine, in other words, the head of the Palestine branch and his sister. Important reasons motivated that trip. So, they had to spend two to three months in Tyrol, and they relied on the hospitality of Finsterbach castle. He added that because the Israelis could not be guests in the noble castle, they would come using Christian names.

- They will tell you their sad story themselves - concluded Misael with a brazen laugh that always showed that he didn't need to disguise it.

The insolent order to offer her castle as a hostel for wandering Jews provoked great anger in Ortruda's spirit. Innate pride rebelled against such violence, but she kept quiet and agreed. She dared neither protest nor refuse, since she was under the sway of that dark sect and perhaps for the first time bitterly regretted having fallen into the nets of that army of evil and darkness.

Two months later, a group of exhausted knights asked for hospitality at Finsterbach Castle. Between the travelers were a knight, a lady, maids, and six warriors. Behind them followed three pack mules.

Ortruda and Greta welcomed them kindly on the grand staircase and led them into the great hall, greeting them on behalf of Guntram, the owner of the castle.

The knight introduced himself as Melchior Laverdac and thanked, on behalf of his sister, Maddalena, for the warm welcome; he then asked permission to retire and rest from his journey.

The travelers only reappeared the next day for breakfast and made the most pleasant impression with their dignified manners and charming conversation.

Melchior was a still young and undoubtedly handsome man, who stood out with a sickly pallor enhanced by his blue-black

[215]

hair. As for his sister, Maddalena, she possessed a charming Asian beauty with a dull tan face color, almond eyes, and abundant black hair.

The costumes of both stood out for their rigid simplicity, but not without elegance, as evidenced by the luxurious sweater of the knight and the Genovese velvet of the sister's dress.

After the meal, Ortruda proceeded to ask the knight about the purpose of his journey, and the knight told her that he had come from Cyprus and was going to France, where he hoped to find some relatives. Seeing the surprise his words caused, he added that his great-grandfather, who had arrived in the Holy Land together with Godfroy de Bouillon,[37] had settled there and owned large estates on the land around Antioch.[38] His ancestors lived there, sometimes rich, sometimes poorer, until the Christians completely lost Palestine.

Seriously wounded in battle along with Joan of Arc,[39] he retired to Cyprus, where he decided to settle permanently with the rest of his possessions, when he suddenly learned by chance through a French Templar that in France there still lived the old Baron Laverdac who considered himself the last branch of his ancient lineage.

---

[37] Godfroi de Bouillon (Godfrey of Bouillon, 1058-1100) - Noble European who was one of the leaders of the first Crusade (1095-1099)

[38] Antioch - Old name of the city of Antakya, Turkey, founded in 307 BC. In 1098, the Crusades made it the capital of a Latin state in the east.

[39] Joan of Arc - Considered a saint by the Catholic Church, she was a simple peasant girl who led the French army to victory in the siege of Orleans by virtue of an excellent military strategy and great personal bravery. Visions that she claimed were divine made her believe that she had been chosen to liberate France from England. During the war, the English imprisoned her in a prison, where she suffered many insults and was tried as a witch. She claimed to the end that her visions and the voices she had heard were of divine origin, but the court condemned her to die at the stake in 1431. In 1456 she was declared innocent by Pope Callistus III; in 1909 she was beatified, and finally in 1920 Pope Benedict XV officially canonized her.

The knight Melchior decided to go to this relative of his to be recognized as his heir, and so he brought all the papers with him to prove his descendants.

- You can understand how I long to see the wonderful country of my ancestors soon, but I am forced to travel extremely slowly, because during the crossing my old wound has opened, and it is making me suffer a lot. As soon as I manage to reach some larger city, I will stay there for a few weeks to rest - concluded the knight.

- But, Baron, if Finsterbach Castle is to your liking, stay here, rest and regain your strength - Ortruda hastened to invite him.

At first, Melchior objected and refused, not wanting to abuse the kindness of the castle's owner. Finally, he agreed, at Ortruda's insistence, who repeatedly stated that it would be a great honor for her to have under her roof a brave warrior who had shed his blood in defense of the Holy Land, and a girl as charming as her sister. Having thus become long-time guests of the castle, Melchior and Maddalena tried to please their new acquaintances: Ortruda and Greta received luxurious gifts on one occasion, and all the castle's servants were also presented with gifts.

In addition, Melchior turned out to be an amazing storyteller, eloquently describing the last battles in Palestine; he knew many details about both the Mohammedan and Christian commanders. Maddalena, on the other hand, sang wonderful Arabic songs and recited fairy tales and Asian sagas, claiming to have heard them from her Saracen wet nurse.

Time passed happily, everyone was enthusiastic about the travelers, and admiration for them spread to the neighboring castles. Meanwhile, Melchior was always gloomy, and often, when visitors came to the castle, he suffered from his injuries. Maddalena, on the other hand, enjoyed great success and had many admirers among the neighboring knights.

Once, while Ortruda was having lunch with her guests, another visitor arrived, unexpected and rare: Arnulf von-Ried.

[217]

Stricken by a storm in the mountains and wet "to the bone" he, accompanied by his squire, decided to seek shelter in the castle.

When he was introduced to the Baron, Arnulf looked at him with attention and surprise. He seemed to have seen somewhere the face of Laverdac. Those dark eyes with their sinister expression and that sonorous, guttural voice seemed familiar to him. He racked his brains to remember where he had seen him, but the memory was not enough, and after a few minutes the impression faded, and Arnulf thought he had been confused by some chance resemblance. Besides, he was interested in something else and told Ortruda how her stepson, the commander of the Templars, Ervin von-Finsterbach, arrived in the region with another knight, accompanying his daughter, Countess Reifenstein, and that they all settled in Castle Zapnenstein.

- You must be mistaken! - said Ortruda. - If Ervin were here, he would come by to see me, since he has never failed in his duty to bring respect to his father's widow. Eliza would also have come with her husband, of course. Even if she had come before him, she would have settled in Reifenstein and would not be alone in Castle Zapnenstein, which after Faleri's luxurious palace will seem like an owl's nest to her.

- But what I have told you is correct. The countess Eliza has been here for a week now and has settled in Zapnenstein with two knights, who must have arrived on business from the Order and are staying temporarily in the castle because of the fire at his command post. All this news was conveyed to me by my chaplain - Arnulf continued, inspired. - As he passed Zapnenstein and saw the Templars' banner in the tower, he entered the castle to rest, but could learn nothing more. The two knights were absent. Eliza was ill, and the guards only said that the knights were staying there temporarily. So worried was I that I decided to visit my mother to find out whether Raymond had returned, and what had happened to the couple who, unfortunately, are such a mismatched pair.

Neither Ortruda nor Arnulf noticed how Laverdac's eyes sparkled upon hearing Eliza's name. Greta turned red and a

[218]

venomous smile appeared on her face, but Ortruda, who was watching her, looked at her with disapproval.

Outside the storm grew stronger, so they invited Arnulf to spend the night in the castle, which he accepted despite his great desire to see Eliza. But the usual joy that reigned at the table did not return and everyone dispersed early.

Greta rushed to her room to devise a plan of revenge against the miserable Eliza, who had managed to get there with Raymond; Melchior felt pain in his wound and Arnulf was not well either.

Arriving in the room they had prepared for him, Arnulf took a cup of hot spiced wine sent by the castle mistress and, wrapping himself in the silk cloak, sat down in the armchair by the lighted fireplace. He was thoughtful, for Eliza's unexpected arrival disturbed him. What did that trip in the company of two Templars mean? Why had she left the house of Fulvio that she considered as her own? Had she seen Raymond and forgiven him again? That thought made Arnulf clench his fists. But, no! It was impossible that the proud Eliza had forgiven such a profound offense, and it would be imbecility to suppose such a thing. If Raymond and Eliza had reconciled, they would have returned together: the young Countess, in choosing the gloomy old castle Zapnenstein as her home, showed that she did not want to set foot in castle Reifenstein. That is right! The hope of happiness was not lost yet; it was necessary to act energetically but carefully. He would now go and settle in his mother's house, visit Eliza, try to find out everything and, the main thing, try to stop stupid Raymond from gaining his wife's grace again. Coming to such a conclusion in his plans, Arnulf was left wandering in magical dreams when the arrival of the old squire brought him back to reality.

- Ouch! I need to tell you about a discovery I have made, which seems so incredible that I wonder if I am not seeing things.

- So, speak up and tell me this mystery! Don't tell me you found the Phoenix [40] bird in Finsterbach or that you have discovered a fairy in one of your towers - laughed Arnulf, happy under the influence of his dreams.

- Unfortunately, the discovery is not at all pleasant, and looks more like a diabolical and deadly deed - said the old squire, shaking his head.

He talked freely with Arnulf whom he had served since Arnulf's adolescence.

Arnulf became serious. Then Anselm leaned toward him and spoke in a half voice:

- The knight Laverdac is an impostor! Not only is he not a noble knight from the land of the Franks,[41] but he is not a Christian, but a Jew from Jerusalem named Uriel; it is clear that he did not come with good intentions to this castle and settled here as if he was waiting for something.

- Have you thought, Anselm, about the significance of such an accusation? - Arnulf remarked, confused. - Do you have evidence to support what you are saying?

- Yes, yes sir! Listen to how all this happened. You remember that in Jerusalem you sent me to the house of the Count, your brother, who lived with the Jew Abdias; and I went there several times to see Ekgardt, Mr. Raymond's old squire. During the visits to Abdias' house, I often saw his son Uriel; Ekgardt and I kept an eye on him when the old squire schemed about the young Count's closeness to this wretch. There I also saw a very suspicious young man, Jewish or Saracen, but in any case, a bandit. I don't know who he was, but he lived in Abdias' house, and from time to

---

[40] Phoenix - A fabulous bird that, according to Egyptian tradition, lasted for many centuries and, when burned, was reborn from its own ashes.

[41] Land of the Franks - That is, Gaul; a Roman name for part of France situated between the Rhine and Liger rivers and the Alps and which was conquered in the 5th century by the Franks, Germanic peoples who had lived in tribes in that region since the 3rd century.

time he disappeared to God knows where, and then reappeared, as always silent and gloomy. I was very surprised when, during the servants' dinner, I recognized Yussuf in Baron Laverdac's entourage. He also recognized me but pretended not to, and I did the same, but now I am starting to suspect. The wretch could, of course, have entered the service of some noble lord, but in that case, it would be necessary to warn this nobleman about the presence in his entourage of this obscure personality. Anyway, I decided to take a look at Baron Laverdac. I learned from the other servants that he and his sister occupied rooms at the end of the gallery leading to your room. I had a reason to stand in the doorway, and I did not have to wait long. The knight and his sister soon left, and two servants were lighting their way. The woman I did not recognize, but in Mr. Laverdac I immediately recognized Uriel, despite his attire. If I still had any doubt, it would disappear upon hearing Uriel's voice; that nasty, insolent laugh of his that gives me shivers on my skin.

Arnulf was silent. Anselm's words reinforced and revived the memories that surfaced in his head upon being introduced to Laverdac.

The old squire was right, Melchior was in fact the Jew from Jerusalem.

The insolence of stealing a Christian name so outraged Arnulf that he immediately wanted to make a scandal and arrest the evildoers; but he was restrained by the following reasoning: such a bold and dangerous disguise must have had a very important purpose, and it was necessary to discover such an intent. However, he should reveal the truth to Ortruda and advise her to quickly arrest her dangerous visitor.

The next morning, before leaving, he asked Ortruda for a few minutes alone and told her about Anselm's discovery, for which she thanked him, embarrassed.

- However unlikely such insolence may be, I will take all measures to investigate the secret and hand over the Jew to the authorities, if he really dared to sully a Christian name and dishonor my house with his presence - she said, shaking Arnulf's hand.

As soon as the knight left, Ortruda went to Laverdac's quarters, under the pretext of visiting the sick man who did not show up for breakfast.

Uriel, whom we will henceforth call by his real name, was sitting at a table reading a manuscript that the castle chaplain had given him. Seeing the concern on Ortruda's face, he quickly stood up and asked what had happened.

- You have been recognized, and if you don't get ready to run away immediately, you will be arrested - she replied, leaning weakly against the wall.

The Jew also turned pale.

- So, did Arnulf recognize me? - he asked, after a certain silence.

- Yes, and also his squire, Anselm. He only did not unmask you because he wanted to give me time to investigate the reason for your coming, but if you do not hide, he will certainly unmask you. Run, Uriel! I will help you in any way I can, even though I am in mortal danger of being accused of complicity with a Jew.

An awkward silence reigned.

- I will wait until tomorrow; the god of my ancestors will protect me - replied the Jew, and seeing Ortruda's surprised look, he added: - Fear not, and remember that I am the head of the Brotherhood, whose branches encompass all societies; it is not easy to arrest me. For the imbeciles, however, I have documents that prove the identity I bear.

Despite her concern, Ortruda had to agree to such a decision. As soon as she was gone, Uriel and Maakha had a long talk.

After noon Arnulf and his squire entered a small forest near Reifenstein. Letting his horse pace, Arnulf thought about how to get rid of his brother who was blocking his way; he was not determined to kill him, since murder terrified him, but it was necessary to drive him away with some clever maneuver, which he fully deserved for his levity.

They were passing through the canyon when suddenly, an arrow from elsewhere pierced the back of Arnulf's head. Death was instantaneous; the body lay for a moment in the saddle, then swayed and collapsed heavily to the ground. Anselm, in desperation, wanted to help his master, but he did not even have time to lift his victim when another arrow, shot with identical skill, smashed into his back; he opened his arms and fell face first onto Arnulf's body. The frightened horses galloped off down the road.

A few minutes later, a man climbed down the trunk of one of the gigantic trees surrounding the clearing and approached the bodies. With skillful gestures, he examined the pockets of the dead, took out their weapons, cut open Arnulf's bag, and removed his gold chain, hat buckle, and gold rings.

During the day, the men returning to Reifenstein found the bodies and brought them to the castle.

Countess Anna was distraught to see her son dead, moreover, the insolence of the murder and the robbery of the knight just a few steps from the castle indicated the appearance of a considerable band of evildoers. As soon as the first burst of maternal doom passed, she regained her usual wit. Ordering the body to be taken to the chapel, she had the castle guard reinforced, and the chaplain, at her behest, informed Count Wolfram.

Arnulf left a very significant fortune. Certainly, the boy, not foreseeing his own death, had left no will, and there were no close heirs on the maternal side. The distant relatives who could claim their rights would be removed. The countess asked her husband to use his influence with the Count of Tyrol to get him to hand over the properties that were left to Raymond, who, as his only brother, was the deceased's closest relative.

Chapter 16

We assume that upon Raymond's arrival in Yafa from Jerusalem, he found the money his father had sent him and the laconic letter ordering him to return immediately. The young Count wanted nothing else, and the land of Palestine burned his feet. From the moment he left Jerusalem, he no longer felt Uriel's malicious gaze upon him, and he got rid of Maakha's fiery passion. So, it seemed to him that the world and hopes were reborn in his exhausted and tormented soul. The pure image of Eliza again dominated him; he remembered with dread the strange vision shown to him by Uriel, telling him that someone else would take his place in his wife's heart.

Raymond was in such a hurry to get home that, without wasting any time, he headed for the port. To his extreme joy he found a Venetian galley leaving in two days and decided to board with all his belongings the next day. Great was his irritation when he learned, when he arrived at the pier, that the galley had already left. After much inquiry, he learned that an hour after he left port, a rich Asian merchant arrived and rented the entire galley for a fabulous price on the condition that the ship would leave the same day at night and take no other passengers on board. The deal was done and before sundown the galley set sail.

Raymond had to return to the inn to wait another opportunity, which did not come so quickly because of the unsuitable time of year for sailing. So, he had to stay in Yafa for another three weeks in anxious waiting. In any case, he managed to find a place on a Genoese *felucca*[42] that had no comforts and was extremely slow.

Tired and ill, he managed to reach Genoa by being about six weeks late, and after a little much-needed rest for himself and old Ekgardt, he decided to seek Eliza in Venice. However, he gave up on the idea; Eliza might refuse to accompany him after he, once again, misbehaved toward her and even caused a real rift between them with his sacrilege.

With a heavy heart, he set out on his way, tortured by the pain in his conscience and the shame of remembering his father, whose trust he had also betrayed.

The further Raymond progressed, the more his journey came to a halt; the sight of familiar places awakened bitter memories in him. He left his father's home, pure, innocent, happy, and carefree, and returned criminal, with a tainted body and spirit.

At the inn, two stops away from Reifenstein, he learned that a couple of times people with horses had stood there waiting for him for several days. He was also informed of Arnulf's death, which was the subject of gossip in a suburb fifty miles[43] away.

Raymond was stunned by this news. Although he had never liked his brother, especially since he dared to fall in love with Eliza, Arnulf's tragic and unexpected end drowned out the petty disagreements and enmity, remembering only the good times. Raymond wept sincerely for his brother. He thought sadly of his mother who must have suffered a terrible blow from that death. Then he became so anxious to get home as soon as possible that he eventually arrived in Reifenstein the evening of the next day.

Seeing the old castle rising proudly above the rock and the flag on the tower, indicating that his father was home, Raymond's heart beat harder. He forgot everything, thinking only of the joy of the meeting and, still far from the castle, blew his horn.

---

[42] Feluca - A light, fast sailing vessel used by the Egyptians and still serving as a means of transportation today.

[43] Fifty miles - About eighty kilometers.

His call was heard and understood; a horn sound answered him from over the walls. By the time he reached the top by the meandering path, the drawbridge was lowered, and Raymond entered the castle hall with his entourage.

The joyful news of the young Count's arrival instantly spread through the castle; from everywhere people ran with torches, and on the threshold soon appeared Count Wolfram himself.

Getting off his horse, Raymond ran into his father's arms, who hugged him tightly.

- You are finally back home, prodigal son! You had us waiting for you too long.

- Ah, Dad! If only you knew! - murmured Raymond.

- All right! All right! Confession and repentance can wait, and now run and embrace your mother; the poor thing has suffered great loss in your absence - interrupted the Count and led him to the stairs, at the top of which appeared Countess Anna.

After the first moments of joy, the desolate atmosphere that reigned in the castle reigned again, and Raymond began to be tortured by pangs in his conscience and repulsive memories. The demonic orgies and mad sacrileges to which he had devoted himself, now seemed monstrous and disgusting to him from the moment his father's radiant, pure gaze examined him attentively and seemed to read what was going on in his soul.

But the evening passed without the slightest uncomfortable innuendo to Raymond. The conversation turned mainly to Arnulf's death, the circumstances that accompanied it, and the possible consequences for the young Count.

Raymond learned that his father had returned home a little over a week ago and that, at his request, the Count of Tyrol had agreed to recognize him as heir to all his brother's property, except for an insignificant part that passed to other heirs. The young Count was soon to go to his suzerain,[44] to swear an oath of allegiance to his new estates, which already made him very rich, even without his father's fortune.

Arnulf's murderers were not discovered. In vain, they searched all around, arrested and hanged many vagabonds, but could not find the real culprit.

With this conversation, the hours passed quickly, and soon Wolfram said that the peregrine needed to rest. And accompanying Raymond to his room, he embraced him, blessed him, and left.

Wolfram returned to his chambers somber and worried and sat for a long time thinking. He did not want to embarrass his son with questions the first night, but he watched him a lot and realized, horrified, how much he had changed. The fresh color of his face was replaced by a sickly pallor; the once pure and open look changed to a feverish and insecure countenance, which sometimes faded, leaving the expression of his eyes opaque; the frank smile became forced and malicious. Wolfram involuntarily felt that a destructive hurricane had passed through his dear son's soul and made him a different person. With a deep sigh, the Count knelt on the choir lectern,[45] next to the crucifix, and in a fervent prayer asked the Heavenly Father to inspire him to heal Raymond's sick soul and put it on the true path.

The next day passed quickly; all morning the countess kept Raymond in his room, asking him questions about the trip, the holy places, and admiring the gifts he had brought her from Palestine.

For Raymond, talking to his mother was easy. In her blind and narrow love for her son, Countess Anna did not look beyond the outward appearance; for her, Raymond's pallor and thinness were nothing more than a consequence of the exhausting trip that

---

[44] Suzerain - In feudalism, one who had dominion over a fiefdom on which other fiefdoms depended; a word of French origin (suzerain); sovereign.

[45] Choir Lectern (facistol) - A large bookcase where books were placed in church choirs.

would disappear after a good rest. She could not see the suffering soul.

The rest of the day was spent distributing gifts to the castle servants and welcoming representatives of the vassals who came to greet the young Count on his return, whom Wolfram covered with generosity.

It was only during dinner that Raymond remembered Greta and was surprised by her sudden friendship with Ortruda. After the meal, Wolfram said goodbye to his wife a little more warmly than usual and said, smiling:

- Now, I am taking our traveler with me to talk to him alone! Come Raymond!

- I am ready, Dad - he replied, pale.

Raymond felt that that fateful moment had arrived, that he had dreaded on the way back; but he stood up from the table with a resolute air.

Wolfram went with him to his dormitory and dismissed the servant, saying that he would undress himself.

- Let's go to my oratory. There we can talk freely, away from any prying ears - said the Count, lifting the curtain and lighting the massive candlesticks with candles on the table.

The oratory was a semicircular room, covered with a fabric printed with figures, showing the "Final Judgment". Besides the choir lectern with the crucifix, there was a table there with a gospel and a prayer book, whose drawings Raymond had admired in his childhood, a folding chair, and an armchair.

Wolfram sat down and pointed at the chair to his son.

- Come, my boy! Let's talk as we often did in your childhood.

But Raymond dreaded crossing the threshold of the holy place; the sacred symbol he had desecrated frightened him. Staggering like a drunkard, he leaned against the door and covered his face with his hands.

- Raymond? You dare not enter the room where you babbled your first prayer? Do you fear kneeling before the Divine Sufferer, who forgave your enemies on the cross? - asked the Count in a deaf voice.

Raymond was silent and shivers ran down his spine. At that instant, his father's hand rested on his shoulder.

- You fool! Even without your confession, I realized that your soul had suffered a terrible desecration; your pale face and blank look revealed many things. But I beg you to tell me the whole truth. No oath can keep you away from your father. Was I not your confidant, the embodiment of your conscience? Are you still silent? Have you changed so much that you have lost confidence in your father? - whispered Wolfram, with such suffering in his voice that Raymond shuddered.

- Dad! Don't ask me what happened! If you, an example of honesty and devotion, knew what happened, you would curse me and reject me with contempt. Yes! I sinned against all divine and human laws, but do not demand confession from me! After that, all that will be left for me is suicide!

In those words, there was despair and a deep sadness. Wolfram's heart squeezed sadly.

- I understand that you would prefer death to the consciousness of dishonor if you had to appear before a worldly trial or a severe church servant. I, however, am calling you to the judgment of fatherly love, to the most lenient of judges, moved only by love, and if the entire world condemns you, only I could pity and forgive you. Fear not, my boy, and tell all. Free your soul from the weight that afflicts it, treat your wounds in front of me so that I can find a remedy and heal them.

Raymond, moved, fell to his knees and in an intermittent voice whispered:

- You are right! I have an obligation to reveal the truth to you no matter how horrible it is. Don't curse me, but free me from myself, if you can!

[229]

Wolfram lifted his son, carried him to the armchair and wanted to make him sit in the chair, but Raymond got down on his knees in front of him. Then, laying his head on his father's shoulder, he began to talk about his life in Jerusalem, about how carelessness threw him into the Jew's hands, and finally described the unbelievable horrors and pleasures he had endured.

Large drops of sweat covered the pale face of the Count, who listened silently to his son's terrible confession; only his heavy, intermittent breathing revealed his emotion.

- Now, Dad, you know everything! Then judge me as I deserve - Raymond concluded in a deaf and downcast voice.

In response, Wolfram pulled him close to himself and kissed him fondly on the forehead. This moment was terribly difficult for the Count; he loved his son very much, he was proud of him, and in his own way made him a complete knight and a good Christian. Suddenly, a band of wandering wretches, whom he was disgusted even to push off his foot, had torn his last son from him, covered him with shame, annihilated him morally, making him a slave to their antics. Such a thought left him choking with rage. But this depressive state was short-lived; his active and courageous nature won out and he regained his usual cool blood.

The Count then straightened up and lovingly ran his hand over his son's head.

- I do not blame you - he said in a normal tone. - You have been punished enough by your conscience, but I feel very sorry for you, and I want to save you!

- Father, do you think it is possible to save a criminal like me? And then, can I avoid eternal damnation?

- Have you forgotten the parable of the prodigal son, which quotes that the doors of the Heavenly Father's house are open to all sinners? Why would you be an exception? At your age you should not despair. You have become a "Luciferian" not by conviction, but by pusillanimity! You can definitely break with the criminal past and start a new life.

[230]

- I swear to you father, that is my most sincere wish!

- With this you are already taking your first step towards salvation, and you just must keep at it! Prayer and repentance will bring you God's forgiveness, while Vart, at my request, will cleanse you of the spell that has contaminated you. But how to free you from the power of that gang will require more thinking. Those wretches must have accomplices around here and will start watching you. But in order to really be able to help you, I must know everything that happens; promise me that you will not hide anything from me and will inform me about the smallest event.

- I promise, father!

- Okay, that should do it! Now, enough of this story. Let's go to the crucifix and pray together as we did so many times in your childhood. I have unshakable faith that God will enlighten us, support us, and restore peace to your soul.

Raymond moved, knelt beside his father and, for the first time after the terrible days in Jerusalem, the ardent, rousing prayer poured out of his torn soul. When he stood up, faith and hope returned to him, and along with them relief that he had not felt for a long time.

They moved on to the Count's dormitory and Raymond, a little quieter, suddenly said:

- Father, I have not yet told you the details of my reconciliation with Eliza.

- Well, after that reconciliation, you did not behave as a husband that is reconciled with his wife, but anyway, tell me what happened between you two.

Raymond told him everything frankly, without justifying himself, including his connection with Beatrice and what happened before his departure.

- I recognize that poor Eliza will need to forgive you a lot more than any other woman in twenty years of married life. If she also disregards these latest offenses, then she will become a true angel of patience and kindness - Wolfram said with disapproval.

- That is why from now on I will be an exemplary husband. For Eliza, the wisest thing would be to be indulgent with me, because I will never let her go; she is fascinating, I love her, and I want her to be mine. After my confession to you, I feel better, and I am going to Venice to bring her back with me - Raymond decided.

Wolfram began to curl his mustache and let out a series of "hum-hum".

- You do not have to go that far to get your wife. Eliza is living in Zapnenstein. Now the question is whether she will want to take you in as her husband!

Raymond jumped up as if he had been bitten.

- Is Eliza in Zapnenstein? How did she end up there and with whom, with Vart or Faleri?

- None of them! I have not seen her yet and I do not know what made her leave Venice.

- But how do you know she is here? Maybe it's just a rumor!

- No, it is true! I was away for a few months, I just returned a short time ago, so I did not know that more than a month ago Eliza arrived here in the company of her father, Commander Finsterbach, and another Templar. Because of the fire at the nearest command post, both knights have temporarily settled in the castle.

- In that case, I will reconcile with my wife tomorrow and bring her here for the duration of the Templars' stay in Zapnestein.

- Don't be in such a hurry, you may be received badly. Listen to how I heard about your wife. A couple of days before your arrival I had to go to Brixen on business. At the entrance to the town, I met some knights, and, to my great surprise, I recognized their chief Ervin Finsterbach. He also recognized me, and we exchanged handshakes. At my request Ervin returned to town, where we talked at the inn. It was Finsterbach who told me about Eliza's arrival, but for lack of time he did not tell me all the details. But what he told me about the way the countess referred to you did not make me very happy. Ervin's friendship for me has not changed, and as a man he is much more condescending to your adventures.

However, he has frankly confessed that Eliza is so offended by you that she has declared her firm resolve to break her unbearable ties with the man she is unable to love or respect. As a result, Finsterbach appealed to my knightly feelings and I promised him that if the countess does not change her mind, I will use all my influence to make you grant her a divorce.

- Oh, Dad! What did you promise that? I am telling you that I will never give Eliza her freedom. Despite all my illusions, I love her sincerely and deeply, and I count on the support of my chosen one, who is equally wonderful in body and soul, to start a new life - Raymond said in a sad tone.

- I am glad to see that you do justice to the qualities of your wife, but unfortunately you have come to this conclusion too late - Wolfram sighed. - The question is: would this evil be irreparable? You can of course force Eliza to live with you, but what will that lead to? She is not a woman like your mother to vent her own dissatisfaction with shouting and agitated scenes. She will give you hell with cold contempt and indifference, which she will openly show. Take these arguments into consideration and think about the separation that perhaps would be better.

- No, never! Don't ever talk to me about separation, Dad! I will go to Zapnestein tomorrow and try to make up. I am dying to reconcile.

- If you want to hear my advice, don't go alone, don't insist! You say that you are dying to be reconciled. But do you really think yourself worthy now to be the husband of a young and pure woman and demand her love?

Raymond paled and bowed his head.

- I want with all my heart to preserve for you the treasure that until now you have valued little - continued the Count in a milder tone, - but to succeed, it is necessary to use docility and persuasion, and not force. I will personally go to Zapnenstein, see Eliza, and try to calm her righteous anger. I will inform her of your arrival and, if possible, get her permission for you to go there and discuss your future life. However, I will not go there for three or four days, because I want Finsterbach to be present during the conversation I will have with her, and I know that he has traveled on business.

Raymond emotionally agreed with his father's decision. The fear that Eliza's anger stemmed from love for someone else tortured him.

The days marked by Wolfram followed sadly and slowly. Finally, the fourth day arrived. The saddled horses were waiting in the palace and the Count was finishing lunch with his wife and son when the sound of the horn announced the arrival of a visitor.

Raymond jumped up, annoyed at the arrival of an unexpected visitor. But to his surprise, he saw through the window a simple stable boy in Finsterbach uniform who burst into the palace at a gallop on a foam-covered horse.

After a few minutes, the confused messenger handed Ortruda's letter to Countess Anna, who hurriedly cut the silken thread that tied it. But she had barely read the first few lines, when she let out a deafened scream and felt senseless into her armchair.

Chapter 17

Let's now see what happened at Finsterbach Castle the day after Arnulf left.

Very agitated and full of anger, Ortruda waited for the Jew and her sister to leave the castle. She could not stand the idea of Uriel insisting on staying in her house, even under the threat of imprisonment, which in those days was equivalent to sentencing to death and torture. So, she was completely dumbfounded when Uriel told her, with a mischievous smile, that Baron Laverdac could now quietly enjoy his kind hospitality.

When, a few days later, Ortruda learned how Uriel had removed the danger that threatened him, she was seized with real horror and bitterly regretted having given herself over to the power of the band of murderers and apostates she had welcomed under her roof.

Greta was not very impressed by the news of Ried's death. She Liked Arnulf so much, but she remembered well his refusal to marry her. When she learned that the deceased's possessions were to increase Raymond's fortune, she considered his death like a punishment and felt a certain satisfaction filled with hatred.

But the news of Eliza's arrival in the country caused Greta's soul a real furor. She began to suspect that the girl had arrived with the aim of joining up with Raymond, whose return was expected at any moment as Countess Anna wrote to her.

Greta immediately decided to prevent any agreement between the young couple, even if it meant unleashing all the demons of hell on them. It was no coincidence that she fancied herself a magician and would not stop at any pain of conscience.

Still, she admitted that Misael was a more powerful magician and asked Ortruda to inform her as soon as he reached the underground.

Greta looked forward feverishly to that meeting. Each day that passed seemed to her a new danger to her plans, and Eliza provoked in her a so wild hatred that she would not hesitate to kill her.

Finally, one afternoon Ortruda informed her that that night Misael would arrive, and she could talk to him at her leisure.

When night came and the whole castle fell asleep, the two women, taking the usual precautions, went down to the underground where the Jew was already waiting for them.

Ortruda talked to him first alone and then said, walking away:

- Now, Greta, I leave you alone with the master! Tell him everything that has bothered you for some days now.

Being alone with Misael, Greta openly told him how much Eliza's arrival bothered her. She asked him to point out a way to separate the young couple, or to bring Raymond to her feet himself.

Misael thought for a while and said kindly:

- Noble Greta, you yourself will trigger the spells that will forever chain the heart of the infidel to you. As for Eliza's arrival, this should not sadden you, but cheer you up, because now that she is separated from the powerful sorcerer who protected her, she becomes an easily removable obstacle. Now, I can reassure you that in two months, the crown of the Counts of Reifenstein will rest on your golden hair.

Three days later, she learned that Raymond had arrived at Castle Reifenstein. Misael told her this news, and added:

The time has come, noble Greta, when I can fulfill my promise: to give you young Count Reifenstein as your husband. You must have enough confidence to submit yourself to all the conditions required by this magic ceremony, whose importance and difficulty you understand, because the moment I place the ring on your finger, Eliza will die of a heart attack. Thus, the obstacle that separates you will be destroyed forever.

Greta heard him trembling with her whole body; her face burned, her eyes sparkled.

- I believe in you, Misael, as in God himself! I know so much of your power and nobility that I will blindly submit to whatever you prescribe. Needless to say, my gratitude will be worthy of the great favor you will render me.

The Jew bowed deeply to her.

- I know that your generosity is equivalent to your beauty and wisdom - he said with a smile, whose double meaning Greta failed to notice in her excitement. - But now, he continued, allow me to tell you the details of the magic ritual. First of all, you will have to leave the castle. I will lead you to my house myself, through the passage I use to get here.

Mr. Raymond will also be there. At home, in the sanctuary that you already know, we are going to perform a part of the marriage rite, more exactly that which is necessary to bind you forever to Mr. Raymond and to break the ties that bind him to Eliza. I have already said that because of this enchantment Eliza will die. When the legal period of mourning for the countess has passed, and the decent norms of society allow it, you will celebrate your marriage with all the pomp you please. This ceremony will take place on Thursday evening. Beforehand, you should wash yourself with pure water and dress in white. In addition, you should bring with you your nightgown, in which you will return home. You are quite familiar with the rules of magic, and you should know that this affair must be kept in the strictest confidence and that only Baroness Ortruda can know that you are going away. I'll be waiting for you here at nine o'clock, beautiful bride of Count Reifenstein! Oh, I almost forgot something important: do you have any holy relics?

- I have a particle of labdanum brought from Rome.

- Perfect! Bring it with you.

When Ortruda heard that Greta was going to leave the castle together with the Jew, she was very frightened and tried to dissuade her from that risky adventure, but Greta just laughed and said that she trusted Misael entirely and that then Raymond's presence would ensure her safety. Ortruda did not dare insist. She was under the thumb of the demonic gang and could not openly contradict them.

On Thursday afternoon, Greta pretended that she wanted to sleep, and went to bed early. As soon as Martha, who had been served a glass of wine, fell asleep, the girl got up, put on a rich brocade dress, sewn for her supposed marriage, put on some jewelry, and hung around her neck the sacred labdanum. Then she wrapped up her sleeping costume, wrapped herself in a dark cloak, put the hood over her head, and went down into the underground. Misael was already waiting for her. He also was wearing a hood and a black cloak, under which he carried a flashlight.

Both, like a shadow, passed through some rooms and down a long corridor that ended in a staircase leading to a second corridor, which in turn led to a gap in the rock, hidden by the shadow of secular trees. This passage was so well concealed that it was impossible for anybody to find it that was not aware of its existence. A few steps away, a man was holding two saddled horses by the reins.

Misael mounted one of the horses, put Greta on the back and, despite the darkness, took off at full speed. The man holding the horses galloped after him. Half an hour later they stopped, got off their horses, and again entered an underground labyrinth a little smaller than the first one. Then they climbed a staircase. The door opened quietly, and Greta found herself in a small, luxuriously furnished room in the Asian manner and lit by a silver lamp.

- Rest here and wait until I come to get you - said Misael, taking off the girl's cloak and pointing at the pile of cushions that served as a divan.

With her heart racing and trembling with a fear that she herself could not explain, Greta sat down and waited impatiently

[238]

for Raymond to arrive. At last, she was reaching the climax of her desires. In an hour at most, Eliza would die, and she, Greta, would become Countess Reifenstein.

Despite the joy and sense of triumph that the realization of her dreams brought, a certain uneasiness and growing sadness filled her soul. This nervous state reached its peak when Misael entered.

- Come on, beautiful bride! Your fiancé awaits you - he said with a smile. - Where is your holy talisman?

Greta pointed to the medallion and stood up hastily. In that instant, all her bad omens that bothered her were forgotten. Now she was going to see Raymond! What did she have to fear?

Misael took the girl by the hand and led her down a corridor that seemed to be a dead end because the door was so cleverly hidden in one of its walls. The room they entered had the appearance of a cave with stone walls and a low, vaulted ceiling. A series of thick columns followed on either side.

In the center of this room there was a huge stone in the shape of a bowl fixed on a foot,[46] a few lamps hanging from iron chains illuminated the gloomy place, dark curtains between the columns, and a group of twelve men standing by the stone, whose evil glances were directed at Greta.

She stared indecisively and turned terribly pale. She saw immediately that Raymond was not there. On the other hand, in the group of Jews she recognized Baron Melchior Laverdac wearing a long Oriental costume. What could the presence of a Christian knight there and wearing that strange costume mean? Could it be that he was Raymond's witness? All these thoughts passed like a hurricane through Greta's mind, but they gave her no time to think.

---

[46] Note from the Russian original: The proof of the existence of such shrines in the Middle Ages is found in the documents of a court case in Regensburg (a German city in the Bavarian region) from the year 1486. In this type of shrine, the corpses of six children were found.

- Brothers! I bring you the bride, a valuable offering to our Lord - said Mishael, pushing Greta toward the stone.

The girl was suddenly seized with horror. She threw herself back and tried to resist.

- Where is Raymond? Let me go! I want to get out of here! - she screamed, struggling.

- You will see him as soon as you lie down on the bridal bed, we have prepared for you - replied Misael with a wild laugh.

He stopped pretending, because he no longer needed to lie now that the victim was in his possession.

Like a flock of birds of prey, the Jews fell upon the unfortunate Margarita. Despite her desperate resistance, she was lifted like a feather and placed on the stone table. A section of the men held her while Misael grabbed her by her long hair, wrapped it in his hand, completely unclasping the girl's neck and throwing her head over the edge of the bowl. At the same instant, Uriel pulled out of his clothes a long, shiny stiletto and made a wide cut across Greta's neck.

A hoarse scream died in Greta's throat as the blood that gushed from the wound covered those present with splatter.

The young woman's body was immediately placed in such a way that the blood dripped into a large glass container, specially prepared for that purpose. Trembling with their whole bodies, their faces distorted like cannibals, those present watched as the red, steaming liquid filled the container more and more.[47]

An hour later, Greta's body, which had become as white as an alabaster statue, delivered the last drop of blood. Then everyone left the body of the deceased and focused on the valuable liquid. The blood was poured into vials that were carefully sealed.

---

[47] Note from the Russian original: The Jewish theological books fall into two categories: Neshat and Kabbalah. To the first category belong the Talmud and the Shulkhan. And according to Shulkhan "it is no sin for a Jew to kill a Christian" (Laws 50 and 81).

The Jews gradually reached a real ecstasy. The smell of blood intoxicated them. Their faces were disfigured; their eyes were bloodshot. Emitting deaf roars and cries of wild joy, they greedily consumed the purple drops that remained on the rims and bottom of the stone bowl.

The others, throwing themselves on the ground, licked up the splashes that had fallen on the stone tiles. It is impossible to convey all the horror of that disgusting scene, the echo of the distant and monstrous cult of Astarte[48] and Moloch,[49] bloodthirsty gods of the Phoenicians, who demanded the blood of children and young girls.

Uriel, who was conducting the ceremony, seemed particularly pleased and excited. His eyes sparkled. With his hands still bloodied, he climbed the stone that served as the altar and, placing his foot on the motionless body of the unfortunate Margarita, he roared:

- Listen to me, brothers and sisters, representatives of our communities are scattered among the cursed goys like flowers that, isolated, grow, bloom, and perfume, lost among roots and weeds! As a representative of the great community of Jerusalem, I believe that I could not choose a more appropriate moment to convey to you the advice and approval of the elders of our people than to make a sacrifice to our god, a victim more pleasant than the most expensive fragrances. I tread on all the Goys in the world with this girl who has just given her blood, and just like her, all the goys must hand over to us everything that is dear to them: their life and their gold, as well. You know that once every hundred years the chosen ones of Israel are obliged to gather at the tomb of the Great Master

---

[48] Astarte- Goddess of fertility, motherhood, and love in Phoenician mythology.

[49] Moloch - According to the Bible, Moloch was a deity worshiped in Palestine, Phoenicia, and Carthage, to whom human sacrifices were made, especially on children.

Kaleb,[50] the holy Rabbi Shimon Bar-Yojai, to give an account of what has been done against the persecutions and to discuss the ways to achieve the only goal we pursue: to reign over the Land as was promised to our father Abraham.[51]

In the Talmud, printed in Amsterdam in 1646, it is written: "The Jews are commanded to destroy the disciples of the Nazarene. After a few pages, we read: It is surprising that the blood of non-Jewish virgins represents such a pleasing offering to Heaven. The shed blood of non-Jewish virgins is an offering as sacred as the most expensive fragrances and, moreover, serves as the best means of reconciling with God and attracting his blessings."

- This year my father was present at this important and secret meeting. He told me to tell you this: stand firm and do not lose heart! In spite of all the persecutions and the terrible slavery we endure, the future of the world belongs to us, and also all the power, which will deliver into our hands the errors, the weaknesses, and the quarrels of our Christian enemies. They are in great numbers and have on their side strength; but we will win by cleverness, patience, and foresight. No wonder Jehovah gave his chosen people the vitality and endurance of a snake, the cunning of a fox, the vision of a hawk, and the memory of a dog.

We are scattered all over the earth because all of it must belong to us. The time will come when we penetrate the disunited ranks of the goys like water that seeps into the smallest cracks in the rock and ends up destroying them. In our hands will be accumulated all the gold in the world and, along with it, the supreme power. Don't forget also that while we drink the blood of our enemies, we reign over them!

---

[50] Kaleb (Caleb or Chelubai) — Cited in the Bible as the principal spy sent to a Canaan, recognized for his fidelity to God.

[51] Abraham - First patriarch of the Hebrews, he symbolizes the definitive break with pagan idolatry and the commitment to monotheism. In Jewish and Christian traditions he appears as a father figure, dignified, humane and firm in his faith.

[242]

After Uriel's speech, there followed a series of advice, orders, and indications on how to apply in practice the measures that were to, soon, submit the whole world to the children of Israel.

The Luciferian's words provoked fanatical enthusiasm in everyone present. Exclamations, shouts, threats, and curses addressed to the goys joined in a general rumble. Such excitement, no doubt, would not have dissipated quickly had it not been for the intrusion of Mishael, who kept his cool more than the others.

- Brothers, you forget that at dawn the body of this woman must be far from here, and that we must destroy all signs of our sacrifice, otherwise we can all die. We can talk and discuss later, but now it is necessary to act.

Becoming sober, as by the touch of a magic wand, the Jews immediately began their sinister work. They took out from behind a curtain a stone bench and some buckets of water. In an instant, Greta was undressed, placed on the bench, and all traces of blood were washed from her. Carefully wiping the body, Uriel placed a colorless ointment over the wound, which emitted a strong aroma. Under the action of the ointment the edges of the wound almost immediately lost the appearance of a fresh cut. Uriel tied a scarf around the neck of the deceased, and then they dressed her in her sleeping clothes. The corpse was wrapped in a wide black cloak, and three men carried her along the same path Greta had passed along two hours earlier, alive, and full of hope.

Uriel, Misael and two other Jews arrived without any problems in the basement of Finsterbach castle. It was very difficult to carry the corpse through the endless passages and up the stairs with it. The Luciferians were panting and covered in sweat, but they kept walking without stopping. A sigh of relief escaped them when they deposited the body by the door that led to the living quarters.

At that spot, they rested and took a breath. The remaining path was the most dangerous and required great speed, caution, and agility.

While three of his companions leaning against the wall were wiping the sweat that ran down their faces, Uriel leaned over the corpse and untied the scarf that was around her neck. The terrible wound was half closed and had the appearance of an old almost closed scar that had opened thanks to a blow or some other accident.

Examining with deep boastfulness that miraculous metamorphosis, the Jew stood up and said:

- Let's go, brothers! It is time to conclude this dangerous expedition.

The three men lifted Greta's body. Under the direction of Uriel, who opened a secret door and showed them the way, they glided like shadows toward Greta's room.

The circumstances favored the evildoers. No floorboards creaked under their bare feet, they didn't bump into any furniture, and Margarita's room was dimly lit by a night-light.

They then placed the body on the large bed with columns. The blanket was still pulled away from the way Greta had left it when she got out of bed to get dressed and follow her fateful fate. Now they covered her with the blanket and gave her the shape of a sleeping person. Then the murderers quickly reached the door and, like evil spirits, disappeared into the dim light of the dawning day.

Only Uriel took another path and headed for the tower, where the knight Melchior's room was. By the secret passage, he exchanged his oriental costume for a silk camisole. Fifteen minutes later, he was sleeping, deep in a deep sleep, in the place he never seemed to have left.

Ortruda slept very badly that night, so badly that two of the maids had to take duty near her. Finally, the Baroness sent for the chaplain to give her soothing drops for her terrible headache, but she strictly forbade disturbing anyone else.

Before dawn, Ortruda felt better, sent everyone to bed, and fell asleep as well. She was awakened by the first maid, who, pale and trembling with her whole body, rushed into the room.

- Noble lady! Excuse me for waking you up! A terrible misfortune has happened! Martha says she found the young lady dead in her bed.

Ortruda jumped up as if she had received an electric shock and turned terribly pale.

- You are delirious, Agatha! Just yesterday Greta was completely healthy.

- Yes, but now she's dead and seems to have cooled off.

Desolate and trembling, Ortruda jumped out of bed, hurriedly got dressed, and almost ran to Margarita's room. The rooms preceding the dormitory were already crowded with people. Every face reflected horror. From afar, covering the roar of the crowd, Martha's cries and shouts were heard.

Upon seeing the Baroness, the crowd opened and let her pass. Staggering and barely able to stand, Ortruda approached the bed where Martha was kneeling. Behind her could be seen a group of weeping women, the old castellan, and the castle chaplain.

- Don't tell me it is true! Is it possible that she is dead? - stammered Ortruda, looking terrified at Margarita's face, white as the pillow on which she lay.

- Yes, noble lady! The poor child is really dead! Her body is already frozen. But this death is a strange mystery. The unfortunate Margarita has a wound on her neck, and I have already sent for the parish priest, Mr. Gubert, who had just arrived at the castle to change the bandage on Andrei's broken arm - replied the chaplain, holding Ortruda, who was barely able to stand up.

A few minutes later, the surgeon arrived, a tall, thin old man dressed in black. He ordered everyone out of the room, and then, helped by the chaplain, thoroughly examined the body.

- I really cannot understand this strange case - he finally said, straightening up. There is not a drop of blood in the veins of the corpse, and if it had come out of the wound, it would have stained the entire bed and part of the floor. Moreover, the wound on the neck is old, already closed and opened by accident.

[245]

- But she did not have any injuries! She was killed tonight - cried Marta out of her wits.

- If this is a crime, then I have never encountered one so inexplicable. Did she leave the castle at night?

- Mr. Gubert, how can you ask such a question? - replied Marta, trembling with indignation. A noble lady, who could not even leave the castle during the day without guards, how could she escape at night to God knows where, and then, in such a way that no one knew or saw her? Here is her cloak! It is hanging the way I put it on after the walk. And there, on the bench, are the clothes she took off when she went to sleep. I slept next to her, and I did not hear the young lady turn over. Oh, the murderers broke in here and...

Tears prevented the old woman from speaking, but quickly mastering herself, she went on:

- This morning I was surprised that the poor thing took so long to call me, because she was always up very early. I entered quietly and approached the bed. Under the dim light of dawn, it seemed to me that she was sleeping peacefully. Then I left. Another hour went by. So, I decided it was time to wake her up. I went in again and took her hand; but her hand was cold as ice. Then I got scared and called for help.

The surgeon and the chaplain exchanged worried glances. The crime was clear, but the mystery surrounding Margarita Ramets' death grew more impenetrable by the minute.

- Noble lady! - said the priest, after a moment's reflection. We must inform the authorities about this extraordinary event. If you allow me, I will send a messenger immediately to Brixen and ask the chief judge to come here and investigate on the spot.

- Of course, Father Hilario, do whatever is necessary. You have complete freedom to order whatever is necessary, because I do not feel able to do it. The death of this poor child, whom I loved like a daughter, struck me in the heart - replied Ortruda, leaving the room on shaky legs.

[246]

In one of the neighboring rooms, Ortruda found Laverdac and his sister. Both were visibly moved. Maddalena, all in tears, asked permission to look at poor Greta; Melchior offered Ortruda his arm to accompany her, since she was about to faint.

Arriving at her dormitory, Ortruda slumped helplessly in the armchair. Her companion kindly placed a stool under her feet and brought her a silk pillow. At the same time, he cast a careful glance into the adjoining room, where the maids were usually kept on duty. The room was empty. All the women ran to see the deceased, who had been taken to the great hall, where the chaplain gathered all the inhabitants of the castle to make a preliminary inquiry and note the answers in the protocol.

Convinced that they were completely alone, Uriel quickly approached the armchair and lightly touched Ortruda's hand, who was sitting with her eyes closed. She shivered and straightened up immediately.

She looked with ostensible horror at the Jew, whose hard, piercing gaze was directed at her with a mocking expression. She had no doubt as to who was to blame for Greta's death, and it seemed to her that the Jew's long, white arms were still stained with the innocent blood of his victim.

- What have you done with Greta? - she murmured, and an involuntary tremor of horror and disgust ran through her body.

A wicked smile slid across Uriel's lips.

- She was the victim of a fatality. You know that the noble Margarita was studying cursed science and intended to kill the countess Eliza. But she pronounced the incantation incorrectly and the vampire fell upon her and suffocated her. Sometimes, it happens that you fall into the grave you have dug for someone else - said Uriel softly.

Then he added, giving Ortruda a stern, threatening look:

- Does the noble lady have any other opinion? Or perhaps Margarita communicated to you some special plan concerning the night that was fatal to her?

Ortruda shuddered. It seemed that she was already feeling the cold steel of the stiletto in her body.

- No! Margarita did not tell me anything, and I have little interest in the night - she replied in a deaf voice.

- You act smart! Remember that curiosity kill the cat! - said Uriel.

He then took out of his pocket a small package and placed it on Ortruda's lap.

- Keep it! Here are some wrapped pieces of the deceased's lost jewelry. Try to put them in the jewelry box before the judge arrives - he said with a meaningful look.

Remaining alone, Ortruda put the bundle in her pocket and put her hands on her head. It seemed that on her neck they had already placed the noose that they could tighten at her slightest disobedience.

In that instant, she was overcome by a terrible despair mixed with a deadly sadness. What was she doing? What kind of masters had she chosen for herself? Despite her own debauchery, despite the criminal adventures to which she was driven by her passions, the series of murders and crimes in which she had become an accomplice horrified her. Every fiber of her being trembled at the thought that it was her fault that a woman's Christian blood had been used for the disgusting Jewish cult. Furthermore, what guarantee did she have that a fatal accident would not reveal her involvement? The continued presence of the Jews in the castle was already an eternal danger for her. Maybe, another person, like Arnulf, might recognize Uriel. But how to resist, how to free herself from that shameful yoke?

A moment later, she stood up, looking gloomy, but determined to carry out the order she had received. However bleak and threatening her future might be, she could not back down, and had to play to the end her role as the "servant of evil" that she had voluntarily chosen.

End of book 1.

Zibia Gasparetto's Greatest success stories

With more than 20 million titles sold, the author has contributed to the strengthening of spiritualist literature in the publishing market and to the popularization of spirituality. Learn more of the author's successes.

Romances Dictated by the Spirit Lucius

The Life Force

The Truth of each one

Life knows what it does

She trusted in life

Between Love and War

Esmeralda

Thorns of Time

Eternal Bonds

Nothing is by Chance

Nobody is Nobody's

God's Advocate

Tomorrow Belongs to God

Love Won

Unexpected Encounter

On the Edge of Destiny

The Sly One

The Morro of Illusions

Where is Teresa?

Through the Doors of the Heart

When Life chooses

When the Hour Comes

When it is necessary to return

Opening for Life

Not afraid to live

Only love can do it

We Are All Innocent

Everything has its price

It was all worth it

A real love

Overcoming the past

<u>Other success stories by André Luiz Ruiz and Lucius</u>

The Love Never Forgets You Trilogy

The Strength of Kindness

Under the Hands of Mercy

Saying Goodbye to Earth

At the End of the Last Hour

Sculpting Your Destiny

There are Flowers on the Stones

The Crags are made of Sand

Books of Eliana Machado Coelho and Schellida

Hearts without Destiny

The Shine of Truth

The Right to be Happy

The Return

In the Silence of Passions

Strength to Begin Again

The Certainty of Victory

The Conquest of Peace

Lessons Life Offers

Stronger than Ever

No Rules for Loving

A Diary in Time

A Reason to Live

Eliana Machado Coelho and Schellida, Romances that captivate, teach, move and
can change your life!

Romances of Arandi Gomes Texeira and The Count J.W. Rochester

Lancaster County

The Power of Love

The Trial

Cleopatra's Bracelet

The Reincarnation of a Queen

You Are Gods

Books of Marcelo Cezar and Marco Aurelio

Love is for the Strong

The Last Chance

Nothing is as it Seems

Forever With Me

Only God Knows

You Make Tomorrow

A Breath of Tenderness

Books of Vera Kryzhanovskaia and JW Rochester

The Revenge of the Jew

The Nun of the Marriages

The Sorcerer's Daughter

The Flower of the Swamp

The Divine Wrath

The Legend of the Castle of Montignoso

The Death of the Planet

The Night of Saint Bartholomew

The Revenge of the Jew

Blessed are the poor in spirit

Cobra Capella

Dolores

Trilogy of the Kingdom of Shadows

From Heaven to Earth

Episodes from the Life of Tiberius

Infernal Spell

Herculanum

On the Frontier

Naema, the Witch

In the Castle of Scotland (Trilogy 2)

New Era

The Elixir of Long Life

The Pharaoh Mernephtah

The Lawgivers

The Magicians

The Terrible Phantom
Paradise without Adam
Romance of a Queen
Czech Luminaries
Hidden Narratives
The Nun of the Marriages

Books of Elisa Masselli

There is always a reason
Nothing goes unanswered
Life is made of decisions
The Mission of each one
Something more is needed
The Past does not matter
Destiny in his hands
God was with him
When the past does not pass
Just beginning

Books of Vera Lúcia Marinzeck de Carvalhoç
and Patricia

Violets in the Window
Living in the Spirit World
The Writer's House
Flight of the Seagull

Vera Lúcia Marinzeck de Carvalho
and Antônio Carlos

Love your Enemies
Slave Bernardino
the Rock of Lovers
Rosa, the third fatality
Captives and Freed

Books of Mónica de Castro y Leonel

In spite of everything

Love is not to be trifled with

Face to Face with the Truth

Of My Whole Being

I wish

The Price of Being Different

Twins

Giselle, The Inquisitor's Mistress

Greta

Till Life Do You Part

Impulses of the Heart

Jurema of the Jungle

The Actress

The Force of Destiny

Memories that the Wind Brings

Secrets of the Soul

Feeling in One's Own Skin

World Spiritist Institute

Printed in the USA
CPSIA information can be obtained
at www.ICGtesting.com
LVHW041322051023
760079LV00007B/1015